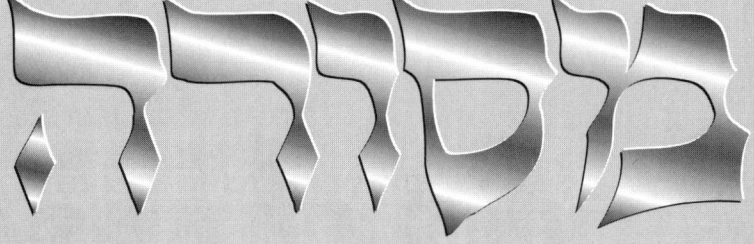

ArtScroll Series®

Rabbi Nosson Scherman / Rabbi Meir Zlotowitz
General Editors

RABBI ZELIG PLISKIN

Building Your

Published by
Mesorah Publications, ltd

Self-Image

and the Self-Image of Others

FIRST EDITION
First Impression ... June 2006

Published and Distributed by
MESORAH PUBLICATIONS, LTD.
4401 Second Avenue / Brooklyn, N.Y 11232

Distributed in Europe by
LEHMANNS
Unit E, Viking Business Park
Rolling Mill Road
Jarow, Tyne & Wear, NE32 3DP
England

Distributed in Australia and New Zealand by
GOLDS WORLDS OF JUDAICA
3-13 William Street
Balaclava, Melbourne 3183
Victoria, Australia

Distributed in Israel by
SIFRIATI / A. GITLER — BOOKS
6 Hayarkon Street
Bnei Brak 51127

Distributed in South Africa by
KOLLEL BOOKSHOP
Ivy Common
105 William Road
Norwood 2192, Johannesburg, South Africa

ARTSCROLL SERIES®
BUILDING YOUR SELF-IMAGE AND THE SELF-IMAGE OF OTHERS
© Copyright 2006, by MESORAH PUBLICATIONS, Ltd.
4401 Second Avenue / Brooklyn, N.Y. 11232 / (718) 921-9000 / www.artscroll.com

---

ALL RIGHTS RESERVED
The text, prefatory and associated textual contents and introductions
— including the typographic layout, cover artwork and ornamental graphics —
have been designed, edited and revised as to content, form and style.

No part of this book may be reproduced
IN ANY FORM, PHOTOCOPYING, OR COMPUTER RETRIEVAL SYSTEMS
— even for personal use without written permission from
the copyright holder, Mesorah Publications Ltd.
except by a reviewer who wishes to quote brief passages
in connection with a review written for inclusion in magazines or newspapers.

THE RIGHTS OF THE COPYRIGHT HOLDER WILL BE STRICTLY ENFORCED.

ISBN:
1-4226-0065-3 (hard cover)
1-4226-0066-1 (paperback)

Typography by CompuScribe at ArtScroll Studios, Ltd.
Printed in the United States of America by Noble Book Press Corp.
Bound by Sefercraft, Quality Bookbinders, Ltd., Brooklyn N.Y. 11232

Table of Contents

	Acknowledgments	10
	Introduction	11
1.	Your Immense Value as a Person Is a Divine Gift	17
2.	Becoming an Honorable Person	22
3.	Why We Need to Feel Good About Ourselves	25
4.	The Importance of Considering Yourself Important	29
5.	"The Almighty Loves You"	32
6.	"I Am a Soul With a Body"	35
7.	Build On What You Did Right	37
8.	What Can I Do to Improve Today?	41
9.	"Thinking Pattern" Versus "Having"	43
10.	Emotional States Go Up and Down; Self-Image Can Be More Stable	49
11.	Act the Way You Wish to Be	53
12.	Upgrading Your Identity Will Have a Global Positive Effect	59
13.	Your Best Moments Are Your Best Teachers	64
14.	If You Were to Meet Hillel and Rabbi Akiva	67
15.	Every Shabbos Can Build Your Self-Image	68
16.	Building Your Self-Image One Tiny Step at a Time	70

17.	Making and Reaching Worthwhile Goals	72
18.	All Inner Strengths in All Contexts	76
19.	Choose to Make the World a Better Place	79
20.	The Young Chazon Ish's Aleph Bais	82
21.	"Choosing Wisely" Versus "Change"	84
22.	"This, Too, Will Build My Self-Image"	86
23.	Focus Exercise: The Great Four	89
24.	Perseverance on the Path of Building Your Self-Image	91
25.	How Long Does It Take?	94
26.	"If I Can Do It Once, I Can Do It Again"	98
27.	"If Someone Else Can Do It, I Can Do It, Too"	101
28.	Expand Your Beliefs About What Is Possible for You	105
29.	Add the Word "Yet" Whenever You Think About What You Can't Yet Do	107
30.	"For a Lazy Person, You Do a Lot"	109
31.	"I Would Never Have Believed That I Could Accomplish What I Did"	111
32.	Stop Thinking Thoughts That Lower Your Self-Image	113
33.	"Next!" to Thoughts That Build Your Self-Image	117
34.	The Power of Teshuvah	120
35.	Being in the Presence of People Who Make You Feel Good About Yourself	123
36.	Authentic Self-Image Versus Projecting an Image for Others	125
37.	Self-Mastery Builds Your Self-Image	128
38.	Thinking About Self-Image: Self-Centeredness and Beyond	130
39.	Humility and Arrogance	132
40.	Realizing the Complexity of Accurate Self-Knowledge	136

41.	"Challenges Strengthen Me"	142
42.	Some Benefits of a Low Self-Image	145
43.	A Purim Parable: A Lesson for the Entire Year	148
44.	On Becoming a Kinder Person	153
45.	Help People Raise Their Self-Image	156
46.	Believing in Other People Can Help Them Believe in Themselves	160
47.	Reish Lakish: Before and After His Encounter With Rabbi Yochanan	162
48.	Create Breakthroughs by Transcending Someone's Resistance	165
49.	Write Short Image-Building Notes	168
50.	Rabbi Preida's Student	169
51.	Let Every Story About the Positive Patterns of Others Add to Your Self-Image	172
52.	Life Isn't a Competitive Game	174
53.	International Committee for Self-Worth (I.C.F.S.W.)	179
54.	"I Am My Choices"	182
55.	We All Start Out as Newborns	184
56.	Consider Yourself a 10 Out of 10	186
57.	On Being Respectfully Assertive	190
58.	Money and Self-Image	193
59.	You Don't Need Permission to Declare, "I Will Live the Rest of My Life With a High Self-Image"	195
60.	Two Patterns: "The Sword Way" Versus "The Healing Way"	198
61.	Speaking Against Others Does Not Build You	200
62.	How a Donkey Sees a Tzaddik	202
63.	Do Things Daily That Are Difficult for You to Do	204
64.	Intensity of Will	206

65.	Resilience: The Art of Bouncing Back	208
66.	Make Health-Oriented Choices	210
67.	A Well-Rested and Well-Nourished Mind Thinks More Clearly	211
68.	Alert Mind, Relaxed Body	213
69.	"What Is the Wisest Thing I Can Do Now?"	215
70.	Become Part of Worthwhile Organizations	218
71.	Store the Entire Book of Psalms in Your Mind's Database	220
72.	Improving Your Courage	221
73.	Building Your Feelings of Confidence Builds Your Self-Image	224
74.	Excessive Confidence Can Cause Many Mistakes	230
75.	Staying Calm Under Pressure	232
76.	Having High Expectations	235
77.	It's Not Over Until It's Over	237
78.	"Does Saying 'I Can' Mean That I Can?"	241
79.	"I Feel Bad About Myself"	244
80.	Rejection and Self-Image	247
81.	Perfectionism	250
82.	What Are the Positive Aspects of Your "Deficiency"?	252
83.	If You Knew That in 10 Years From Now…?	255
84.	What Might Have Been	256
85.	Sometimes a Tough Coach Is Better	258
86.	Overcoming Discouragement	260
87.	On Developing the Attribute of Happiness	263
88.	Smile at Mirrors	271
89.	Negative Anchors to Positive Anchors	274
90.	A Joyful Pessimist	278

91.	A Positive Self-Image Prevents Much Anger	280
92.	On Being Self-Conscious Around Other People	283
93.	Forgiveness Releases Resentment	285
94.	Changing Your Memories of the Past	287
95.	"I'm Glad You Have Feelings"	290
96.	How African Violets Transformed Someone's Self-Image	292
97.	Respect the Elderly – Even When It's You	294
98.	Limited Education	296
99.	The Dave Farrow Story and Your Memory	298
100.	Keep a Victory and Success Journal	302
101.	Some People Enjoy Finding Weaknesses in Others	303
102.	People Who Are Angry And Blaming	306
103.	Note to People Who Are Frequently Angry and Insulting	309
104.	Just Plain Stubborn	312
105.	Boosting Yourself by Lying and Exaggerating	316
106.	"Albert Einstein Never Won Any Football Games"	318
107.	If a Jewish Doctor From Vienna Would Have Spent a Month in a Yeshiva	320
108.	A Formula for Self-Development: G.T.S.S. = B.R.A.I.N.	324
109.	Positive Play-By-Play Self-Commentary	326
110.	Positively Alphabetical	330
111.	Daily Affirmations to Build Your Self-Image	345
	Index	351

Acknowledgments

I am grateful to the Almighty for His constant kindness. I pray that this book be a source of inspiration and happiness for many.

I am grateful to the entire ArtScroll staff for all they have done to publish this book and my previous ArtScroll books. I am especially grateful to Reb Shmuel Blitz and Reb Avrohom Biderman.

I am grateful to Mrs. Sarah Shapiro for her insightful and cogent comments on the manuscript. Her input was very helpful.

I am grateful to Mrs. Tova Ovits for her excellent editing. I appreciate her professionalism.

I am grateful to my late father, a disciple of the Chofetz Chaim at his yeshiva in Radin. My father's love for Torah, his exemplary character traits, and his wisdom all radiated great light.

I am grateful to my mother for her constant love.

I am grateful to all my many teachers throughout my life.

I am grateful to Rabbi Noah Weinberg, the Rosh Hayeshiva of Aish Hatorah, from whom I have gained so much.

I am grateful to my dear friend Rabbi Kalman Packouz for his friendship and encouragement.

I am grateful to my dear brother-in-law, Rabbi Hershel Weizberg, for his ongoing kindness and compassion that are greatly appreciated.

May Hashem bless me, my wife, and our entire family with the unlimited kindness He has bestowed upon us until now.

Introduction

Considering yourself important is an essential mindset. Feeling good about yourself is a basic human need. Knowing your inner strengths and positive qualities enables you to use them again and again. Acknowledging your past accomplishments and achievements gives you a happier life and enables you to continue to accomplish and achieve much more.

Your self-image creates the quality of your life. Therefore, the goal of this book is to help you continuously build your self-image. As you build your own self-image, you may even have a greater positive influence on the self-image of others.

It takes an entire lifetime to live one's life. Building your self-image is a lifelong process. Throughout your life there will be factors and events that build your self-image, while other experiences do the opposite. The positive and elevated thoughts, words, and actions that you think, say, and do are all part of the process of building your self-image.

Your self-image is your identity. It is how you answer the question, "Who am I?" It is also your answer to the question, "Who am I becoming?" It is your self-concept; your thoughts about who you are.

Your self-image is your general sense of worth and value. It is also how you feel about your many specific character traits and patterns, including the many emotional states that you experience regularly. It is your awareness of your strengths and weaknesses. It includes your accomplishments and achievements, and your plans for the future. Your goals and dreams and wishes are all part of the picture.

Many factors shape our self-image. The way we think important people view us has a great effect on our self-image. Major life events, our daily challenges, and the way we project how our life will be in the future — all these influence our self-image. Friendships or the lack of friends, positive or negative comments from others, and those to whom we compare ourselves, also impact our self-image.

There have been many outside influences on your self-image. But since you are the ultimate chooser of your self-image, how you personally think about yourself is the main ingredient. After you read this entire book, the ideas you have read will be part of your thought process.

As you focus on the thoughts, words, and actions that build you, your choices in these areas will become higher and greater. Your thoughts, words, and actions create your spiritual life. They create your character traits. They create your emotional states, your happiness and joy. The right thoughts, words, and actions will enable you to reach the goals you strive for. They will enable you to live in harmony with others.

Regardless of what thoughts, words, and actions you have chosen before, you can make wiser choices this very moment. Therefore, regardless of whatever your self-image was a moment ago, you can — right now — begin rebuilding your self-image.

Your emotional state or mood at any given moment will influence your thoughts about yourself. When you are calm and happy, you think more clearly. When you are in a good mood, it is easier to be aware of the positive aspects of who you are, the positive things you have already done, and the positive things you can do in the present and future. Throughout the book you will find thoughts and ideas that will be conducive to gaining a greater ability to be calmer and happier.

It is common for people to be told, "Your problem is that you have a low self-image." Such statements usually lower a person's emotional state and make him feel worse about himself.

It would be much wiser and kinder, and more beneficial, for people to say, "You have infinite value and worth. You already know you have strengths and inner resources. But you have even more strengths and resources that you are not yet fully aware of, and they will enhance your life as you become more aware of them. There are many more strengths and inner resources that you can gain and build up from now on. As you keep building your self-image, it will have a positive impact on all your future thoughts, words, and actions. You will be calmer, happier, and more self-confident."

Turn "problems" into "goals." Don't say, "My problem is I have a low self-image, a low self-concept; I lack self-esteem, and self-confidence. I'm excessively self-critical, and have insecure thoughts and feelings. In general, I feel bad about myself." Instead, think, "My goal is to build my self-image, develop a higher self-concept with balanced self-esteem, more self-confidence, and balanced self-criticism. I should have more secure thoughts and feelings, and in general master greater happiness and joy as I pursue worthwhile goals."

Your every thought has an impact on your present emotional state and your entire future. Every positive thought is a tiny piece in the entire picture of your life. Keep traveling in the right direction and you will eventually go far.

Whether or not you choose to continue reading this book, you can think, "I am a person who is in the process of building my self-image." Some might think, "My sense of self is so high and great that I don't need to read a book on the topic." Or some might sigh, "My self-image is so low that nothing I read and nothing anyone says to me can build or raise my self-image."

Those with the high self-image listed above might be right that this particular book is not what they need. But every human being has room to grow and develop. The greater someone is, the more he realizes how much more there is to grow and develop. Even those whose self-image is super great might find ideas and suggestions in this book that will help them build the self-image of others.

And to those who think that their self-image is so low that they can't do anything to build it, my response is, "I disagree." There are positive and elevated thoughts they can think, words they can say, and actions they can take that will automatically lift their self-image.

Every person in the world has a self-image, whether he is clear about it or not. And everyone's self-image is one of a kind. When it comes to reading ideas about building your self-image, you would really need a book tailor-made for how you are feeling at the moment that you are reading it. Sometimes our minds are clear and other times our minds are tired and less clear. Sometimes we feel calm and sometimes we might feel stressed. Sometimes we are happy and sometimes we are not. Sometimes we feel basically good about ourselves and just want to read ideas to add to our positive self-image or help others build their self-image. At other times we might feel bad about ourselves. Sometimes we feel hope and sometimes we might feel discouraged.

Each idea in this book has been helpful for many people. It is impossible to know in advance which ideas and which sections will be what you need most at a given moment. Your mood or emotional state when you read will make a major difference in how you see yourself and how you react to the material. You might read the book one time and not benefit as much as you will after rereading it a second and third time. I hope readers will be encouraged and motivated to continue growing and developing themselves in ways that they personally need the most.

This book has ideas and stories to help you grow. Those who imagine how they can apply what they've read and appreciate the images they visualize will experience positive feelings. They see themselves building their self-image. Some readers, however, might find themselves feeling sad about what they've read, and feel less hopeful or less positive about themselves. They might feel disappointed that they don't feel much better much faster. If this has happened to you in the past, I hope you think many thoughts that give you greater happiness and joy, thoughts that create more hope and empowerment, thoughts that lead to positive accomplishments and achievements, both while you read this book and in the future. Be patient and build yourself little by little. Let this book point you in the right direction, but realize that a long and worthwhile journey takes time. Appreciate each bit of progress.

Many people would benefit greatly from having a personal teacher, coach, mentor, trainer, or an insightful friend who could help them bring out their best traits; someone to help them set and reach positive goals in the important areas of their lives. They need someone to guide them to thinking the thoughts that will increase their level of happiness and joy, their level of confidence and courage, their level of inner calm and serenity. They need someone to help develop their minds and their thinking patterns; someone to help them on the path of continuously building their self-image by upgrading the level of their thoughts, words, and actions. They need someone to frequently ask them, "What could you think, say, and do now to enhance your life even further?"

Throughout your life you will find teachers for further growth and development. You already have had many. Remember what you've already learned from them. Keep your eyes open and you will continue to find more teachers and role models. Make an effort to be around people with positive character traits, positive mindsets; people who speak respectfully, and who act in ways that you admire and respect.

After you read through the book once, go through it again, this time underlining sentences you find helpful. Mark off paragraphs that were especially meaningful to you. Then you can zip through the entire book whenever you wish to review your personalized, condensed, highlighted version.

You are unique. You are the only person in the world who is exactly who you are. The Almighty has not made anyone else like you. Only you have your unique genetic makeup and your unique life circumstances. No one alive now, and no one who ever lived before, and no one who will ever live in the future was, is, or will be just like you. You are the only person in the world with your unique positive qualities and challenges. You are the only person in the world who has your particular life mission.

You, like everyone else alive right now, are a work in progress. You have a multitude of positive choices you can make throughout each and every day. Choose life! Choose positive thoughts, words, and actions. With every positive choice you make, you build yourself. Keep making positive choices.

Your Immense Value as a Person Is a Divine Gift

According to the Torah perspective, you have tremendous value. You are created in the Creator's image (Rabbi Akiva in *Pirkei Avos*, ch. 3). You are a child of the Almighty (ibid). The Talmud (Sanhedrin 37a) states, "You are obligated to say, 'The world was created for me.'"

When you are asked, "Who are you?" let your answer be, "I am a grateful child of the Almighty, Creator and Sustainer of the universe. I am created in His image, and He created the world for me to fulfill my ultimate life mission."

How much is an expensive diamond really worth? What is its true value? To the diamond itself, the whole concept of worth and value is irrelevant. A diamond can't think or feel. When people think about the diamond's value, they really mean, "How would an expert evaluate the financial value of the diamond?" This is not a question about how much the diamond is worth to itself. Rather, it is a question about how much money a buyer would have to pay for it.

However, there is a context to this value. If someone were starving, food would be more precious than a diamond. If someone needed medicine to save a life, the medicine would be worth more. On the other hand, if someone needed something of financial value that is light and easy to carry, the diamond could be worth a lot to him.

Who can reliably assess that value? A diamond appraiser can. But when it comes to the true value of a human being, who can tell us how much that human being is actually worth? Only the Creator!

How much any human being is worth to any other person is subjective. Different occupations are paid different amounts of money. Professional athletes, entertainers, and performers are paid a fortune by those who anticipate financial gains from their talents. Creative geniuses may receive high salaries from the heads of companies who expect to make large profits from their mental talents.

But the amount of money involved is not at all based on how much any given person is worth to him- or herself. It is based on the market value of someone's skills or ideas. You are worth all the money in the world to yourself. Don't let anyone's limited perspective lessen your sense of personal value.

The Almighty's perspective is the ultimate perspective. It is the basis of reality. The real question we need to ask ourselves is, "What does the Almighty consider my true value to be?"

From the Almighty's viewpoint, the answer is, "You are My child and you are precious. You are created in My image. In essence you are a Divine Soul. I have created the world for you. Your entire being and your value are a gift from Me. When you see yourself from My perspective, you know that you have infinite value. Your intrinsic worth is greater than anything that can be measured materially."

Some people are experts at putting themselves down. They keep saying derogatory things like, "Who am I anyway?" "I'm nothing special." "I have a low self-image because I'm a nobody." "I don't see myself living a meaningful life."

There is a story about a man who came to the rabbi of a synagogue and said, "Rabbi, I have a request to make. Can you please make me a kohain so that I can enjoy the special rights a kohain has in the synagogue?"

"I'm sorry," the Rabbi replied. "I can't make you a kohain."

"But, Rabbi, I'll pay you $1,000 to make me a kohain!"

"I would like to help you out," the Rabbi said, "but I have no way to make you a kohain."

"Rabbi, I will make an offer that I don't think you will be able to refuse. I will give you $50,000 if you make me a kohain."

"I'm sorry, but I can't make you a kohain no matter how much you offer me," said the Rabbi. "But I'm curious. Why is it so important for you to be a kohain?"

"You see," said the man, "my father was a kohain, and my grandfather was a kohain, so I want to be one also."

He doesn't need to do anything special to become a kohain, because one is born a kohain if one's father is a kohain.

The same concept applies to having immense inner value and worth. Anyone who is born a human being automatically has tremendous value and worth. You don't need to be born with a high I.Q. or have a brilliant mind to have infinite value. You don't need to amass money or property, or have great skills and talents, or accomplish great accomplishments. You exist; therefore you have unlimited value.

If the knowledge that you have inherent, immense value is just an abstract idea and you don't actually feel that you have infinite worth, what can you do? Make this knowledge a basic part of your self-concept by calmly and gently repeating many times, "Who am I? I am a being created in the image of the Creator. I am a child of the Almighty. The universe was created for me. The Almighty loves me. Each and every day, I will think, speak, and act in ways that build my character and my self-image."

If you repeatedly say this with strong emotion every day, eventually this idea will be internalized. It will be a foundation of your sense of self, even if it was an abstract concept when you first started.

Some people may repeat it a few times, but when they don't see immediate results, they give up. "This won't work," they claim. Or they think their negative self-image is so strong that repeating positive messages is "just fooling myself. I am really a nobody. Repeating words doesn't make me feel better about myself."

People who keep putting themselves down usually have done so many times over a long period of time. They need patience and persistence. They need to continue to repeat this message over a long period of time: "Who am I? I am a being created in the image of the Creator. I am a child of the Almighty. The universe was created for me. The Almighty loves me. Each and every day, I will think, speak, and act in ways that build my character and self-image."

You do not have the right to decide your own value. The Almighty has given you value as a gift. The gift is yours, whether you claim it or not. Your awareness of this value will make an immense practical difference in all aspects of your life.

Each and every day, gain a greater realization that you are a child of the Creator and are created in His image. Every blessing you make adds to this awareness. Every prayer you say adds to this awareness. Every mitzvah you do adds to this awareness.

Knowing that you are a child of the Creator makes you recognize that greatness is stored in you. You have the ability to become a person who thinks, speaks, and acts in ways that bring out more and more of your awesome potential.

Don't needlessly limit and block yourself from being all that you can be. Don't wrongly assume that you can't be a magnificent human being with refined character traits. Don't mistakenly think that your awesome brain's billions of neurons can't learn and know a massive amount of knowledge and wisdom.

The way you think about yourself creates who you are. The way you think about your happiness and joy, your confidence and courage, your intellect, and your potential talents and skills, creates your self-image. Be open to more and more possibilities for yourself. Be willing to develop yourself and your self-image tiny step by tiny step.

Maintain self-respect at all times. Keep your composure even when things don't go the way you would have wished. Let the thoughts you think, words you say, and actions you take throughout each day build your character and your self-image.

Be willing to meet the challenges of life with heartfelt prayer and trust that the Almighty, your Father and King, Creator and Sustainer of the universe, will lead you along the path that you wish to go (Makos 10b). You choose the road to your life's mission and destination. Make a profound decision to choose a fulfilling and meaningful life. This decision will become your self-image. Besides creating a great life for yourself, you will have a positive influence on many other children of the Almighty.

> *Someone once came to me with the complaint, "I have a serious problem. I consider myself to be worthless. I'm not very bright. I have a poor memory. I'm not talented or skilled. Almost everyone I know is better than I am in many ways. I feel bad about myself most of the time. I've tried to accomplish, and I've failed*

over and over again. How can I possibly feel good about myself when I am so inferior to others?"

"Can I ask you a few questions?" I asked him.

"Of course," he replied. "If they are too difficult, I probably won't be able to answer them. But you can ask."

"If someone grew up on an island that was far from civilization and found a priceless antique washed ashore after a shipwreck, how much would he consider it to be worth?"

"Not very much," he replied.

"And if no one told him that a certain museum would pay over $3,000,000 dollars for this antique, could he possibly guess its financial value?"

"Certainly not."

"Did you ever hear about the Native Americans who sold the island of Manhattan for a few dollars worth of trinkets?"

"Yes, it's considered one of the most undervalued evaluations of all time."

"And have you ever heard about publishers who didn't realize the potential value of manuscripts that eventually sold millions of copies in book form?"

"A number of times."

I replied, "Even if everything you told me about yourself is true, you are making a colossal mistake. I would love to discuss this with you and show you how you already have much more potential than you can imagine. But even if you don't want to talk about that now, I must say that you are underestimating yourself even more than those people who underestimated the value of Manhattan.

"The islander in the first story didn't know the value of the antique he found, because he didn't have the data necessary to evaluate its worth. If he had spoken to the curator of the museum, he would have had greater knowledge and he would have had a more accurate awareness of the antique's value. Anyone reading about Manhattan today would have a greater appreciation for the value of its real estate."

I continued, "Studying the Torah concept of the Almighty's perspective of the value of each and every human being will give you an inkling of the great value you and every other human being actually have. Once you realize that you aren't qualified to evaluate how much you are worth, you will open up to the immense potential of your true worth.

"Since the Torah concept is that the entire world was created for each and every person individually, your value is greater than that of all the billions of galaxies in the universe. This is mind-boggling.

"Once you realize that you have such awesome worth as a person, even without accomplishing any more than you have already accomplished, you will be much more open to recognizing many of your hidden strengths that you will begin to reveal to yourself and others as you become aware that they are there," I concluded.

"You have given me much food for thought," the fellow acknowledged. His face and his body language now expressed the sense of self-worth that he always had had a right to feel. He had needed this bit of encouragement to make a major difference in his life.

Becoming an Honorable Person

Someone always treated with great respect and honor could easily consider himself honorable, especially if he was treated this way since he was a young child. Even then, new and old acquaintances all treated him with tremendous respect. He was told by everyone he met, "You are special. You are important. You are honorable." Again and again he heard, "You are an important and honorable person now. You have been important and honorable from the day you were born. And you will always be an important and honorable person."

This individual will have integrated and internalized, "I am important and honorable." If someone were to try to put him down in any way, it would be easy to respond, "That person is wrong. I know that I am important and honorable."

The Sages in *Pirkei Avos* (4:1) define the honorable person as "someone who shows honor and respect to other people." They are teaching us that it's not how other people treat you that makes you important and honorable. Rather, it's how you treat others.

When you realize that every human being is created in the image of the Almighty, you realize that right from birth every human being is important and valuable. By being respectful to other human beings, you add to your self-respect. You recognize that when you treat others with respect, you are expressing respect to the Creator.

Each time you speak to someone with honor and respect, you become more and more honorable. What is making you more honorable? The way you treat others. This is an ongoing process that you continue daily.

Many people feel better about themselves if they have a very expensive house or car, or make a large profit in a smart business deal. You can feel better about yourself by treating other people with respect and honor, especially when it is difficult to do.

Some people feel better about themselves if they win a sports championship game, appear on *The New York Times* bestseller list, have a banquet in their honor, or receive a standing ovation for a difficult achievement. "I am a champion," they each proclaim to all who will listen. You can feel even better about yourself by treating other people with respect. And you don't need to boast about this to others.

Others feel good about themselves only after winning an Oscar, Pulitzer Prize, Nobel Prize, or important election. All you need to feel better about yourself is to treat other people with respect.

Treating everyone with respect makes you honored and respected by our Creator. Any human honor pales in comparison to being considered honorable by our Father, our King, Creator and Sustainer of the universe.

The more people you respect, the greater you become.

Imagine that everyone you meet wears a sign saying, "Please treat this child of Mine with great respect. Your Father, Your King, Creator and Sustainer of the universe."

What does it mean to treat other people with respect and honor?

Think of the times you've noticed people being treated and spoken to with respect. How do you speak to people you greatly respect? What do you do to treat them with respect? Speak to many more people this way, and treat many more people this way.

You will become more aware of the potential of each and every person, and know that they can continue to develop themselves further. Your belief in others will make it easier for them to believe in themselves. When you treat other people with authentic respect, you will have a positive influence on their self-image. They will see themselves in a more positive light.

After you consistently treat other people with respect, your self-image can be, "I am considered an honorable and respectful person by my Father, my King, Creator and Sustainer of the universe, because I treat other people with respect."

> There was a fellow who went around complaining, "I don't get the respect that I deserve. It's awful and disgraceful that people don't understand how great I am. They don't give me the respect that someone of my caliber should receive."
>
> The poor fellow thought that if he whined and kvetched enough about not getting respect, others would say, "Yes, this person should really get more respect. Let's all treat him with much more respect."
>
> But the fellow's strategy was failing. Instead of respecting him, people began to pity him.
>
> Someone sincerely wanted to help this person out. He approached the complainer and said, "Can I be straight with you about how I see the situation you are in?"
>
> "Of course you can," the fellow responded.
>
> "You want to be treated with more respect, don't you?"

"That's exactly what I've been telling everyone."

"If you want to fix a situation and you go about doing it the wrong way, what do you think will happen?"

"It obviously won't work."

"Whining and demanding honor and respect won't get you what you want. I strongly advise you to stop telling other people that you aren't receiving the respect you feel you deserve. Stop focusing on whether or not others are respecting you. Instead, make it a high priority to speak to others with respect, whether or not they to speak to you with equal respect. Keep this up for at least a month and come back to me with the results."

A month later the fellow who used to complain about not being respected reported, "I wouldn't have believed it if I hadn't experienced it myself. As I treated more and more people with respect, I found it became less important that others treat me with respect. I actually experienced more pleasure in treating others with respect. And even though I didn't demand respect at all, others treated me better than ever before. I'm grateful for your suggestion."

There are many people who would gain by following in this person's footsteps.

Why We Need to Feel Good About Ourselves

The essence of human beings is the Divine gift of value and worth; every human being is important. When we feel bad about ourselves, we are cut off from this sense of value. But when we feel good about ourselves, we are more open to realizing this sense of value and worth.

When we feel good about ourselves, we speak and act on a higher level. We have more harmonious interactions with others, are more cheerful, and act as better friends.

When you are in the presence of people with a Torah awareness of their own greatness as children of the Creator, people who have an authentic love for kindness, you may feel emotionally and spiritually uplifted yourself. And as you develop and create this inner consciousness as your constant attitude, you may become a source of light and life for others, too.

Sometimes a person might feel bad about himself because of wrongs that he has committed. He focuses mainly on those wrongdoings and therefore considers himself to be a much worse person than he actually is. This can cause a person to become depressed and discouraged. This takes away the joy of doing mitzvos. However, even when someone feels bad for doing too many wrong things and not enough good things, he can still feel positive: He has a high sense of his own value. This will balance out those negative feelings and add to the motivation to stop doing wrong from now on.

Anyone can right his wrongs by doing teshuvah now; he can repent for those wrongdoings. As we will write later on, when one sincerely repents out of love for the Almighty, the Talmud states that those bad deeds are retroactively transformed into being considered good deeds.

A person who has done bad things in the past should resolve to do much more good in the future than he would otherwise have done. He should ask, "What can I do to make amends?"

The Torah (Vayikra 25:17) prohibits us from insulting people and causing them pain with words. This, says the Talmud (Bava Metzia 58b), is worse than financially cheating someone. If someone steals another person's money or otherwise causes monetary loss, the harm is outside of the person. If someone causes another person pain with words, he is hurting and belittling that person, which is more painful than a financial hit. That person is likely to feel that his self-image has been lessened. This takes a person away from feeling his Divine value and worth.

Embarrassing a person in public is considered an even worse crime (Baba Metzia 59a): The Talmud equates public humiliation to murder. Why? When the person feels the intense distress of being belittled when others are present, his self-image might be temporarily destroyed. He may feel worthless. Outside of physical pain, this is the most excruciating distress that a person can feel.

People worry about the many ways that others can lower their self-image. They're afraid others will disapprove of them, look down at them, or make fun of them. They're afraid of being laughed at, of "making fools of themselves." They're afraid of looking different from others, or of being embarrassed by a parent, teacher, or classmate in front of others. They're afraid of speaking in public and not speaking well. They're afraid of being considered unimportant, unliked, and unloved.

Beginning at a very young age, people appreciate being praised. Children smile and feel good when they are told that they are good, that they are smart, that they are "big," that they have done well, that they are important. Telling children these things builds their self-image. They feel good about themselves. Human beings always need to feel good about themselves.

A number of years ago, I heard a guest lecture by the head of a Chassidic yeshiva. He was known as an exceptionally brilliant scholar. Everyone who attended that lecture smiled widely when he said in passing, "I can live for two whole weeks on a good compliment." Many people of his stature would be embarrassed to say this in public. I think that he wanted to encourage his audience to make sure to praise other people.

People boast to feel good about themselves. They want others to know something positive about them. They want to feel important. It is only a rare human being who feels so important that he doesn't need anyone else to say that he is important.

Someone might even boast, "I don't need anyone else to say anything positive about me." But why did he feel a need to say it?

Some people won't boast about themselves, but they will tell you how special their children and grandchildren are. They will tell you how special their students are. They will tell you how great and grand the groups, institutions, and organizations that they are affiliated with are.

When a young child says that he is three-and-a-half, four-and-a-half, five-and-a-half, he is making a statement. "I am big. I am not just four or five; I am so big that I have another half added to my age." Never make fun of children who say this. They have a valid need, and so does every other person you meet.

The need to feel good about yourself is a highly powerful motivator. Much of what people do in life comes from this motivation. People use different items or events to help them feel good about themselves. Some are motivated to accomplish a lot, attend prestigious schools, be considered knowledgeable, receive excellent grades in school, and win elections. Others want financial wealth, a large house, an expensive car, and clothing that others will admire. Still more are motivated by other displays of honorable status.

It is highly problematic and counterproductive to make seeking honor and praise a goal in itself. There is much in Torah writings about the harm and danger of depending on honor and praise given by others (see *Gateway to Happiness*, pp. 268-292). The ideal is to do good for the sake of the Almighty. The ideal is to realize your own value and worth to such a strong degree that you don't need to be honored and praised to feel good about yourself. But this is a level that takes mature thinking to reach.

Living life with a Torah outlook on the meaning of life and the great importance of every human being will automatically bestow upon a person a healthy sense of self. But building one's self-image is not an ultimate goal in itself. The goal is to fulfill the will of the Almighty. The goal is to accomplish positive accomplishments, each person in his own way.

> *When Rabbi Simcha Zissel of Kelm would wake up his young children in the morning, he would gently say to them, "Children, wake up. You have a kingdom to rule. The Almighty gave humans command over the entire creation" (Hameoros Hagdolim, cited in Growth Through Torah, p. 144).*
>
> *I once told this story to someone who responded, "That's what I have been doing wrong. I have been way too stern and severe with my children. I have come across as a tough army sergeant. I would say to them. 'Get up! Don't be lazy. Hurry up or you'll be late!'"*

A number of days later, the fellow called me up to tell me, "The next day I spoke to my children in a loving, cheerful tone of voice and I said, 'My beloved precious children, the Almighty loves you and I love you. Good news! It's time to wake up. I wish you a happy and joyful day. We want to be on time, so let your great energy flow and let's start the day off right.'

"My children thought that I had flipped out. But they smiled. When I repeated this the second and third day, they were in much better moods in the morning than they had been in a long time. I used to blame them for dawdling and going too slow. I now realize that the way I think about the situation and the way I talk creates the emotional atmosphere."

The Importance of Considering Yourself Important

Considering oneself important is one of the most important mindsets that a person can have. As Rabbeinu Yonah, author of *Shaarei Teshuvah*, wrote in *Shaarei Avodah*: "One who wishes to elevate himself must be aware of his own self-worth, and recognize his stature and his ancestors' stature. Awareness of the greatness of his ancestors gives an incentive to reach their level of greatness. He doesn't want to embarrass them by doing anything improper. He will say to himself, 'I am too great and important to lower myself to do this wrong act.' If a person is unaware of his value, it is easy for him to behave in a lowly manner."

Let the words, "I am important and therefore I must speak and act in ways that reflect my intrinsic importance" resonate in your mind. This is meant in an elevated, spiritual way, not an arrogant or narcissistic one.

"A person is obligated to say, 'The world was created for me' (*Sanhedrin* 37a), and 'When will my deeds reach those of Abraham, Isaac, and Jacob?' The Torah requires us to be aware of our greatness. Feel proud that you are created in the image of the Almighty. Pride in the awareness and elevation of your soul is not only proper, but is actually an obligation. It is a binding duty to recognize your virtues and to live with this awareness" (*Toras Avraham*, p. 49).

The great Chassidic master, Rabbi Aharon of Karlin, said, "If a person does not consider himself an 'important person,' he will not free himself from his negative habits" (*Dor Deah*, vol. 1, p. 167).

In *Gateway to Happiness,* p. 116, I wrote, "What people believe about themselves and their abilities serves as a self-fulfilling prophecy. Believing oneself to be inferior, untalented, unimportant, or incapable influences one's actual abilities. One's self-concept greatly determines what one can actually do. If you view yourself as unable to do things, you will be unable to do them. On the other hand, if you see yourself as talented, capable, and important, your self-concept will open up powers and talents that would have remained dormant had you thought of yourself in lesser terms. We have the ability to change our self-concept. Therefore, Rabbi Aharon of Karlin advised people to consider themselves as important, which enabled them to strive for greater accomplishments. Hardly anyone utilizes their entire capabilities. Most people use a low percentage of their potential, and could accomplish much more than they realize. By deciding you are capable of accomplishing more, you will accomplish more."

I wrote this twenty-three years ago. With more life experience, I have a much stronger appreciation of what Rabbi Aharon of Karlin told us.

"Negative character traits come from discouragement. People with faulty traits do not think of themselves in elevated terms or as being distinguished. They think they do not have the inner strength and potential to reach elevated levels and virtues. Only when people recognize they have the potential to reach the most elevated levels will they strive for greatness" (*Hashlamas Hamidos*, p. 3).

The Chazon Ish once told a close student who was very humble, "It would be preferable if you had a bit of conceit. This would help you fight fatigue and laziness. It would be preferable if you would use both your good and bad inclinations" (*Toras Hanefesh*, p. 99).

The Chazon Ish himself was very modest and humble. The advice to that student is a lesson that can be very helpful to many students. This doesn't mean that someone should rationalize his own conceit by claiming that the Chazon Ish said it was all right. Rather, each person needs to know himself; he must consider which character traits to use to a greater or lesser extent. It might be helpful to ask oneself, "If I were speaking to the Chazon Ish, would he tell me to be more modest, or would he say that I need a little more conceit?"

Rabbi Moshe Rosenstein of the Lomza Yeshiva said, "Only a person who inwardly feels good about himself will be able to fulfill the commandment of 'love your neighbor as yourself'" (*Ahavas Meisharim*, p. 109).

People who have feelings of inferiority and frequently feel bad about themselves need to strengthen their sense of self. They need to build their self-image. Having modest self-confidence will enable you to be kinder to more people.

The classic mussar book *Chovos Halevavos* reads: "The type of humility the Torah advocates comes only after you realize how elevated you really are. Then there is value to humility. A lack of this awareness is not a virtue, but a major fault (6:2)."

Rabbi Yehuda Leib Chasman wrote, "Your awareness of your worth is not a contradiction to the obligation to be humble. Humility is not a lack of awareness of your positive accomplishments and abilities. Only a fool is not aware of who he really is, and this is not humility. Humility is the internalized awareness with every fiber of your being that everything you have is not your own. Rather, it is a gift from the Almighty who bestowed His kindness on you. The more a person actually feels that what he has is a gift, the greater his humility" (*Ohr Yahel*, vol. 3, p. 93).

Rabbi Elchonon Wasserman was asked if his teacher, the extremely humble Chofetz Chaim, was aware of his own greatness.

"Yes," Rabbi Wasserman replied. "Although the Chofetz Chaim was imbued with humility, he nevertheless frequently said he personally has the responsibility for the spiritual welfare of his entire generation" (Ohr Elchonon, vol. 1, p. 64).

Study the biographies of the great Torah scholars Rabbi Moshe Feinstein and Rabbi Yaakov Kamenetzky. They were both humble but realized that they were great in Torah knowledge. If you had the merit of being in their presence, you felt their greatness and elevation along with their modesty. They had modest self-confidence, a quality that even young people should emulate.

"The Almighty Loves You"

"The Almighty loves each person more than each person loves his own self" (*Shmiras Halashon*, vol. 1, ch. 2). This statement by the saintly Chofetz Chaim gives us a powerful message for our self-image: "I am a person who the Creator and Sustainer of the entire universe loves and considers valuable."

What do people who love themselves do? We take care of our needs. We drink when we are thirsty. We eat when we are hungry. We do what we can to get what we want. We spend much time thinking about what we can do to make ourselves happy and live a good life.

People spend much of their life trying to earn the money that they hope will enhance their lives. They spend years trying to learn the skills and talents that will get them the jobs that will help them earn money. People spend a great deal of time trying to improve the quality of their homes and dwelling places. Why? Because they care about their own well-being and want to do what they can to feel better. Even people who don't value themselves properly still spend much time and energy trying to improve their lives. They do what they can to be more comfortable.

This is because human beings care about themselves. People are important to themselves. People love themselves.

Parents love their children. They are committed to spending an enormous amount of time and energy on the welfare of their children. This is unconditional love in action.

The Almighty's love for you is unconditional, infinite, and eternal. How would you feel if you recognized that the Eternal and Infinite One loved you? The feelings would be indescribable. Even a tiny amount of awareness of what this would mean would be magnificent.

As you reflect on what it means to be loved by the Almighty, let these feelings become a part of your self-image. If you ever question your basic sense of extreme value and worth, challenge it. Remember, "The Almighty loves me. The Almighty considers me valuable and important. Even if at present I don't feel worthy, who am I to argue with the Almighty's unlimited perspective?"

There are some people who feel so extremely bad about themselves that they feel a sense of self-hate. A person who feels self-hate needs to make it a high priority to change that hate into love. Adopting the Torah awareness that each person is loved by the Creator and Sustainer of the universe can start them on a path of self-respect and balanced self-love. "If the Almighty loves me, I have a right, even an obligation, to love myself as a child of the Creator."

Someone with negative feelings towards himself should pray to the Almighty, "My Father, my King, Creator and Sustainer of the universe, I pray that You grant me love for You, for all of Your children, and for myself, Your child." Even people with very positive feelings towards themselves can elevate themselves with this prayer.

Every time you enter and exit a house with a *mezuzah* on the doorpost, you have a reminder of the Almighty. You have the ability to develop the habit of thinking, "The Almighty, Creator and

Sustainer of the universe, loves me. I am created in His image and I am His child." This way you will have frequent reminders of this lofty, image-building thought.

> Someone once told me that when he was a young child his father frequently said to him, "You are valuable and precious. You are important to me. You have infinite value. The Holy Creator loves you and so do I."
>
> He heard this hundreds of time. His father would sing it to him as a lullaby to help him fall asleep at night.
>
> This young boy had a learning disability and had a rough time in school. During those days, many teachers weren't yet aware of how to teach children with learning disabilities. A number of teachers verbally humiliated this boy. The other children often made fun of him.
>
> Although he found the comments of those teachers and those boys highly distressful, he would repeat to himself, "I don't care what they say; they are wrong. I am valuable and precious. My father said so, many times. My father told me that the Creator loves me. If these people would have any sense in them, they would understand that I am important, and they wouldn't speak to me this way."
>
> Growing up with an inner appreciation for his great value and worth, this boy had a high spiritual soul. His level of love for the Creator was extremely high. His love for others as children of the Creator helped him become someone who loved to do kindness for others. The pain and distress he suffered from others gave him a great sensitivity to help save others from distress any way that he could.
>
> Some people develop resentment and negativity towards others if they grew up being humiliated as young children. This boy developed differently because his father frequently expressed his love and connected it with the love of the Almighty. This boy grew up with a highly developed self-image that enabled him to feel much empathy and care for others.

"I Am a Soul With a Body"

Some people identify more with their body but know that they have a soul. Other people identify more with their soul and realize that they have a body.

When someone realizes that he is a soul with a physical body, his spiritual identity has a major impact on how he lives his life. His connection with the Almighty is a major element in how he sees himself, in how he views the purpose and meaning of his life, and in what gives him a sense of fulfillment and satisfaction.

We need to nourish our bodies to stay healthy and alive. We need our bodies to carry us though this life. We need to nourish our souls for our eternal well-being. Those who realize that they are souls with bodies make it a higher priority to nourish their souls.

In everyone's life many dilemmas will arise: "Should I do this or that?" "Should I say something or not?" "What are my highest priorities and what are much lower priorities?" "How should I spend my time right now?" "Should I do this act of kindness for someone who needs it, or should I do what I was planning to do to have a good time?" Someone who sees himself as a soul with a body will resolve these dilemmas in a much more elevated and spiritual way.

People who identify themselves with their bodies are more concerned about their body image. How they will look to others seems like a tremendously high priority. Everyone wants to look presentable, but a person who considers himself just a body will want to look better than others, as an ego issue.

A person who identifies himself with his soul will take good care of his body to keep it safe and healthy, but he will keep his main focus on nourishing his soul. A person who sees himself as being a soul, someone who has a body just for the duration of his stay on this planet, will tend to view other people as essentially being souls also. This will raise his view of others. He will automatically treat others with greater respect.

The more you see yourself as a soul with a body, the higher your self-image will be. Who am I? "I am a soul who is living in this world within my body."

When you don't know what to do, ask yourself, "What course of action would my soul want me to choose?"

> When I met someone at a wedding whom I hadn't seen in a while, he seemed totally different. Because he knew that I cared about him and his welfare, I felt comfortable asking him about what had inspired him to become a more spiritual person.
>
> "There is one major thought that has made an incredible difference in my life," he told me. "I now view myself as a soul. My body is just along for the ride."
>
> I asked him if he could elaborate, so he added, "There is hardly anything in my life that is the way it used to be. Everything about me feels different. I used to care way too much about trivial, material things. Then I heard someone describing himself as being a soul with a body, and I realized that it would be wise for me to adopt the same mindset. I greatly admired and respected that person, and if he acted the way he did because he identified himself as a soul, I, too, would try it.
>
> "I feel that a tremendous amount of needless pressure has melted away. I used to worry a lot about money and about having all the things that I felt I needed. Now that I identify myself as a soul, I still need some money, of course, but material things seem less significant.
>
> "My praying has become a very important part of my life. It's much more important to me now to nourish my soul. My likes and dislikes have a much higher spiritual component. The inner happiness that I now experience is way beyond anything that I experienced before I saw myself the way I do now."

Build on What You Did Right

I have heard one of my favorite self-image building stories from the student himself and I have repeated it in public to many teachers.

There was a fifteen-year-old student who was studying in a yeshiva in Jerusalem. The boy was bright, but he tended to be a bit dreamy. He didn't concentrate as well as he potentially could.

At the beginning of the school year he earned a fifty percent grade on a weekly test in Talmud. The teacher called him over, and the boy expected the teacher to reprimand him for not doing well.

Instead, the teacher said to him, "You received only a fifty because you only answered half the questions on the test. But let me show you how wonderfully you did. Look at what you answered for question number five. This was a difficult question and you answered it excellently! Look at what you answered to question number fourteen. You understood the intricacies of the entire section, and you explained yourself very clearly. Keep up the good work."

The boy felt good, but didn't change. The next week, the boy again received a fifty on the weekly Talmud test. The teacher called him over. The boy thought, "Now the teacher will really let me have it for not doing well."

To his surprise, the teacher said to him, "Your mark was only a fifty because you didn't answer all the questions on the test. But look at how well you answered the questions that you did answer. Look at question number six: Your answer shows a complete grasp of the material that this question asks. Look at question number nineteen. You explained the complex Tosafos with total clarity. Keep up the good work."

This time a major transformation occurred. The boy said to himself, "I see that I do have the ability to understand what we are learning in class. I need to focus better in class when the teacher is explaining the lesson. I also need to review what we learned a number of times. I believe that I have the ability to understand what we are learning in class."

The next week, the boy focused well during the actual class. The entire week he diligently reviewed the material that was covered in class. At the end of the week, when he received the results of the test, he had scored one hundred percent. He had answered every single question correctly. The same thing repeated itself with the next test, and the next test, and the next test. After four straight hundreds, his self-image was totally transformed.

He now realized, "I am someone who understands all that we learn when I concentrate and review."

That fellow is now married with a nice family. He is considered a scholar by all who know him. When he first entered the large Mirrer Kollel, he received a perfect score on a difficult test.

How long did it take for that insightful and clever teacher to totally change the student's self-image? Just a couple of minutes, two weeks in a row.

"I didn't realize how much that teacher's remarks helped me until a year or two later," the beneficiary of that teacher's wisdom told me. "It was amazing what it did for me. I now try to help other students with the same pattern that this teacher applied with me."

All parents and teachers can learn from this. Please note that the teacher did not say, "What's the matter with you? If you can answer some of these questions, why can't you answer all of them that way?" This approach would probably not have been helpful. It focuses on criticizing the student. The approach the teacher used was inspiring and motivating. If focused on what the student did right.

The parents of that student had a very positive attitude towards their son. "But that was too global for me," the student explained. "The reason the teacher's approach was successful was because he pointed out specifically what I did right. I saw it clearly, right before my eyes."

We can all do this for ourselves. You can build your own self-image by noticing what you do well. "Since I see that I can do this well, then there are many more things that I will be able to do well, too."

There was a rabbi who consistently brought out the best in people. When people would tell him that they saw themselves in a negative light, he would ask them these questions:

"What do you like about yourself?"

"What do other people like about you?"

"If you would have greater self-mastery, what would you like about yourself?"

"What are your highest dreams and aspirations for yourself? Don't be shy about saying what you really would want. If you would actually be, do, and achieve all that you would wish, how would you be?"

Then he told the person he was speaking to, "Every day, pray for the Almighty's help in being all you would wish to be. Then feel good about yourself because you want to be that way. A sincere effort to improve is immensely valuable. Keep up these prayers each and every day and you will find yourself becoming more like you wish to be."

> *Someone told me, "I used to have an extremely negative self-image. I looked at myself as a person with a huge amount of faults. I didn't have a fraction of the Torah knowledge I wished to have. My praying wasn't as focused as I wanted it to be. I wanted to improve and develop my character traits, but there were so many details that I still needed to work on. I found the entire process so overwhelming that I felt lost.*
>
> *"I spoke to a rabbi known to bring out the best in those who consulted him. I told him about how bad I was feeling about myself, and he put me at ease right away. This is what he told*

me. 'You are very sincere about learning Torah and developing your character traits. Your situation is not so bad; rather, you are looking at the whole picture in a way that is excessively self-critical.

"'Imagine that you are climbing a tall mountain. One way of making the climb is to keep telling yourself how high you still have to go, how tired you are already, how uncertain you are about getting to the top, and how slow your progress is. Constantly complaining about the weather and the food, and voicing other negative thoughts, are guaranteed to make the entire climb distressful. Can you see how thinking these thoughts will ruin the entire climb?

"'Now imagine that you decided in advance to enjoy the trip. You appreciated every aspect of the climb, and focused on progress. You thought about what you accomplished already, and other positive aspects of the trip. After each step you said, "I can celebrate another step towards my destination. I am enjoying all the effort I am putting into this. As I look back, I feel great about the amount of progress so far. Since I made this much progress already, it means that I will be able to keep making more and more progress."

"'The thoughts create a positive or negative way of looking at things. It's all up to you. Keep building on what you did right. This way you will keep making more progress your entire life and you will be creating a joyful life for yourself.'

"After my talk with that rabbi, I gained a much greater awareness that I choose what to focus on. From then on I resolved to focus on my progress and on how much I have accomplished, with a total commitment to keep developing myself my entire life. This new way of looking at my life situation totally improved my entire outlook on life. Instead of being stuck on the thoughts of how far away I was from where I wanted to be, I focused on thoughts of appreciation and gratitude for all the knowledge I had already gained, for how I was already working on my character traits, and for how grateful I was for the opportunity to keep developing myself."

What Can I Do to Improve Today?

Throughout your life, you are writing your autobiography through all that you do. You are in the middle of writing the story of your present and future life. Your current self-image tells the story about yourself until now. Since you are still in the middle of this life story, at any given moment you can speak and act in ways that elevate the story of your life and make it more meaningful. You can choose to do much more good than ever before, become more spiritual, gain wisdom, be kinder, influence others, and refine your character traits. The positive things that you can do now revise the entire picture of your life.

Each minute, hour, day, week, month, and year, you write new sentences, paragraphs, pages, and chapters. The positive choices you make, what you think, say, and do, add self-image-building content to your entire life. Every entry in your autobiography adds to the entire picture. Many entries make just minor additions. At times, an important entry can change the entire picture of where you are now and what direction you are headed.

At this very moment, and at every moment, you have the ability to make great choices. What will you say and which actions will you take to positively impact your own life or the lives of others?

We all have many positive qualities, traits, and behavior and thought patterns, and we all have faults and deficiencies. It's important to identify with your positive qualities. For a positive self-image, focus on what you already do right and keep developing yourself further in these areas. Resolve to correct your faults; self-improvement is a lifetime project.

Focus on reaching your goals. What is important for you to accomplish? Like many people, you may need to improve your ability to focus on your highest priorities. In order to reach the goals you most want to reach, clarify the areas you need to improve.

A valuable question to ask yourself each and every day is: "What can I do to improve today?" Early in the day you might think of some specific things to improve that day. You might want to enhance certain thoughts, words, and actions.

Throughout the day, you might find yourself in various situations that give you opportunities to develop in some way. Different challenges might arise that could help: You might meet someone today from whom you can learn something valuable. Speaking to this person and gaining from his knowledge and experience can help you improve and grow. Or you might come across an article or book that could help you improve. What you read could have a very positive impact on your life.

Not thinking about improving might cause you to overlook a great opportunity to move forward. By asking yourself frequently, "What can I do to improve today?" you focus on improvement, and you pay attention to things you focus on.

If you ever think detrimental thoughts, ask yourself, "What can I do to improve today?" Those negative thoughts could serve as positive reminders that you want to improve yourself.

Just making this question a habit will enable you to improve in many ways. Now that you are thinking about asking yourself, "What can I do to improve today?" you are already on a path of improvement.

As you make this question a habit, your self-image can be, "I am a person who frequently asks myself, 'What can I do to improve today?'"

One way to constantly improve is to frequently imagine yourself being the way you wish to be. Keep repeating this vision. Make your mental pictures colorful with intense emotion. Make these pictures so real that you feel them.

Visualize yourself being a joyful, kind, courageous, self-confident, enthusiastic person who reaches goals. Visualize yourself being a patient, serene, harmonious person. Visualize yourself being a grateful person with a great self-image.

One of the main ways to constantly and continuously grow and develop your positive qualities is to apply your knowledge and wisdom. Every time you apply what you know, you add to your self-image: "I am a person who applies more and more of what I know."

When you ask yourself, "What can I do to improve today?" add the question, "What new knowledge and wisdom can I apply today?"

As you continue to apply more of your knowledge and wisdom, you improve the entire story of your life. Let this thought motivate and inspire you to be and do more.

> *"I am a procrastinator," someone once told me. "I keep thinking that about so many important things to do that some of the more minor things don't get done. I feel guilty about not doing some of them, and this was always on my mind.*
>
> *"Then you told me about the benefits of asking yourself, 'What can I do to improve today?' It was really helpful: I thought of my common procrastinating pattern and decided to take care of a few items on my to-do list. Even before I actually did those things, I immediately felt better about planning to do them. They were no longer just minor and trivial things that I had to do. Rather, now I viewed them as things that I would be doing in order to improve myself. I felt great."*

"Thinking Pattern" Versus "Having"

Let's look at two sentences: 1: "I have a low self-image," 2: "The way that I'm thinking limits me and makes me feel bad."

There's a great difference between the two.

People who think in terms of "having" a low self-image might think that a "low self-image" is something they actually "have." They might see this as a description of who they actually are.

We "have" a heart, a brain, lungs, hands, feet, and so on. These are "things" that we actually have. They are part of our body. Someone might also "have" the flu, a strep throat, or an ear infection. These are illnesses that one might "have." A person might "have" a house, a car, a telephone, a pen, and a book. Here the word "have" refers to something we own. However, when it comes to the way we view ourselves, "have" refers to our patterns of thinking.

One might think of oneself in a positive or negative way. When we view this as a "pattern of thinking," it is much easier to improve the situation. We don't have to change what we have or who we are; we need to improve the way we think of ourselves. As we do this, we will be more open to speaking and acting in ways that help us accomplish more and feel better.

For example, a person might feel that he lacks a sense of importance and worth. It's easy to see why he might say, "I have a low self-image." But if he realized that this is a pattern of thinking, he also can realize that it would be beneficial to think, "Right now I don't think of myself as having sufficient value and worth. Instead, I focus more on what is wrong with me, rather than on what is right with me and how I can continue to improve. What can I think, say, and do that will enable me to increase my sense of value and worth and build my self-image?"

Let's repeat the last sentence: "What can I think, say, and do to increase my sense of value and worth and build my self-image?"

Repeating this thought many times strengthens your resolve to think and act in a way that leads to a better self-image.

Realizing that the entire issue of self-image is an issue of thought, we can and should commit ourselves to improving our thinking. Throughout this book, you will find ideas to help you "think your way" to a better self-image. And once you know these different, positive patterns, you will be more aware of other ideas that can continue building your self-image, ideas you read, hear, and think of yourself.

People frequently ask, "Why do I have a low self-image?"

There are many possible answers that one can give, even though there is only one valid and real answer: "If you have a low self-image, it is because of the way you think about yourself. Think better thoughts and you'll change your self-image."

People have given many reasons to justify "having a low self-image." If you feel that you have a low self-image, see if any of your reasons are included below:

- "My parent(s) didn't believe in me."
- "My parent(s) believed in me so much that I became discouraged and gave up, because I could never fulfill their expectations."
- "I was treated badly."
- "I was ignored as a child."
- "Someone told me, 'You have a low self-image.'"
- "I know people who are brighter and more successful, and I look down on myself for being less than they are."
- "I don't have some talents or skills that others have."
- "I am dissatisfied with the way I look, or the way that I'm afraid others think I look."
- "I keep focusing on a handicap that I have."
- "People around me have verbally put me down."
- "I didn't have friends."
- "I felt rejected."
- "I was very different from the other people around me."
- "It's my physical appearance."
- "An older sibling made fun of me."
- "I was younger than my siblings."
- "Others laughed at me."
- "My accent is funny."
- "I was called bad names."
- "I lost a number of games and decided that I'm a loser."
- "I considered myself stupid."
- "I had more life challenges than others."
- "I'm shy."
- "I'm afraid to speak in public."
- "I'm obsessive-compulsive."
- "My teachers didn't believe in my potential abilities."
- "I received low grades in school."

- "My many fears hold me back and limit me."
- "I've made many mistakes."
- "I feel guilty about the past."
- "I shared a problem with someone, especially someone in authority, and I was told, 'Your problem isn't really this or that; your real problem is that you lack self-esteem.'"
- "I was always around people who didn't have high aspirations. Without a role model for accomplishing more, I keep accomplishing less."
- "I was told, 'You have a low self-image because of heredity. You were born with low self-image genes.'"
- "I was told that I'm like someone else who has negative traits."
- "I'm a perfectionist and I'm never perfect."
- "I wasn't good in sports and in my school (or neighborhood), sports were the key criteria."
- "I felt I had a poor memory."
- "I was told that thinking positively about myself would be considered arrogance and conceit."
- "Someone read a book or article on self-hate and told me that I have some of the symptoms of self-hate." (The same people forgot to tell you that you also have some of the symptoms of positive feelings about yourself.)
- "People who were envious of me had a vested interest in putting me down so they could raise their own self-image."
- "I have an angry spouse."
- "I'm very emotional and others see this as a major fault."
- "Even though I'm very bright and intellectual, I don't have the type of emotions I wished I had."
- "I had great plans that didn't work out the way that I'd hoped."
- "I lack the patience necessary to master ideas and skills. I give up, thinking that I'm not as intelligent as I would like to be."
- "Even though I have many skills and talents, I lack some that I wish I had."
- "I can't sing well."
- "My memory is not as good as I wish it was."
- "I don't have as much money as some other people do. Even though other people might have less, I still look down on myself."

- "I don't have any money at all and think that money is what gives a person a sense of self-worth."

Even if these statements are based on partial truths, thinking of yourself in a consistently negative way is the only way to have a low self-image. Improving your thoughts improves your self-image.

The way you think of yourself now is your present self-image. Regardless of your past self-image, you have free will and the ability to build yourself and your self-image.

There is a tremendous feeling of relief to be free from the debilitating effects of "having a low self-image." It is one's personal *"Yetzias Mitzrayim"* to let go of negative thoughts about oneself.

People who say they "have a low self-image" might be referring to their usual behavior patterns. Thinking of the positive behaviors, instead of believing they "have a low self-image," will be much more beneficial and will change the way they look at themselves. They should decide to speak and act in better, higher, and more elevated ways.

Even a person with many positive behaviors and actions can look at himself in an inferior way. Therefore we need a total package. We need to change our patterns of thinking, our patterns of speaking, and our patterns of what we do and don't do.

Some people who say they "have a low self-image" might be referring to a lack of confidence and courage. Confidence and courage are attributes that we can all improve by changing our thoughts, words, and actions. When we raise our level of confidence and courage we will feel better and do more, and we will build our self-image. These are both very important qualities to develop, and each one will be dealt with in separate sections of this book.

Some people "have" a low self-image, and find that nothing helps improve it. In that case, they may benefit greatly by not thinking about the entire topic of self-image for a while. That's right: Don't think about self-image at all. There's no obligation to think about it.

There is much to gain by focusing on the positive actions they can do without considering their self-image. Most people lived their lives this way in the past. Not thinking about a negative self-image frees their minds to think about developing positive thought patterns, such as gratitude and appreciation for all the good in their lives. Instead of feeling bad about who they are, they think about things in the past and present for which they are grateful, thereby increasing their general level of happiness.

> A number of years ago, someone told me, "I used to feel awful about myself. I would often complain, 'I can't imagine feeling better about myself. I have many faults. I haven't accomplished a fraction of what many people I know have accomplished. I frequently make mistakes. Even if I do feel happy every once in a while, I know it won't last because of who I am. My self-image stays low. I heard about how self-image is a key part of who you are. I can't do anything about my height, my fingerprints, and many other characteristics. A low self-image is one of those integral parts of me. Even though I try, I see that I can't do very much to change it.
>
> "Someone said to me, 'After talking to you about trying to improve your self-image, I see that nothing I am telling you is changing your self-image.'" He suggested that I stop thinking about my self-image for the next two months and added, "I know this will very difficult for you. But every time your mind thinks about your self-image, move your thoughts to positive, general things you can do. Don't do this to improve your self-image. If you do, then it will be easy for you to convince yourself not to feel better. Just live your life in a normal way, without considering your self-image.'
>
> "I argued, saying that it's not easy for someone like me to stop thinking about my self-image. He told me that he agrees that it won't be easy for me to stop thinking about my self-image. But if I build up the habit of switching my thoughts to more enjoyable topics, eventually it will become easier for me to master this habit.
>
> "The first week was a constant battle. I kept thinking about my self-image. But since I had agreed to follow this person's advice, I changed the focus of my thoughts again and again. The more times I did it, the more I realized that even though it was difficult, I was able to do it!
>
> "Not thinking about my self-image was like taking a great vacation. I began feeling better. I wasn't feeling better about myself, but I was feeling better.

"That person called me up a number of times to encourage me to keep changing my mental channels. He told me to make a list of many topics to think about; any positive or even neutral topic that had nothing to do with my self-image could go on my list.

"As time went on, I saw the benefit of not focusing on my self-image at all. After the two months that I was committed to do this, I had a stronger realization that what I had been saying so many times—that I have a low self-image—wasn't something that I needed to keep focusing on. I saw that this was just a pattern of thinking that I had become accustomed to repeating. I gained a greater awareness that self-image was just a pattern of thinking, and that I didn't really have to think about it at all to function well in my life.

"Not thinking about my self-image for two months made it seem less of an issue. I had made it a higher priority to focus more on gratitude and the positive things that I could do.

"Instead of focusing on my self-image, I ended up doing and accomplishing more positive things and feeling much more happiness in my life."

Emotional States Go Up and Down; Self-Image Can Be More Stable

The feelings and emotional states that one experiences can fluctuate. Many internal and external factors influence our emotions, including how rested we are, the weather, and the quality of background noise. (Listening to your favorite music and songs will raise your emotional state, but annoying, loud noise will cause distress.) Whether we were just successful or unsuccessful changes our mood; being treated well also does. Whether we just made or lost a lot of money, and whether we were recently praised or insulted, impact our emotional state, too.

Feelings during any given day can vary greatly. With some people this is more drastic and pronounced. People who view their self-image as the way they feel about themselves can easily find that their sense of self is similar to a roller coaster ride. Some of the time they feel tremendously high, and some of the time they feel tremendously low.

Stabilize your self-image by seeing it as a Torah idea. You are always a child of the Creator, created in the Almighty's image, even when you feel awful. Therefore, you are always valuable and important. Remember that you have already done many positive things in your life, and will do many positive things in the future.

"But if I experience failure and loss, won't that lower my self-image?"

It can only lower your self-image if your subjective thoughts let it. Instead, decide that your self-image will be based on the Torah concept of your infinite worth and value. You might feel bad that things didn't work out the way you wanted, or you might recall that each life challenge is an opportunity to develop your character. But your feelings after a failure do not reflect on your ultimate value and worth. Focusing on this will enable your self-image to remain high, regardless of how various events unfold.

When teaching self-development, I like to focus on four factors: Goals, Traits, Emotional States, and Self-image. The initials of these factors are: G.T.S.S.

Goals are all the many things that you wish to do and accomplish in your life. You have major life goals and minor ones. When you have a positive self-image, your goals will be higher and you will be more likely to reach them.

Your *traits* are your patterns of thinking, feeling, speaking, and acting that create the positive qualities of happiness, kindness, courage, patience, serenity, enthusiasm, harmony with others, and gratitude.

Your *emotional states* are your feelings at a given moment. Your states are not the totality of who you are; your states are how you feel. Even if you feel miserable, you are not a miserable person. You have intrinsic value of immense proportion, regardless of how you happen to feel.

Someone once told me that he is such a miserable person. I responded, "You are not a miserable person. You are just in distressful states because a frequently angry person mistreats you. *You* are a kind and compassionate person. Now let us work on improving your life's situation." Years later, he told me that this had a tremendous effect on building his self-image.

Your brain's billions of brain cells store every positive state you ever experience. I recommend "collecting" positive emotional states by naming them as you experience them. Labeling the positive states stored in your brain makes it easier to connect with those positive states at will. This is a skill that can take time to gain. But you can have a positive self-image whether or not you master this skill.

Your self-image is your sense of identity, the way you describe yourself. It is the way you answer, "Who am I?" Your feelings about yourself might vary depending on the emotional state you are experiencing, but your basic view of yourself can consistently be, "I am a valuable human being, and it is up to me to live my life in a way that brings out the best in myself."

When you think about your self-image in the context of these four factors, it makes it easier to realize that your emotional feelings may rise and fall or be high and low; you will feel good at times and bad at others, but your self-image is in a different category. It is the category of *states* that changes, not your self-image. The category of self-image is a statement of your mindset about your basic value and worth. Remember that your value and worth are always high.

> *"Some people make me feel good about myself and some people make me feel bad about myself," someone told me. "I feel a bit silly that my self-image flip-flops so drastically."*
>
> *I said, "Your problem is that you see yourself the way others happen to see you. You feel good when people see you in a positive light. But these good feelings are not just feelings for*

you, because they become your own vision of yourself, putting you at the mercy of others. Those who have an ayin tovah — a good eye — will see you in a positive way. But those who tend to focus on the negative and what they can criticize will see you in a negative way. The way they speak to you will make you feel uncomfortable. Since you easily see yourself the way these other people see you, around them you feel worse about yourself.

"To consistently see yourself more positively, realize that your essence is valuable and worthwhile. Different people speak and act towards you in various ways. Some make you feel good and some make you feel bad. Your feelings in the presence of these people will change. But your self-concept can and should always be positive."

A while after this conversation, the fellow said to me, "I now realize that I was confused about the topic of self-image. I mixed my feelings together with my actual thoughts. While it was actually my feelings that were frequently changing, I thought my entire self-image was twisting and turning. Now that I am trying to view my feelings separately from my thoughts, it is easier to me to keep my self-concept positive. I have a goal: to feel better even in the presence of critical people. But even when I do feel bad about what they say and how they say it, I realize it is a matter relating to my feelings, not to my entire sense of self. This makes it much easier for me to rebound and gain a more objective look at myself.

"Based on what you told me, I also have gained a greater appreciation for my fluid emotional nature. While this does make me more vulnerable to fluctuations in how I feel at a given moment, it also gives me special strengths that colder personalities lack. I feel the distress of other people on a deeper level, which gives me a greater level of compassion and understanding. I can read people better and enter their world to a greater extent than many others. Because of this tendency, I am able to help many people in ways that I wouldn't be able to if I didn't have such a deep emotional nature. My goal is to gain greater mastery over my emotional states. But knowing that my temperament has many advantages when it comes to being kind and caring makes it much easier for me to handle the extra challenges."

Act the Way You Wish to Be

There is a basic principle found in the writings of the Rambam (*Hilchos Daos*) and other classic Torah sources about turning ourselves into what we want to be. The principle can be summarized as: "Act the way you wish to be and you will become that way."

We human beings are influenced by our actions. Take, for example, someone who wants to become a kinder person. By doing many acts of kindness over time, the person actually becomes a kinder person. Even if the person doesn't consider himself to be kind at the start, after many kind actions, he will authentically become kind.

Each day write down at least ten positive actions that you did. Write down kind words and acts, blessings that you said mindfully, and other things that you did even though they were hard to do. Write down when you felt grateful, and when you refrained from saying something that would cause another person distress. Write down an encouraging telephone call that you made.

What will happen when you are resolved to write down ten positive actions each day? You will go out of your way to do them. There are always ten positive things you can say or do or think. This will have a cumulative effect on your self-image. You will know that you are a person who does these positive actions.

When it comes to being confident and courageous, some people feel that they need to "really" be confident and courageous before they can act and speak that way. Others know that it's possible to *act* brave even without really *feeling* brave. The self-creation rule is: Act the way you wish to be. After acting that way over time, you self-create yourself.

When it comes to having a positive self-image, some people feel that first they must already have a positive self-image before they can speak and act the way a person with a positive self-image would speak and act.

There is some truth here. Self-image is based on your thoughts. So to actually be a person with a positive self-image, you need to think the way a person with a positive self-image would think. But you may start behaving like someone with a positive self-image would behave, even before you actually think of yourself in a positive way. Keeping this up over time will teach you that you have what it takes to be a person with a positive self-image.

Start to speak and act the way you would if you already had a positive self-image. Even if it is difficult for you to speak and act this way in the beginning, force yourself to do it.

You can keep repeating to yourself, "I will speak and act the way I would if I already had a positive self-image. Speaking and acting this way will help me build my inner feelings of actually having a positive self-image."

As you speak and act positively, you have a choice of how you will view what you are doing. Some individuals might say to themselves, "I am speaking and acting like a person with a positive self-image, but I don't really have a positive self-image. I am speaking and acting like a person who has a high level of self-confidence, but I don't really feel self-confident." Someone who keeps on thinking this way is negating the mental strengthening accomplished by his positive speech and behavior. That is the power of thought. Negative thought works against someone, while positive thought works for that same person.

It's better for a person who starts off feeling this way to say, "I see that I *can* speak and act like a person with a positive self-image, like a person who has a high level of confidence and courage. The more frequently I do it, the more this will become who I actually am. As I keep this up, I will keep building my self-image."

Every time you repeat self-image building sentences, you will be conditioning your mind. Your thoughts and actions are working in harmony to build your self-image. You can repeat, "Every time I speak and act like a person with a positive self-image, I am building my self-image. Every time I speak and act as if I had a high level of confidence, I become a more confident person."

The principle of speaking and acting the way you wish you were can also be worded, "act as if."

As in, "Act as if you had a great self-image."

When you keep acting "as if" you had a great self-image, it will eventually be your natural way of being.

Speak and act "as if" you were highly confident and courageous. Over time, this will increase your authentic level of confidence and courage.

Speak and act "as if" you were a joyful, kind, and serene person. Over time, this will make you a more joyful, kinder, and serene person. Be patient and you will actually become more patient.

This principle is also called "pretend."

"Pretend that you have a great self-image, and speak and act that way." As you keep "pretending" you have a great self-image, you will eventually make it true.

When you interact with others in challenging situations, pretend that you are highly self-confident and courageous. Be self-respecting and respectful of others the entire time. Keep this up and you will actually become that way.

Some people need to keep "pretending" and acting "as if" for longer periods of time before it becomes automatic and spontaneous. Then they integrate and internalize this way of thinking, speaking, and acting.

There are individuals who find that after a relatively short period of time of acting "as if," and "pretending," they already feel they are actually changing.

Regardless of how short or long it takes until "pretending" works for you, it's worthwhile to speak and act this way. You will gain tremendously just knowing, "I am a person who *can* speak and act the way I wish to be. Since I can speak and act like a person with a positive self-image, I might actually be better than even I realize."

The reality is that as soon as you can "act as if" and "pretend" to behave a certain positive way, you really and truly have the ability to do it. One act of confidence and courage means that this behavior pattern is now stored in your brain, and your brain is always with you. Some people realize this faster and sooner than others.

Some people need positive feedback to believe that they really have increased their level of confidence and courage. Someone might spontaneously say to such a person, "I see that you're really brave." In the "old days" he might have argued, "I'm really not." But after realizing that he really has this confident and courageous pattern in his repertoire of behavior, he will be able to say, "I might not have seen myself this way before, but clearly I have the ability to be this way now."

Some people who might be envious or a bit mean might comment, "You really aren't like this. You are just speaking and acting this way."

I would *like* to suggest that the recipients of these attempts at putting them down retort, "And you aren't really envious or mean, you are just speaking and acting this way." But since that wouldn't be the way to win friends and influence people, it's better to say, "When you study the Rambam you will see that speaking and acting in a positive way is the way to integrate and internalize a positive pattern." And it could be much better to say, "You're right. This pattern isn't my automatic pattern yet. My goal is to keep it up and little by little there will be progress."

Since we have the free will to choose our present thoughts, words, and actions, we therefore can choose positive patterns in a moment of a profound decision. Then, when we continue the positive pattern every day, the neural pathways in our brain make this behavior more automatic.

Some people claim, "I'm not a very good actor. I can't just act like a person with confidence and courage. I can't just act like a person with a positive self-image."

It is true that some people seem to naturally have greater acting abilities than others. But the vast majority of young children are skilled at acting. Most three-year-old and four-year-old children "act" when they play with their toys and their dolls. They can play "make believe" with great skill. You were once three and four years old. Most likely when you were too young to be self-conscious about the way you acted, you were able to speak and act like the way you wanted to play.

You can still play as if you were a great actor, if you will stop judging yourself. Don't make any negative comments and just act like a person with a great self-image. Do this for a few minutes when you are by yourself.

Say to yourself, "I can act like a super-confident, empowered person. I can speak like this when I am by myself. I can raise my hands and say out loud to myself, 'I am a person who can choose to speak and act the way I wish' when I am by myself."

Keep repeating this until you sound convincing.

When you feel comfortable doing this when you are alone, you can keep practicing and mentally seeing yourself being this way when you are around others. One day you will feel confident to do this in the presence of others. If it goes well, then you will know with greater clarity that you can be this way. If it doesn't go as well as you wished, then you can continue practicing and visualizing.

If you claim that you can't act this way, you should realize that you are just *acting* as if you can't do it. I'm positive you really can. All human beings can. Because you've acted another way for so long, you've convinced yourself that you can't act this way. But it's only an act now, too. And the reason you are so convincing is that you've repeated this negativity often enough that you believe it. Stop playing this limiting role. For just a short while, play the role of someone who can speak and act like a person with a positive self-image. Just play this role for three or four minutes. If that's too long, do it for two minutes, or for thirty seconds. But keep doing this over and over until you are ready to say to yourself, "I see I can do this for thirty seconds."

Once you are able to speak and act as if you have a great self-image for even thirty seconds, you will have this pattern stored in your brain for a lifetime. And since your brain is always with you, you can repeat this behavior pattern many times.

Your self-image will then be, "I am a person who can speak and act as if I had a great self-image for a short time."

Let me share a secret with you. If you can consistently speak and act as if you have a great self-image, and you are happy that you have received the gift of being able to have it, you'll always be able to enjoy playing this role throughout your life. It won't matter if you can "really" do this, or if you can just feel happy that you can play the role: You will always be able to speak and act this way, with inner good feelings.

Imagine if you had a great personal coach who would constantly be there to whisper inspiring, encouraging, and empowering messages in your ear, reminding you to speak and act the way you wish to be. This great coach believes in you and knows that you have great abilities. This would make it much easier for you to be the way you wish to be. Your inner mind knows what you want to be like. Let the whispering of your inner mind inspire, encourage, and empower you.

> *I've asked many people how they developed a positive self-image.*
>
> *I told someone with the most positive self-image that I was writing a book on self-image. "You probably always had a positive self-image," I said to him.*
>
> *"What makes you think that?" he asked me.*
>
> *"Your positive way of being looks totally natural. You don't look like someone who is trying to seem more confident and self-assured than you really are. You probably grew up with a positive self-image."*
>
> *"I'm afraid that you're wrong about that," he replied. "I had a strong inferiority complex. Years ago, someone I shared this with retorted, 'You don't have an inferiority complex. You are inferior!'*
>
> *"That was a cruel joke. I felt very down about myself, and this statement just added to my feelings of being inferior. A sentence I once heard from a rabbi helped me: 'You become the way you act.'*
>
> *"I repeated this to myself over and over again, 'You become the way you act.'*
>
> *"This was a turning point in my life. I wanted to become much more than I already was. I made a list of the ideal traits and qualities that I wanted to make my own. I decided to behave the way I would if I actually had these behavior patterns. I kept this up for many years. I enjoyed the process and I saw progress. I appreciate that you say that my self-image looks natural. It is spontaneous now. I'm sure that anyone who acts the way he wishes to be and keeps it up will successfully become more like his ideal."*

Upgrading Your Identity Will Have a Global Positive Effect

Every individual has many positive qualities and strengths, as well as faults and weaknesses. Be aware of your positive qualities. Identify yourself with them. The more you identify with what you already know how to do and what you do right, the more positive your identity will be. Then look at each fault and weakness as something that you plan to overcome.

Like ducks, we are different in different elements. When a duck walks on land, it does so awkwardly and slowly. When a duck swims, it becomes more elegant. And when a duck flies, it becomes a beautiful sight. The duck flies or swims much faster than it walks.

If a duck would judge itself only by its walking ability, it would see itself in a limited way. But the duck also has the ability to swim and fly! You might be deficient in some areas, but you have other strengths. Let those strengths raise your view of yourself.

Your mindset about what you are able to do in life will have a global effect on your entire way of being. Most people view their perceived limitations as real. The reality is that every single person has a tremendous amount of potential.

When you believe that you can do something, you will be able to do more and better than when you believe you can't. Although it's possible to believe that you can when you really can't, you will never know which are real limits and which are imaginary limits until you try to make breakthroughs.

Some business consultants have a full range of marketing expertise that can improve their client's bottom line. Some businessmen know how to expand their profits, but other business owners need to hire consultants. Most people limit their financial possibilities on their own. By expanding the awareness of what they could be doing, consultants show their clients how to gain more in less time.

The same applies to expanding what is possible for you when it comes to developing yourself and your self-image. You will gain tremendously when you expand your knowledge and self-image in important areas such as developing your character traits, mastering your emotional states, studying and remembering, concentrating and focusing, bringing out the best in yourself and others, and influencing or motivating yourself and others, among many other important areas in your life.

When you do positive actions, allow them to improve your mindset about yourself. Every time you are successful at doing something, let it add to your self-image. Every time you receive sincere, positive feedback, allow it have a global positive effect on your identity.

Some people start off in life with a needlessly low self-image. They might have had excessively critical parents. They might have compared themselves with other children who outdid them in various ways. They might have had a sibling or neighbor or classmate who was envious of them and purposely said negative things to put them down. They might have found it difficult to make and keep friends. They might have been very different from others in their environment. They might have had health and physical challenges. They might have had unrealistic expectations for themselves and therefore always felt that they were inferior.

When someone has a negative self-image, it is easy to think that others look at him more judgmentally than they actually do. When others laugh in his presence, it's easy to think that they are making fun of him. When others make a slightly negative remark, it is easy to think that they meant it in a much stronger and deeper way than they actually did. When others don't include him in their games and activities, it is easy to feel distressfully rejected, way out of proportion to what really is going on. Mistaken assumptions are wrong, but they still can have a very negative effect.

When negative self-thoughts have been going on for a long time, the negative mindset seems like reality. A person who grows up with this inferior attitude doesn't view it as just the thoughts he happens to be thinking. Rather, he views it as the reality. He thinks of himself as unworthy, insecure, and having less value than others.

Having strong negative feelings about oneself can be such an integral part of a person's identity that it isn't easy to help him raise his self-image. Not realizing how strong these negative thoughts and feelings are, some people might say positive things, but those positive messages don't register.

Some people might discount the positive statements of others by claiming:

- "This person doesn't really know me. If he did, he wouldn't be saying these positive things about me."
- "This person is just saying this positive statement to be nice. But he doesn't really mean it."
- "Yes, I do have some positive qualities. But my faults and mistakes are so many and so strong that they greatly outweigh the positive aspects."
- "This person isn't very insightful. He could say these good things about me only because he doesn't realize how inferior I am."

When this person improves his general sense of identity, he will realize that he has needlessly thought less of himself. He will realize that looking at himself so negatively wasn't an accurate view. Rather, it was a bad habit, and bad habits can sometimes last for a long time.

- Many events can inspire people to take the major step out of negativity to realize that they're basically better than they had imagined: Someone might do such a positive thing that he finally says to himself, "Since I did such a positive thing, it shows that I really am much better than I thought."
- Someone might hear so much positive feedback from others that, over time, the sheer weight of those positive statements adds up.
- Someone might meet a wise and insightful individual who sincerely tells him that he sees many positive qualities or a few major ones. This person is highly credible and the positive picture he paints changes the negative self-image.
- Someone might realize that he created his low self-image with immature thoughts when he was younger, and it doesn't make sense for him to use his childish thinking as his present reality.

- Someone might decide, "My negative way of thinking was valid for the way I was when I was young. Now I am totally dedicated to changing my way of thinking, speaking, and acting. Now I am creating myself in new and better ways."
- Someone might read a book on the topic of self-image and realize that some of the ideas make so much sense. He would recognize that he is a work in progress, constantly creating himself and his identity. Since he is the sum total of his choice of thoughts, words, and actions, he decides to revise his view of himself.

Many perceived limitations and blocks are only imaginary. But an imagined limitation or block still limits what one actually is able to say and do. Since these limitations are only imaginary, use your imagination to picture yourself going far beyond those unnecessary limitations. The new, upgraded, positive pictures about what you will be able to do create greater potential for you. Spend time visualizing yourself being the positive person you wish to be. Let your developing mental pictures become part of your self-image. As you improve your self-image in this way, you will find that your thoughts, words, and actions will enhance your life.

Human beings are infinitely changeable. You are a human being; therefore, you are infinitely changeable. This classic form of logic is true for all human beings and it is true for you.

When you speak to credible people who believe in your abilities more than you presently believe in yourself, you will find it easier to modify your own picture of your capabilities.

Think of people you consider highly successful. They might be people you know well, or have once met, or have read about or heard of. They might be successful in an area that is not important to you, but the very fact that they were able to excel teaches you that you too can excel in your own endeavors.

People who became billionaires on their own had to raise their sights high and keep doing whatever it took to reach that level. Most likely wealth is not your personal goal. But when you search for Torah knowledge, character excellence, and high spiritual attainments with the same drive and motivation, you will greatly expand your own level of success.

As you improve your mindset about who you are, you will notice more and more positive changes in your life. Look for them and let them register. Then you will have a greater awareness that you have actually raised your self-image on a deeper inner level.

> *Someone told me that he had read about raising the financial mindset of wealth, and it was very helpful in raising his spiritual and character trait identity.*
>
> *He read that people who won large amounts of money in lotteries or suddenly inherited wealth still thought about themselves with their previous financial mindset. Even though they knew that they now had a lot more money than ever before, they still thought like people who didn't have very much money. They made poor investments. They wasted large amounts of money. And much sooner than they would have thought, they had financial difficulties.*
>
> *If someone earns his money a little at a time, the slow process of building wealth becomes part of his mindset. Step by step he begins to consider himself wealthier and wealthier, and this becomes an integral part of his thinking. But some people who suddenly become wealthy still view themselves as not being wealthy. Those who are able to change their mindset and think, "Now I am a wealthy person," are able to make wiser decisions about how to save their money, and how to spend it in a way that makes the money last for a long time.*
>
> *My acquaintance realized that when he made spiritual and character trait advances, it was important for him to develop his mindset as well. He needed to realize that his self-image was growing. The old, limiting mindset was outdated. The progress he made in his life was an integral part of who he was now and he needed to internalize this information.*

Your Best Moments Are Your Best Teachers

Your best moments are your best teachers. We each have moments that are special in our lives, moments when we go beyond what we are usually able to do. Moments when we are especially spiritual and elevated, self-confident and courageous, happy and joyful, kind and compassionate, calm and serene, persuasive and influential, insightful and intuitive, forgiving and understanding, and creative and innovative.

During our best moments, we go beyond our own selves in almost unbelievable ways.

Each best moment in our life sheds light on what we can possibly do and who we can possibly be. Our best moments raise our self-image to a degree that our ordinary moments can't and don't. There are many stories of how in emergencies some people exhibit qualities that are usually hidden even from themselves. Mothers lifted cars to save their children. Individuals were quick-witted to save themselves or others from potential harm or danger.

In the field of athletic achievements, world records are broken all the time. For the rest of their lives, even if the athletes never repeat their record-breaking achievements, they are known as the holder of the record. It was their best moment. It wasn't a moment that they could repeat over and over again, but it becomes part of their self-image. "I am the person who did this outstanding feat." The first person who climbed Mount Everest solo didn't do it as a weekly activity. But after one time, this was his self-image: He could do what no one had done before. And this self-image stayed with him his entire life.

We all have our "I can"s and "I can't"s. There are abilities, skills, and talents that we know we know and we know we can do. There are other abilities that we feel that we can't do. Every time you transform an "I can't" into an "I can," you raise your self-image. After enough transformations, you will have a greater understanding that whenever it's important for you, you will be able to turn an "I can't" into an "I can."

Be aware of some best moments that you have already experienced. Because that best moment was out of the ordinary for you, you might not yet have added the significance of that moment to your ongoing self-image.

Make your best moments part of your identity.

Look back at your life history: Which best moments can you now add to your self-image? "I am a person who once…" We aren't referring to boasting about this to anyone else; we are talking about viewing yourself regularly as a person who was able to do what you actually did. This will help you realize that you will be able to do even more special things in the future.

Think about some great things you can do now or in the near future to make a breakthrough about your self-image. Even if you do this just once, you now have this accomplishment as part of who you are. "I am a person who did this difficult feat."

I had heard that to be a student of the great Torah scholar, the Vilna Gaon, one needed to repeat the first verse in the book of *Divrei Hayamim* for four hours straight. The enthusiasm in reciting this verse needed to be continued with the same passion as at the beginning of the four hours. The first verse contains just three words: the names Adam, Shais, Enosh. For some people, repeating this verse with a steady level of enthusiasm for four hours will be four hours well spent.

The great teacher Rabbi Praida repeated a lesson four hundred times to a student who was especially slow. Perhaps you can find someone to repeat a lesson to four hundred times. You could repeat a lesson four hundred times to yourself! Think of something that you would be willing to repeat to yourself four hundred times. Then this feat is added to your self-image.

Regardless of *why* you do something, if you did it, that means that you were *able* to do it. People do all kinds of strange things to get into the *Guinness Book of World Records*, in order to build up their egos. If they would do something strange just to build up their own self-image, they wouldn't need to try to get into a record book. So it makes sense that if you do something difficult just to build up your self-image, after doing it you have a personal right to add that accomplishment to your own list of personal "records."

Be on the lookout for future best moments. This can serve as an added incentive to do things you usually consider too difficult to do. Now that you are doing this for the lasting, positive effects of a personal breakthrough, you will have the extra motivation to do things you had considered too difficult.

When you want a special lift, ask yourself, "What would my best moments tell me right now?"

Review your best moments; now feel the inspiration of those moments uplift you and allow you to speak and act with the elevated and empowered thoughts and feelings of those moments.

> *I suggested that an acquaintance think of something constructive to do to create a special achievement. He decided to read twenty biographies of great people. He was usually a slow reader and found it challenging to concentrate for long periods of time. He usually wouldn't have had the patience to read twenty biographies, but since he wanted to add this achievement to his self-image, he read with much greater focus and concentration than usual.*
>
> *After finishing the twentieth biography, he felt tremendous. For him, that was a major achievement. Now his self-image was, "I have these twenty biographies stored in my brain."*
>
> *Having the life stories of twenty great people stored in his brain had a very positive influence on him. His next goal was to read fifty biographies of great people.*

If You Were to Meet Hillel and Rabbi Akiva

Imagine what it would be like if you were to meet Hillel and Rabbi Akiva. They both were highly elevated, spiritual scholars who treated everyone with great respect. Regardless of who you were and what you had done or not done, they would have treated you with the ultimate respect.

Hillel taught us to be a disciple of Aharon, Moshe's older brother and the first High Priest. Aharon treated everyone with tremendous love and respect. Treating people with respect motivated and influenced them in positive ways. They said to themselves, "If Aharon treats me with this degree of respect, it means he sees me in a positive light. I need to elevate myself to deserve this treatment."

Rabbi Akiva taught that every human is precious because each one is created in the Almighty's image. Rabbi Akiva saw the good in every situation and he saw the Divine in every person.

If you ever feel bad about yourself because someone didn't treat you with the proper respect, imagine what it would be like if you had just had an encounter with Hillel and Rabbi Akiva. They would have spoken to you in a way that would help build your self-image. Allow yourself to feel the positive feelings you would have experienced after talking to them.

Although we can't really meet them in person, we have their wisdom recorded in the Mishnah and the Talmud. From them we can learn how to treat other people with tremendous respect. This way we will have a positive influence on the self-image of people we encounter.

I have often imagined what an encounter with the Chofetz Chaim would have been like. My father, of blessed memory, was a student of the Chofetz Chaim in Radin. The Chofetz Chaim sent him on a special mission to Grodno to convince the owner of a factory to keep it closed on Shabbos. When he returned and reported that he had been successful, the Chofetz Chaim patted him on the cheek and said, "So young and so clever." These few words had a major impact on my father. As he would tell me about this incident, he patted his own cheek the way the Chofetz Chaim did to him. These were a few seconds that lasted a lifetime.

> Someone once remarked to me, "After hearing about imagining an encounter with Hillel and Rabbi Akiva, I thought to myself, 'Let me imagine how I would feel if I would have been a guest at the home of Abraham and Sarah. They would have both greeted me, "Welcome, my dear grandchild. It's such a pleasure to have you as our guest. Let us see what we can give you to eat and drink." My soul soars when I reflect on what that experience would have been like for me and my self-image.'
>
> Which great individuals of the past would you want to speak to for inspiration and for raising your self-image? What do you think they would say to you?

Every Shabbos Can Build Your Self-Image

Shabbos is a weekly celebration of the creation of the universe. When we observe Shabbos each week, we increase our recognition that the Almighty created the world. The Talmudic opinion adds to the depth of this appreciation: Each person is obligated to say that the universe was created for him. It's not merely that the world was created, but that it was created for me. The vast universe is my universe. Every single person has a right to think this way. This gives us a glimpse into our true stature in the world. It also obligates us to plan to make the world a better place for others in our own, unique way.

The realization that "the vast universe with all of its billions and billions of galaxies and billions and billions of suns in each galaxy was created for me" is so elevating that nothing in our tiny planet can compare to this lofty thought. Everyone else can have this thought also. The world was created for each one of us to meet our life mission.

People celebrate many things in life. But any celebration is relatively small and minor compared to the ultimate celebration: Celebrating the creation of the entire universe.

On Shabbos we gain a greater appreciation for all the specific aspects of creation in our planet. We are grateful to the Creator for the mountains and oceans, flowers and trees, animals, birds, and fish, fruits and vegetables, and all the raw materials that are used in building homes and other structures, among other things.

Every single Shabbos you have another opportunity to gain a deeper appreciation of the fact that you are tremendously valuable and important. You celebrate the creation that is yours to enjoy. The fact that others also benefit and gain from creation can add to your spiritual awareness that you are happy for the good fortune of others.

Each and every Shabbos your self-image can expand. "This Shabbos I am gaining an even greater awareness that the vast universe and all of the beneficial things on our planet were created for me. And I feel happy that others also benefit."

> *"Someone suggested that I rejoice that others also benefit from the world," a student told his rabbi. "But this really took away from some of my pleasure. I'm not special. The world was created for others also. They too benefit from the sun and the water and the food and the flowers. I feel bad that I don't feel happier for the happiness of others."*
>
> *"Your feelings are the normal feelings that a person will have until he works on developing more happiness for the happiness*

of others. The very fact that you feel bad that you aren't happy for others is a positive step forward. You realize the ideal and you wish to experience it.

"I suggest that you turn your highest aspirations into a prayer. Pray to the Almighty, 'I wish I could feel happy for the happiness and joy of others. Please grant me the feelings that I wish I had. I realize that others are Your children also. Let me experience pleasure because You are bestowing Your kindness to all your children.'

"As you pray this prayer in your own unique way, you can feel good that you are praying for more elevated feelings."

Building Your Self-Image One Tiny Step at a Time

There are special occurrences, situations, and opportunities that help build your self-image in a short time. However, it is more common to improve one tiny step at a time every day than to have quick progress in this area.

The daily question to ask yourself is: "What small improvement can I make now?"

You might be able to improve in one area a little bit by a little bit every day. Or you might have a few different areas where you could improve a little bit each day.

Your areas of improvement could include studying Torah, concentrating on prayer, performing kindness, or developing various character traits. Or you might strengthen areas of confidence and courage, happiness and joy, being calm and serene, or any other qualities that you wish to keep developing.

Add every small improvement and development to your total sense of identity and self-image. When you regularly improve yourself, you will have a self-image of, "I am a person who regularly keeps improving myself."

Focus on the improvements that you are making. Let those improvements register in your mind. Allow yourself to feel positive feelings for those improvements. Consciously add each small improvement to your self-image.

Even someone who feels that he has a long way to go will see that he is making progress. Instead of having a self-image of, "I am far from the way I wish I was," the self-image will be one of growth and development.

When you want to help others build their self-image, don't suggest that they set a goal that appears too far from their current state. It might appear unrealistic and overwhelming. Your suggestion might be ignored because it seems far too difficult. But when you suggest a tiny bit of improvement, it's more likely to be accepted as realistic and possible.

> *I heard a person who constantly develops himself say, "I am highly motivated to do all I can to improve in many areas. This is my greatest pleasure in life. But I become frustrated when I try to help others build their self-image and reach higher goals. At times, the more enthusiastic I am, the less motivated the people I try to motivate become. They think I am asking them to do something almost impossible.*
>
> *"I listened to a lecture given by someone who made it a life mission to constantly improve himself and help others improve. Edward Deming was one of the top people in the field of improving businesses. The key to his success: telling people to break down their goals and projects into a number of parts, then focus on tiny improvements in four or five areas. Each small improvement was relatively easy. But it added up. The fact that small improvements were made each day and the fact that the improvements were in a number of areas made tremendous overall progress.*

"I focused on what I could do to apply this to my own life, and then I started teaching it to others. Celebrating small successes made the entire process enjoyable. The people who were committed to making these tiny steps built up their self-image tremendously. They knew that they would be able to make consistent progress on whatever was important to them. Their level of personal happiness grew greatly together with their positive self-image."

Making and Reaching Worthwhile Goals

Life is a process of setting and reaching goals. Formulating and achieving worthwhile goals add meaning to life. Even if one's life is very challenging, having worthwhile goals raises the quality of life. The happiest people are those who strive for worthwhile goals, not those whose life is just fun and games.

People with a positive self-image believe in their ability to attain meaningful goals. Someone who has already accomplished worthwhile goals will have an even more positive self-image.

Part of successful goal making and reaching is an awareness of your life mission. People who are clear about their life mission are clearer about their goals. Developing a life mission that inspires and motivates you is one of the most important things that you can do in your life.

What is your vision for yourself? People of great vision set and reach great goals. What are your dreams for yourself? Even if a particular dream seems too far in the future or too lofty, knowing our dreams can help us aim for more meaningful goals.

An essential part of thinking goal-reaching thoughts is to have the self-concept: "I am a person who is able to attain the goals that I planned."

The book you are reading now was part of one of my goals. Every book you ever read was a product of the goals of a number of people. Every product you ever buy was once someone's goal. Someone had to invent it. Someone had to make it. Someone had to sell it. Every school and every teacher is the product of people making and reaching goals. The telephone was a goal, cars are the products of goals, and airplanes and airlines are products of goals. Every supermarket product comes from a goal that was set and reached. Everyone who ever accomplished and achieved anything made a goal and reached it.

Learn from other goal-setters and -reachers. You have a multitude of people from whom to learn.

Experts at bringing out the best in people start with the assumption: "Every single person has every single basic inner resource that is needed. It's just a matter of finding it."

As long as you can read, you can find and read the information that you need. As long as you know how to ask questions, you can find knowledgeable people to find the answers that you need to know. As long as you can find someone who can show you how to do something, you can learn to do anything. You need patience and persistence. With these qualities you can learn anything.

To set and reach goals, you need to take action. Without taking action, no matter what you might wish to accomplish, nothing will happen. Small steps towards goals add up. Every step you take gives you the momentum to continue. Picture all the benefits of reaching your goals. Let these potential benefits motivate you to get started and to keep going.

To accomplish anything in life we need ambition and energy. As you continue to increase your level of ambition and energy, you will find yourself reaching more and higher goals.

There is a well-known goal-setting question: "If you knew that you would certainly be successful, what goals would you make for yourself?" This question is also phrased as: "If you knew that you couldn't fail, what goals would you set?" These questions help point you in the right direction.

Some people don't yet believe in their ability to accomplish the goals that they would wish for. I advise them to make a list of inner strengths, resources, skills, and talents that would help them reach the goals that they wish to reach.

Clarify your goals. What would you like to achieve and accomplish? Ask yourself and others, "What positive qualities do I need to reach the goals that I wish to reach? What specific skills and talents do I need?"

Gain greater awareness of the inner resources that you already have. Think of the major undertakings that you have already accomplished in your life. Think of things you accomplished in school. Think of interests and hobbies. Write a comprehensive list of all the inner strengths, resources, skills, and talents that enabled you to complete whatever you have accomplished. Don't take anything for granted.

Visualize yourself planning and reaching worthwhile goals. Picture yourself accomplishing your goals. As you make these mental pictures, think about what you would need to learn and develop in order to reach your goals.

Find a teacher, coach, or mentor who could help you set and attain your goals. Those teachers can help teach you the tools that you need. Get together with some friends and like-minded people who will encourage you to make and reach your goals and dreams. Some people call these types of groups "mastermind groups." Those who belong to such groups credit them with the motivation and inspiration that helped them accomplish as much as they did.

Remember the goals that you've already reached. Even if you reached them a long time ago, let them be part of your self-image: "I am a person who has already reached these goals. I have already accomplished and achieved so much."

Every goal that you reach builds up your self-image: "I am a person who can make and reach more goals."

> *"I am an expert at not reaching goals," someone over forty years old once told me. "I have heard many talks and read many books about the importance of making and reaching goals. I talk*

a lot about it, but deep down I feel that I don't really have what it takes to reach my goals. I don't have the time needed to reach some of my most important goals."

"What are some of the goals that you have tried to reach?" I asked this fellow.

He gave me a whole list of things that he tried but didn't accomplish.

"What do you really love to do?" I asked him. "You have been involved in many worthwhile activities, but you probably weren't really excited about doing those things. Unless you are truly enthusiastic about your goals, your positive energy won't last."

"I really want to change careers, but I don't think that I will be able to earn a living doing what I really love to do. It's not practical. I have a family and I need to make enough money to support my family," he explained.

"I am going to give you a homework assignment," I told this fellow. "Do some research. Find people who are doing things that are similar to what you want to do, and find out how they earn enough money to support their families."

The fellow contacted me a couple of months later and reported, "I found out that I could earn more money than I had thought by doing what I truly love to do. After talking to other people, I realized that I was wasting a lot of money. By making a number of changes in my lifestyle, I could cut down on a lot of needless expenses. Since I began doing what I love to do, I found similar things that I enjoy doing. Now that I am doing what I love to do, I have much more energy and I am thinking in more creative ways. I now have a much stronger sense of accomplishment, and I feel much better about myself."

All Inner Strengths in All Contexts

Each and every person who reads this section has many inner strengths. The truth is that everyone who knows how to read has many inner strengths. But since you are the one reading this, I want you to become more aware of your own inner strengths.

The vast majority of people utilize some of their inner strengths sometimes, but not always. This is certainly true for me. It's probably true for many people who are reading this.

People might be kind, courageous, confident, patient, harmonious, happy, or relaxed in some contexts, but not in others. People might be able to concentrate well and stay focused in some contexts, but not in others. People might be able to stay centered and flowing in some situations, but not in others. It would be wonderful to be able to access all of your inner strengths in all contexts. In other words, if you can be calm and relaxed, confident and courageous, centered, focused, and flowing in some contexts and around some people, it would be wonderful to access those mental and behavioral states around all people, all the time.

An important facet of every human being is the brain. Our brain is always with us wherever we are. It's impossible to forget to take our brain along when we go out, no matter how absent-minded we are.

Another important idea is that, according to the latest understanding of the brain as I am writing this, we each have over 100 billion neurons (brain cells) and each neuron contains a large amount of data.

Every positive behavioral pattern that you've applied even once is stored in your brain. Every inner strength that you've ever manifested is stored in your brain. All you need is one moment of being confident and courageous to have confidence and courage "on file." The same applies to moments of happiness and joy, inner calm and relaxation, feeling centered, focused, and flowing, and communicating with clarity, self-respect, and respect for the other person.

You can tell your inner mind, "I want to be able to access all the inner strengths that I have in my brain, in all contexts with all people." Then you can have a self-image of: "I am a person with many inner strengths stored in my brain. I want to utilize more inner strengths in more contexts. And right now I am telling my inner mind to automatically apply all my inner strengths in more contexts and with more people."

Some people object, "But I don't yet use all my inner strengths in all contexts!"

That is probably true. But you can still say, "I am a person who is constantly improving more inner strengths in more contexts."

This self-image will be true as long as every once in a while you say to your inner mind, "Please automatically upgrade more of my inner strengths in more contexts. Perform this upgrade when I am awake and when I am asleep."

If you are the type of person who doesn't want to have to remember to do this, you can say, "Dear inner mind, I don't want to have to keep reminding you. I trust that if I tell you just once, you will be able to do it on your own. Please, constantly apply all of my inner strengths in more contexts."

After doing this only once, your self-image can include: "I am a person who once told my inner mind to utilize all my inner strengths in all contexts."

You would be better off repeating once a day: "Let my inner mind apply all my inner strengths in all contexts."

But if you don't want to do this once a day, at least do this once in your life.

Roger Bannister ran a mile in less than four minutes just once to be considered a person who ran the four-minute mile. I'm certain that as he got older he wasn't able to keep this up. Nevertheless, since he did it once he was able to think, "I am a person who ran a mile in less than four minutes." I personally have never been able to run a mile in four minutes. I have never tried to and don't plan to. While this is part of my self-image, it doesn't really cause me any lack of happiness and joy. I have told my brain to apply all my inner strengths in all contexts.

So even though my brain is still in the middle of upgrading, I still have a positive self-image because I have told this to my brain. I am happy that my brain still works. So even though my brain doesn't do everything I want it to, it does some of the things. I am grateful for this.

Every time you see that you have a new inner strength, you can say, "Inner mind, I see that I have this strength right now. Please refresh my brain so that I will apply this inner strength in many more situations in the future."

If you ever find yourself in a situation where you need an inner strength like courage, joy, serenity, enthusiasm, concentration, empowerment, or creativity, ask yourself, "What inner strength would I need right now to be able to do what I want to do?"

Then you can ask yourself, "In what time and place have I ever had the inner strength that I need now?"

If you recall any time in your life when you had the inner strength that you want now, it means that this inner strength is stored in your brain. Access it.

Access that inner strength by speaking and acting the way you did when you had that confidence, courage, joy, inner calm, enthusiasm, or other inner strength.

If you can't recall even one moment of acting this way, then you can *pretend* that you were able to behave like you have that inner strength stored in your mind. Speak and act that way just once, pretending you can do it. The moment you do this, you give yourself that inner strength, available to access again and again and again.

> *I once met a person who kept telling me what he wasn't. "I'm not as happy as I want to be," he said.*
>
> *Throughout the conversation he said many similar sentences. "I'm not confident." "I'm not courageous." "I'm not calm and relaxed." "I'm not creative."*
>
> *"Wait a minute," I said. "How many banks does a person need to rob to be considered a bank robber?"*
>
> *"One would probably do it," the fellow said.*
>
> *"And how many beautiful paintings does a person need to paint to be able to consider himself someone who knows how to paint well?"*

"One would do it," he replied.

"So all you need is one moment of confidence to consider yourself as a person who has confidence, and one moment of happiness to be considered someone with happiness stored in his brain. The same applies with every positive trait and pattern.

"Stop making statements about what you are not. Each time you repeat this, you are conditioning your mind negatively. Conversely, each time you remember that you have many inner strengths stored in your brain, you are conditioning yourself positively.

"From now on, every time you catch yourself saying that you don't have a specific positive strength, let it remind you to say, 'As long as I have experienced this positive quality even once, it means that this inner strength is stored in my brain. Inside my brain, this positive quality is always with me.'"

I asked this man to please contact me in a month to let me know how he was doing. He called me and told me that sometimes he still starts to say that he is not courageous or not patient. But in a short while he remembers to think of a time that he did have the positive quality in question. Besides this being helpful in increasing the amount of time he experiences the positive quality, his own self-image has improved.

Choose to Make the World a Better Place

Each and every day, choose to make the world a better place in your own unique way. When you do something with this pattern each and every day, your self-image will realize, "I am a person who chooses to do something each day to make the world a better place."

When you pick up a little litter each day, you are choosing to "make the world a cleaner place." What you picked up might be just one small piece of litter. But when you have the thought, "I am making the world a cleaner place," you have raised your sights.

When you do a small act of kindness a day, you are choosing to "make the world a kinder place." What you said or did might be just one tiny act of kindness, but you remembered to think, "I am making the world a kinder place." This builds your self-image.

When you say or do something to raise the self-image of another person, you are choosing to make the world a better place. That person is now going to see himself in a better light than before. You are helping humanity, one person at a time. You build your self-image to include: "I am a person who makes the world a better place, one person at a time."

Some people challenge this. "Isn't this a bit overdoing it? All I'm really doing is one small action. I'm not really doing anything heroic. I'm not making a major change in people's lives. I'm not really changing the entire world."

If you look at what you are doing as one small action, then that is its reality for you. It doesn't affect your self-image very much. But take a more global look at what you are "really" doing. You are truly helping humanity. You are truly making the world a better place. This is the greatness of your thoughts. This is the greatness of your action. This is how you are truly building your self-image. When you think in this more elevated, global way, you will continue to find more and greater things that you will be able to do.

You will improve every aspect of your life. Your thoughts and feelings about yourself will be higher and greater. You will end up speaking and acting in higher and greater ways.

One act of kindness might seem like a minor accomplishment — but not to the person you were kind to. To that person you have done a major service. And when you keep acting with kindness, after a while you will have done 1,000 acts of kindness, then 2,000 or even 10,000 acts of kindness. And with both the one act and with the 10,000 acts, you have improved the total picture of the world.

This entire consciousness is included in the Talmudic statement, "A person is obligated to say, 'The world was created for me.'" (*Sanhedrin* 37 a).

Keep on thinking this way and you will see yourself in a much greater light.

Wish the world well. Then you are a person who wishes the world well. Say out loud, "I wish the entire world peace and prosperity." Then this becomes part of your self-image.

> *"I usually have a positive self-image," someone said to me. "But once in a while I get stuck in a rut. Although I have a lot of happiness in my life, and have much to be grateful for, when I feel emotionally stuck I'm not in touch with the inner strengths that I know I have. My self-image at that time drops greatly. I realize that this is just based on a temporary feeling; I know when I feel better emotionally, I will feel better about myself, and I will have much more energy. But I would like a suggestion to help give myself an emotional pickup that will also give my self-image a boost."*
>
> *"If you knew that you were making the world a better place, would that give you an emotional and spiritual boost?" I asked him.*
>
> *"It certainly would," he said. "I would get a strong feeling that I am doing something meaningful. Even though I know that I have already done a number of constructive, meaningful things, it's like I get hungry for more when I feel that I haven't done anything significant lately."*
>
> *"This is my suggestion for you: Ask yourself, 'What can I do to make the world a better place, person by person?'"*
>
> *"I can immediately think of two things that I can do for two people. Viewing it as making the world a better place adds to the meaning of what I am thinking of doing. I feel much better already," he said enthusiastically.*

The Young Chazon Ish's Aleph Beis

The Chazon Ish (1878-1953) was known by the title of his profound Talmudic works. His actual name was Rabbi Avraham Yeshaya Karelitz. Thousands sought his guidance at his modest apartment in Bnai Brak. Although he held no official position, he became a recognized worldwide authority on all matters relating to Jewish law and life.

The Chazon Ish is the subject of one of my favorite self-image stories. When he was a three-year-old boy he had finished learning the Hebrew alphabet. He told his father, who was a great scholar and the rabbi of their town, "I know the entire Talmud. I know every single letter that you will find in any volume." It would be so easy for the three-year-old to think, "I can't read even one page of these holy books. I don't know and can't understand what's written here."

Instead, what did this precocious child say? "I have the building blocks of all that is written here. I know the entire alphabet. I know every single letter. I can tell you what is an *aleph* and what is a *bais*. I even know what is a *shin* and what is a *tuff*. Therefore, I know the entire Talmud," even though he couldn't read a word, or understand the concepts in it!

Do you know the alphabet? Do you know how to read words? If you are reading this, of course you do! Then you have the building blocks of all knowledge. It's just a matter of spending the rest of your life gaining more knowledge.

The Mishnah states in *Pirkei Avos* at the end of Chapter Two, "You are not required to complete the task. Yet you are not free to withdraw from it."

When you are in the process of learning more, you have the choice of choosing your self-image. One self-image is: "I don't know that much. There is so much more that I need to learn. All that I've learned already is only a drop in the bucket. I feel so bad about this." A much better self-image is: "I feel so wonderful that I am involved in the process of studying and learning more. Regardless of how much I already know, I don't know that much. There is so much more that I need to learn. All that I've learned is only a drop in the bucket. I feel wonderful that I am in the process of constantly learning more. Since I know how to read and how to listen, I will continue to study more."

Let the three-year-old Chazon Ish be your teacher. His approach worked for him. He realized that he had the basic building blocks. Therefore, he felt great about himself because he would always be able to continue learning.

This is a great lesson for parents and teachers. Repeat the story of the young Chazon Ish to children and students. Show them that they have the building blocks. Of course there is so much more to learn. That is what life is for. But for now, "You are a person who knows the basics."

> *I once heard about a teacher who was great at developing his students. He was a great motivator. Students who didn't do that well with other teachers did magnificent work with him.*
>
> *I asked this teacher, "What is your secret?"*
>
> *"I don't have a secret," he said. "Anyone can do what I do. After we learn new information, I tell my students, 'Now you have added more wisdom to your mental knowledge library. You know more now than you ever did before. You can be happy today because you're going to end the day knowing more than when you started. Keep this up and you will have a massive amount of knowledge stored in your brain.'*
>
> *"When I said this, I could see the looks on the faces of my students. They constantly felt progress. There was a happy atmosphere in my class."*
>
> *If someone reading this doesn't have a teacher who takes this approach, he can create this approach himself. After reading the story about the Chazon Ish you can repeat this message to add to your self-image, "I am a person who knows that the Chazon Ish felt that knowing the alphabet meant having the building blocks of all knowledge."*

"Choosing Wisely" Versus "Change"

Making choices every moment of our lives is a very important facet of life. We keep choosing our thoughts, our words, and our actions. It is wise to make wise choices. The Torah (*Devorim* 30:19) tells us, "Choose life."

Each and every moment you choose what to think at that moment. Regardless of what you have chosen to think about a moment ago, this moment you are making a new choice. Your new choice might be to continue thinking the same thing. That is still a choice, even if you never realized it before, because you can always choose to think about something else.

Each and every moment you choose what you will say or do at that moment. Regardless of what you have chosen to say or do a moment ago, this moment you are choosing what to say or do now. You might choose to continue, or might choose to do something different. You might choose to do something you have never previously done, or you might choose to do what you have been habitually doing.

The Torah tells you, "Choose life." Wise choices are life-giving choices.

When people talk about "change," they are referring to the choices that you make now that are different from earlier choices.

Different people have different attitudes towards the concept of making changes. Some people are motivated and inspired by the term "making changes." Those who enjoy "making changes" should keep using the term.

However, I have often heard people say, "It is difficult to make changes," or "It's not easy to make changes." I have also heard people say, "Making changes is painful," or "It's not pleasurable to make changes." They find it difficult or distressful to "make a change." I suggest that they think of it as "making wise choices now."

Choosing new and beneficial thoughts, words, and actions, and continuing to keep choosing to think, speak, and act that way, could be considered making positive changes. For many people, it's easier to look at them as "wise choices."

When you decide to frequently ask yourself, "What is a wise way for me to think, speak, and act now?" you can recognize, "I am a person who wants to think, speak, and act wisely," and then add the realization to your self-image.

When that question motivates you to actually think, speak, and act better than ever, you can become more aware of the positive changes that you are making, regardless of how you feel about the term "changing."

> An older person was trying to positively influence someone much younger. That younger person really wanted to improve, so he put in much thought and effort. He thought he was speaking and acting better, and wanted to continue improving.
>
> One day, he bumped into that older person who meant well. "Did you change already?" that older person asked him.
>
> "Yes, I did," the younger fellow replied.
>
> "But did you 'really' change?"
>
> This question surprised the younger fellow. "How can I prove to him that I 'really' changed?" he sincerely asked me.
>
> When a person thinks in terms of "changing" and "really changing," the way to prove that one has actually changed is to wait for time to pass. When someone speaks and acts differently over time, we can say that the person has really changed.
>
> However, when we look at the first steps of someone trying to better himself, our main goal should be to motivate and inspire him to continue on the improved path. This applies to how we view others, and it also applies to how we view ourselves.

"This, Too, Will Build My Self-Image"

Each and every day you will have many opportunities to build yourself and your self-image. Every positive thought, word, and action builds you.

When you see that you have behaved in a positive way, you can say to yourself, "This, too, will build my self-image."

If you have not behaved the way you would have liked, you can think about how you wished to have thought, spoken, and acted. Thinking about what you want to be like conditions your mind to think, speak, and act more in that way. You can say about this pattern of thinking, "This, too, will build my self-image."

Every small strength builds your self-image. Every time you do something difficult, correct a mistake you caught, gain spiritual awareness, or overcome laziness, you build your self-image.

Even when you lose or fail in some way, maintain your dignity. All losses and failures are temporary experiences. They are not your essence as a person. When you realize your basic value and worth as a person even after failing at something, you build your self-image.

Repeating the sentence, "This, too, will build my self-image," reminds you that not only are you doing something positive right now, but you are also building your entire self-image. Someone who is committed to say, "This, too, will build my self-image," 100 times a day for a month will find a unique way to build his self-image on each of those days.

People who keep putting themselves down usually do it many times a day. They might do it so automatically that they don't realize how often they say needless putdown statements to themselves.

If you just practice repeating, "This, too, will build my self-image," even without any special reason, the repetition will make this a sentence that easily comes to mind. Then your inner mind will search for and find ways each day to actually build your self-image.

> *I met someone who was frequently critical of himself.*
>
> *"I've had a rough life," he frequently said. "There is something wrong with me."*
>
> *"What exactly is wrong with you?" I asked him.*
>
> *"Everything!" he replied.*
>
> *"Nobody who is even slightly normal has 'everything' wrong. What exactly do you consider wrong with you?"*
>
> *"I am very insecure. I never feel good about myself. I am always nervous that I am doing the wrong thing. My children are much more nervous than other children their age."*
>
> *"To focus on your current issues and on what you would like to accomplish, you should make a list of the problematic patterns and your specific goals," I suggested.*
>
> *"There is something wrong with me," the person kept repeating.*
>
> *"That's a self-image statement," I said. "So is your goal to upgrade your self-image?"*
>
> *"No. Just changing the way I think about myself isn't enough. I feel down most of the time. I feel nervous most of the time. I feel awful most of the time."*
>
> *"So if you would feel better about your total self, and felt happier, calmer, and more confident, then you would consider that existence better than this. Does this make sense?"*
>
> *"Yes, I see how it could be put that way," he acknowledged.*
>
> *He gave me a lengthy description of his entire day and how he lived his life. I asked many questions and saw that he did many things right, but they didn't register in his mind. He didn't realize that he was already doing many positive things.*
>
> *"We will work on any and all of the issues that you want to work on, but I would suggest one pattern that will be a key to helping you improve your entire self. If it makes sense to you, will you be willing to try it out?"*
>
> *He agreed.*

"Every time you feel good about what you do, repeat to yourself, 'This, too will build my self-image.' You do numerous positive things each and every day. When you repeat about each one, "This, too, will build my self-image," it will help you realize that you already are doing many things that can help you feel better about yourself. When you are in the process of building your self-image, you will be motivated to do even more positive things.

"You already feel good a number of times a day; let them register in your mind. So whenever you smile, laugh, or feel good about some accomplishment, say to yourself, 'I feel a bit happy right now. This, too, will build my self-image.' Whenever you are feeling even a bit calm, say to yourself, 'I feel a bit calm right now. This, too, will build my self-image.' Whenever you are feeling even a bit confident, say to yourself, 'I feel a bit confident right now. This, too, will build my self-image.'

"Be patient. This will take time. But after a couple of months of reiterating this pattern, you will see that you have repeated it hundreds, even thousands, of times. You will realize that you are making progress. Instead of telling yourself, 'Something is wrong with me," you will be repeating, 'I am building my self-image.'

"There might not be a magical moment when you will joyfully exclaim, 'My self-image is much higher than before!' But by keeping this up, you will certainly realize over time that you are consistently in the process of building your self-image."

When he understood how much he would benefit from making it a habit to repeat, "This, too, will build my self-image," he felt a great sense of relief. This episode gave him a stronger awareness of how his pattern of thinking had a major influence on his life.

Focus Exercise: The Great Four

As I have written repeatedly, we all make four choices each and every moment of our lives by choosing our thoughts, feelings, words, and actions.

Since we must make these four choices all the time, we can improve our lives if we improve our level of choosing in these four areas.

Here is an exercise to help you focus on four key elements that will enhance your choices:

A number of times a day, repeat to yourself:

Great thoughts
Great feelings
Great words
Great actions

As you keep repeating these eight words, you will find that they have a positive influence on your thoughts, feelings, words, and actions.

How often should you repeat these words? Until they become part of your automatic way of thinking. People serious about improving themselves should repeat the four elements for two minutes at a time, ten times a day. Someone who tends to think in counterproductive ways or tends to feel bad for a good part of the day should repeat them more often. Before judging how much you personally could benefit, I would suggest that you try repeating them for at least two weeks.

It is especially valuable to repeat them in the morning and in the evening.

You can say them when you are walking.

You can say them when you are waiting for someone.

Individuals who keep repeating distressful thoughts would be wise to make it a habit to repeat these eight words, which will fill their minds with positive thoughts and feelings.

Along with this exercise, here are a number of similar uplifting exercises:

Joyful thoughts
Joyful feelings
Joyful words
Joyful actions

Kind thoughts
Kind feelings
Kind words
Kind actions

Elevated thoughts
Elevated feelings
Elevated words
Elevated actions

Courageous thoughts
Courageous feelings
Courageous words
Courageous actions

Calm thoughts
Calm feelings
Calm words
Calm actions

Grateful thoughts
Grateful feelings
Grateful words
Grateful actions

Empowered thoughts
Empowered feelings
Empowered words
Empowered actions

Cheerful thoughts
Cheerful feelings

Cheerful words
Cheerful actions

Wonderful thoughts
Wonderful feelings
Wonderful words
Wonderful actions

Self-confident thoughts
Self-confident feelings
Self-confident words
Self-confident actions

I've found that many people who would gain greatly from this kind of exercise don't even give it a sincere test. They argue from a place of logic. This isn't in the realm of logical or not. This is a meditative exercise that has a very positive effect on your thoughts and feelings. I hope that you will be able to benefit from it.

Perseverance on the Path of Building Your Self-Image

The classic story about how the great Talmudic Sage Rabbi Akiva began to study Torah at age forty has been an inspiring story for many. When he learned an idea he quickly forgot it and eventually became discouraged. He was ready to give up, but then he passed a rock that had water steadily dripping onto it. The persistent dripping of the water had made a hole in the rock.

Rabbi Akiva realized, "A few drops of water couldn't make such a hole. It is the *persistence* of the water that carved the hole in the strong rock. When I study Torah persistently, the ideas that I study will be engraved in my mind and I will eventually understand and remember."

The wisdom of Rabbi Akiva has shed much light in the world for many generations. Without persistence, he wouldn't have become the great scholar that he became.

Rabbi Yisroel Salanter commented that Rabbi Akiva learned that each repetition makes a dent in the rock. If the first drop of water would have done nothing, then the second and third drops would have done nothing, and there wouldn't have been a hole in the rock. Each drop must have done something, even if it wasn't noticeable.

This thought has the power to motivate us. Each time you review Torah concepts and ideas you are accomplishing something. It could be just a tiny accomplishment not noticeable to the human eye, but persistence makes a difference.

Persistence and perseverance are qualities that make a major difference in people's lives. They make you keep going.

You keep going even when good things take much longer to accomplish than you thought they would.

You keep going even though you face disappointments and reversals.

You keep going even though things become more difficult.

You keep going even though others try to discourage you.

Making and reaching goals enables you to accomplish, and this builds your self-image. When you persevere, you reach more goals.

Every time you persevere, you build up your identity as a person who is able to persevere. By viewing yourself as a person who perseveres, you're more likely to persevere in the future.

Every toddler who walks had to persevere in order to advance from crawling to walking to running well.

Every young child who has learned to speak his first language had to persevere until he was able to speak clearly.

Everyone has had many experiences of when they persevered. Think of more instances when you persevered and didn't give up.

People with a low self-image find it easier to give up too soon.

They are likely to say, "Why should I keep trying? I probably won't be able to accomplish what I want to accomplish. It's all just a waste of time anyway."

By persevering, you tell yourself, "I have the inner strength to keep going. I believe that when I persevere, I will be able to accomplish."

When you persevere, you can't be certain that you will reach all your goals. But when you don't persevere, you can be certain that there are many goals that you could potentially reach that you won't reach.

There is a well-known riddle: How do you eat an elephant? The answer is: One bite at a time. This is exactly how you eat an apple, a banana, or a cookie. As long as you eat a bite at a time and keep it up over a long period of time, you will succeed in your goal.

This is the same way you read a long book: One sentence, then one page at a time. You read an entire encyclopedia, or an entire library, the same way: One sentence and one page at a time.

Learn from the stories of people who accomplished great things in life because they persevered. If other people have persevered, you too can persevere.

We have light bulbs today because Edison, the inventor of the light bulb, persevered. He tried one filament after another until he found one that worked.

Whenever I meet people who survived the Second World War, I ask them, "What enabled you to survive?"

One elderly gentleman replied, "I decided that I only need to keep on going one hour at a time. After I made it through one hour, I said to myself, 'I only need to persevere now for another hour.' I kept doing this hour by hour. I felt a sense of victory for every hour that I was able to keep going."

Persevere in your quest to build your self-image. Some people try to build their self-image for a short amount of time before they get tired of trying and give up. Building your self-image is a goal with guaranteed success when you persevere. As long as you keep on thinking, saying, and doing the things that build up who you are, little by little you will make progress.

> *I frequently ask people who believe they are stuck with their low self-image, "How long have you worked on building your self-*

image before deciding that this is who you are and this is how you will stay?"

There is one common factor in the answers that I hear: They haven't persevered long enough.

Some people in the process of doing what they can to raise their self-image don't view a low self-image as a final statement. Instead, they view their present self-image as something they want to improve. Even if they have tried many times and haven't yet succeeded in reaching their goal, they know that by persevering they will keep developing themselves.

One person who made major progress in becoming more than anyone thought possible said, "I decided to keep on going as long as it takes."

The words, "As long as it takes," reverberated in my mind.

In what area of your life would you gain tremendously if you were willing to work on it "as long as it takes"?

How Long Does It Take?

Many people wonder, "How long does it take to build one's self-image?"

Since it takes our entire life to live our entire life, one can say that it takes a lifetime to fully build our self-image.

Often, people who ask, "How long does it take?" really mean, "How long does it take to change from having a low self-image to a higher self-image so I will be able to feel better about myself?"

It's not really a matter of time. Rather, improving a self-image is an individualized process. It takes a change of thought. Once you change your thoughts about yourself, by definition your self-image will be changed.

If you thought that you didn't have a certain talent, how long did it take you to realize that you actually have that talent?

I know someone who frequently said that he wasn't able to sing songs because he was tone-deaf. Decades ago, a choir leader in his school implied that he was totally incompetent as a singer. One day the man told this to a professional *chazon* who also gave singing lessons. That *chazon* said to him, "I will make a sound. You repeat it."

The forty-year-old man repeated the sound exactly.

"You aren't tone-deaf!" the *chazon* proclaimed. "The way you repeated the exact tone that I used shows that you have the potential to learn to sing. I could teach you if you are interested in taking lessons."

The fellow didn't become a great singer or a professional *chazon*. As a matter of fact, he didn't even want private singing lessons. But his self-image about singing totally changed. Now he no longer viewed himself as tone-deaf. Instead, he immediately began to look at himself as someone who had the potential to learn to sing well if he ever wanted to. One day this fellow decided to make his elderly mother happy and composed his own tune, without following the notes of any established song. His mother said to him, "You sound great. I love the way you are singing."

I spoke to that fellow recently and he told me that although he doesn't sing for others, he makes up joyful and majestic tunes in his own mind for himself. He doesn't have great control over his vocal cords, but he does have great control over his mind and the tunes that go through it.

There are many people who sincerely want to build their self-image, but it takes them a long time before they actually feel better about themselves. People who have viewed themselves negatively for a long time have repeated negative self-statements many times every day for many years. Now they need to be willing to repeat life-enhancing messages over and over again.

The first step in building one's self-image: Resolve not to put yourself down. One shouldn't repeat to oneself or to others overall self-belittling statements.

Then, even before realizing the full extent of your hidden talents and skills, realize that your value and worth as a child of the Creator is immense.

I frequently tell people to imagine that an emperor's young son was kidnapped by his enemies. Those enemies kept telling the boy that he is a lowly slave, was always a lowly slave, and will always be a lowly slave. For years the captured prince was treated like a slave and he thought, "I am being treated like a slave because that is who I am."

Many years later, the emperor found out where the bandits were holding the prince. The emperor sent in his army and freed his beloved son. The son was taken to the royal palace and treated like the prince he really was.

How long will it take the prince, who was now dressed royally and treated royally, to realize that he was born a prince and deserved honor and respect? This transformation will happen rather rapidly, won't it?

Be patient in the process of conditioning your mind with image-building thoughts. Be willing to repeat positive ideas many times. If you find that this book has a positive effect on you, read the book many times until you find yourself integrating the thoughts and ideas.

Regardless of how long it will take for you to build your self-image, it's still a road that is wise to travel.

> *I once met someone in his early fifties who told me that someone said to him, "Since it took you about fifty years to create your low self-image, it will take you a very long time to improve your self-image."*
>
> *After a couple of years of hardly making any progress on his self-image, the man wondered how to speed up the process. It was suggested that he speak to a coach who viewed self-image as a subjective way of thinking.*
>
> *At the first visit to this "joy coach," the man was asked, "How do you create joyful states for yourself?"*
>
> *Having been conditioned for so long to talk about all his sad memories, failures, and all the reasons why he was unhappy and had a low self-image, he was confused by the question.*

"It's not so easy to create joy just because one wants to," the man argued.

"If you don't know how to do something, of course it's not easy to do it. If you know how to do something the right way, it might be easy or it might be difficult, but at least you will be able to do it," the coach told him.

"But I have all these life experiences that get in the way," the fellow argued.

"It's not your life experiences that get in the way," said the coach, "it's that you constantly think about them in a way that blocks you. When your thoughts focus on gratitude and appreciation for all that you can appreciate, you will find yourself feeling much better. And when you keep your focus on the thoughts, words, and actions that build your self-image, you will find your entire self-image becoming better from day to day."

"But won't the past thoughts get in the way?" the man asked.

"They will certainly arise in your mind from time to time, but they don't have to get in the way. Whenever you find your inner mind flowing to unhappiness-producing thoughts and to thoughts that create a lower self-image, change your focus to thoughts of gratitude and appreciation, and thoughts of building your self-image from now on."

"But I'm not certain that this will work for me," the man argued.

"If you don't apply my suggestions, they can't possibly work for you," the coach said. "The more time you spend arguing why this won't work, the longer you delay applying these suggestions. I know for certain that this works when people apply these thoughts. And I also know that just hearing what I am saying to you won't make a change, unless you change your thoughts. So you have a choice now: Keep arguing, don't apply it, and it won't help you; or apply it and there is a strong possibility that you will make progress."

"It makes sense that I should try to do it," the man agreed.

"It will probably be easier for you to keep appreciative thoughts and thoughts of raising your self-image if you speak them out loud to someone. I will listen to you now as you think your thoughts out loud. When you go home, find a friend who will listen to you talking in this happiness- and image-upgrading way. If you can't find anyone with the patience to listen to you, record your self-talk on a recorder. Even if you erase it soon afterwards, talking out loud will make it easier for you to keep your focus on beneficial, life-enhancing thoughts."

After two weeks of applying the suggestions every day, the man in his fifties reported, "I wouldn't have believed that in such a short time, I was able to create a much happier way of being and feeling much better about myself."

"If I Can Do It Once, I Can Do It Again"

An important self-image includes the realization, "If I can do it once, I can do it again." In other words, any positive pattern applied even once is stored in your brain, which allows you to apply that pattern again.

If you can be assertive in a calm, clear way even though you usually find it difficult to be assertive, then you can have the self-image that you will be able to act this way again and again.

A person who is finally able to concentrate well because he decided to concentrate will gain very much by thinking, "Since I can focus my mind on what I want to concentrate on now, I also have the ability to concentrate again in other situations."

When your self-image includes, "If I can do it once, I can do it again," every time you do something positive, you gain not only by doing the good thing, but by adding the knowledge that you will be able to do this positive thing more times.

This attitude is the opposite of thinking, "If I can't do something every single time I want to do it, I don't really have the ability to do it."

The danger of this "all or nothing" attitude is that any failure to do something immediately lowers one's self-image. "Since I couldn't do it this time, it means that I can't really do it." So every failure to do something positive will not only be considered a failure this time, but will lower one's sense of self for the future.

When you have the attitude of, "If I can do it once, I can do it again," it is more likely that you will be able to do those positive things more times than if you were to have the limiting attitude.

We need to be realistic. If you can never do a specific task each time you try, it means that you've never been able to do it. But knowing that you can do it *sometimes* is much more helpful than thinking that you basically can't do it. You will eventually be able to do it more often by viewing yourself as a person who *can* do it.

Think of a few ways that you will benefit from realizing that you can do anything that you've already done once.

> *When I coach people to raise their self-image, I find that the mind-set of, "If I can do it once, I can do it again," is a powerful self-image booster. Some people are shy and timid. They feel that they aren't able to speak well in front of a crowd, and even five people might be considered a crowd for them. I know that if they are able to speak in public even once in a way that they themselves are totally satisfied with and they get positive feedback from the audience, they will be able to make a breakthrough.*
>
> *"Would you like to have a positive influence on the lives of other people?" I ask them.*
>
> *"Very much," is the general response.*
>
> *"What are some of the major ways you would like to influence others, if you could? Imagine that you had a great audience. The people in the audience are totally open to listening to what you have to say. They are eager to develop their lives. What are five positive traits and positive patterns that you would suggest that they develop?"*
>
> *We write down the traits and patterns.*
>
> *"Now I will read this list in a tremendously enthusiastic way. All you have to do is repeat it after me in the most enthusiastic way you can imagine. You don't actually have to do this in front*

of others. We are not rehearsing an actual speech. We are just practicing being able to speak in an enthusiastic way when you are by yourself."

This takes away pressure.

For example, I will say, "I feel privileged to speak before you right now. Life is for growing and developing yourself. Our goal is to create a great you. We want to bring out the best in ourselves. So let us commit ourselves to develop the following positive traits. Let us develop our quality of happiness and joy. Let us appreciate all the gifts that the Creator has given us. Let us have gratitude from the moment we wake up in the morning, throughout the entire day. Let us develop our trait of kindness. Let us consistently think about how we can help others. Let us do many acts of kindness joyfully. Let us develop our level of courage. Let us have the courage to do all the positive things that we would wish to do. Let us develop more and more patience. As we develop patience we will be able to keep on developing ourselves in great ways. And each and every day let us think, speak, and act in ways that keep enhancing our lives and the lives of others."

I read the sentences with enthusiasm. The person I'm coaching repeats it as enthusiastically as he can, for now. This is repeated over and over again, with more enthusiasm each time.

This is done in an exaggerated way. The person practices in a way that he feels is impossible to do with anyone else present.

Once even one sentence is said in a way that is clearly confident and enthusiastic, I repeat a number of times, "You just did this in a powerful way. Since you did it once, it means that this pattern is in your brain right now. Since you can do it once, it means that you can do it again."

Some people rightly say, "But I can't do this in front of a crowd!"

Since they think they can't, they really can't.

"But you just did it once, right?"

This is obviously correct, and they agree.

"Now let's repeat over and over with great enthusiasm: 'Since I can do this once, I can do it again.'"

Everyone who keeps practicing will be able to do it. Often, young children are able to do this more easily than adults. They rely on their own experiences of being able to do it, rather than going into the mental fiction of, "I can't really do what I just did. I could just do it now."

If you really couldn't do it, you wouldn't have been able to do it now. It's just that you have a self-image that you can't do it, so you think you can't. Keep repeating this enough times and your inner mind will have to agree that you are really able to do what you have just done.

"If Someone Else Can Do It, I Can Do It Too"

We might think that we won't be able to do or accomplish something. But seeing that someone else can do it tells us, "If this person can accomplish that, I will be able to do it also."

The Sages (*Pirkei Avos* 4:1) define a wise person as someone who learns from every person. Develop the habit of interviewing people you meet to find out exactly how they learned to do what you would like to learn to do. What are the thoughts that go through their minds? What are the actions they take? What are their attitudes and mindsets? What are the mental pictures they see? What are the books they read? What are the classes and recordings they heard?

People with a low self-image might say to themselves, "Others can do it, but I can't. I'm not intelligent enough. I'm not talented enough. I'm not disciplined enough. I'm not patient enough. I'm just not the kind of person who can accomplish these sorts of things."

They should accept the realization that, "If someone else is able to do something and I try to do the same things that they do, I will be able to do it, too."

This is one of the most powerful attitudes and mindsets that someone could have. When you view every positive pattern of speaking and acting as a role model for your behavior in that pattern, you constantly develop yourself.

Every especially confident person teaches you how to speak and act with more confidence. Every courageous, joyful, kind, or calm person teaches you how to be more courageous, joyful, kind, or calm. Every great speaker or motivator teaches you how to be a better speaker or motivator. Every person with positive character traits who influences you teaches you how to develop your own character traits and positively influence others.

Interview people who do things well, especially if they do something exceptionally well. Ask them what they believe enables them to do what they do. Ask them about the entire sequence of their thoughts, their feelings, and their actions. Ask them, "What do I need to know to do what you do?"

Will you always be able to do what others can do just because you observed them and interviewed them? Certainly not. But you will be able to do a lot more than if you hadn't learned from others.

There definitely will be things that others can do that you won't be able to do. There are genetic factors, there are issues of size, there are innate gifts of genius and talent, there are personal interests and inner motivations. There might be reasons that you don't yet know about that enable this person to do what he does and they might not apply to you.

But there are a multitude of things that others can do that you, too, could learn to do — if you are dedicated, patient, persistent, and open to finding teachers, coaches, tutors, books, and recordings, etc. As you keep gaining more knowledge and learning more skills, you will be able to do many more things than you are presently able to do.

Right now you might say to yourself, "I would never be able to learn to do that so skillfully." But if you had the proper training, you could learn how to be skillful. When you gain more knowledge and skills and talents, your entire self-image will change for the better.

Many people started off thinking that they couldn't possibly achieve what others have achieved, but were strongly committed to learn. They were successful beyond their initial dreams.

Every young child applies this process naturally and automatically. That is how we all learned how to speak and pick up our basic vocabulary. We heard others speak and we picked up speaking. We picked up the accent of those around us. Children who grow up in New York, in London, in Johannesburg, and in Melbourne all speak English, but they all speak with a noticeably different accent.

We learned to write by copying how a teacher or parent wrote. Mistakes were pointed out and we were told how to correct them.

Some skills we learned from others without giving much thought to it. Other skills took a lot of effort and practice. Some skills we realized right away that we would be able to learn. Others we weren't certain. And with yet other skills we thought we would never be able to learn but actually did.

We are all limited by the time factor. We have a limited amount of hours a day, a limited amount of days a week, and a limited amount of days a year. So we don't have all the time we need to learn all that we might want to learn. But in the time we do have, we can learn a tremendous amount.

Keep repeating, "If someone else can learn to do something, I can learn to do it also." This attitude about learning to do anything that anyone else can do won't guarantee that you will be able to literally do all that others can do. But it will guarantee that you will eventually be able to do a lot more than you can do now.

Each time you learn more new skills and gain greater expertise, you build your self-image.

Be on the lookout for people who already believe, "If anyone else can do it, I can do it, too." Learn from them.

Refuse to allow handicaps to stop you. People have overcome a wide range of handicaps. Learn from them. And learn from other handicapped people that your own perceived limitations don't need to limit you any more than absolutely necessary. Every handicap creates various limitations, but there are always a multitude of things that any given handicap won't stop a person from being able to do.

A prime example is the presidency of Franklin Roosevelt. Polio handicapped him and confined him to a wheelchair, but did not stop him from running for the position of president of the United States, from campaigning, and from winning. He helped the United States overcome the Great Depression. He led the United States during World War II.

I recently read an article about a blind man who received his medical degree. Adjustments needed to be made since he couldn't see, but he was determined to successfully do all he could. And he overcame a challenge that not everyone would even try.

The worst handicap anyone could have is a handicap of attitude. Limiting oneself is a handicap that most of us need to overcome. Let us all learn from those who don't needlessly limit themselves.

Be on the lookout for people who don't yet have the attitude of, "If anyone else can do it, I can do it, too." Be resolved to help others build their self-image. Teaching them this limit-breaking attitude will transform their lives.

> *While writing this book, I frequently asked successful people what their self-image was like when they were children.*
>
> *On an overseas flight, I joined a conversation with a surgeon and an international salesman of jet planes. When I asked them about their childhood self-image, the surgeon said that when he finished high school, he didn't really believe he had the necessary intelligence to become a surgeon. But when he considered going to medical school, he met a number of fellows who weren't especially brilliant and they had become surgeons.*
>
> *"If they can do it, I have no question in my mind that I can do it also," he said to himself.*
>
> *This thought kept him going when he faced challenges. His many years as a successful surgeon proved to him that he was right.*
>
> *The fellow who sold expensive jet planes said, "I met a large number of salespeople. I had average grades in school. I figured that there's not a major difference between selling planes and other things. It's just that the price is different. If others can sell all the things that they sell, I, too, can get the training to sell these expensive items."*

Many of the most successful people in the world became that way because they saw that someone else was able to do it. Leaders in all fields have this attitude. May you have it also and then be a positive influence on many people's lives.

Expand Your Beliefs About What is Possible for You

Every single human being has tremendous potential to gain a great amount of knowledge and accomplish a lot. The vast majority of people needlessly limit themselves. When we have a limited belief in what we can learn, know, do, accomplish, and achieve, we limit ourselves in life. Some individuals don't needlessly limit themselves, but most do. You, too, are probably even more capable than you believe.

Do you feel that you are using your full potential? Most people reply that they aren't. By answering "no" you are making a statement: "I believe that I have a lot more potential than I am actualizing."

The good news is that you *can* do a lot more than you think you can.

Learn from your own moments of peak performance. Sometimes you will read and understand faster and better than usual. Sometimes you will be much more creative than usual, or have more courage and take greater risks than usual. Sometimes you will be much more assertive and accomplish more than usual. Sometimes you will get a great job you thought was too difficult, and then do the job really well. Sometimes you will have a surprisingly great positive influence on more people than usual. Sometimes when you try raising money for a worthwhile cause, you will ask for and receive a much larger amount than you expected.

Perhaps you thought something would be impossible to accomplish, but you were pressured into trying. To your surprise, you were highly successful. Another time, you were certain that you wouldn't be able to satisfactorily perform a task you were asked to do. You felt you should try anyway, even if just to show that you tried. Then you surprised yourself, because it was so easy to do much better than you had thought possible.

Every moment of peak performance sheds light on the potential you have for doing more and better than what you believed you could do.

Look for teachers and coaches who are experts at helping people expand their beliefs about what they can do. Since they personally know others just like you who are now able to do and accomplish more, they might be able to convince you, too, to expect more from yourself.

Sometimes a one-time encounter with a person who sees your unrecognized inner strengths can open you up to new possibilities in yourself.

Think about it: Is there a good possibility that you can really do and be more than at present? Your instinctive response shows that your mind knows something positive about you that you don't fully realize.

Some people already accomplish a good deal and do what they do exceptionally well. Unless they keep on expanding their awareness of what is truly possible for them, they might feel they are living up to their potential. But with expanded awareness, in the same amount of time, they might be able to accomplish exponentially more.

Have the courage to ask people who might know the answer: "In what ways do you think that I could do, be, and accomplish more than I am at present?"

> *I spoke to a personal coach who is an expert at bringing out the best in people. I asked him for the major secret for his success.*
>
> *He said, "I work with the following premise: The Almighty gave each person tremendous abilities. Even people who seem*

to be highly successful are really limiting themselves in many ways. I feel certain that if I were to stop people on the street at random, I would be able to show most of them that they are not doing all that they could be doing. But my problem is that I don't like to argue with people. I don't like to tell people that they can do much more than they are doing now; they will argue with me. So I don't stop people in the street at random; I wait until people come to me and hire me to help them. I feel bad about not doing all that I could be doing. Nevertheless, those who come to ask for my professional services and are willing to pay me are willing to believe that they have inner strengths just waiting to be used. When they agree to use everything within to be and become more, they will go way beyond what they used to believe about themselves."

Add the Word "Yet" Whenever You Think About What You Can't Yet Do

"**Yet**" is a short word that can be a great boost to one's self-image. When you say that you can't do something, add the word "yet" to the end of the statement.

Compare these two sentences: "I don't know that," and "I don't know that yet."

Also compare: "I don't have that skill," and "I don't have that skill yet."

Similarly: "I don't have the self-confidence and courage to do that," and "I don't have the self-confidence and courage to do that yet."

When you add the word "yet," you are implying that you will eventually be able to know something, you will eventually gain the skill, and you will eventually have the self-confidence and courage to do what you want to do.

The word "yet" reminds you that you are a person who can learn more and do more. Whatever you don't yet know, you can learn. If you need to talk about what you aren't able to do, talk about it in the past tense. To talk about the future, talk about what your goal is.

Make it a regular habit to consistently add the word "yet" to statements about what you don't yet know and what you can't yet do. Or use the two phrases, "until now" and "my goal is."

For example, "Until now I haven't mastered that skill. My goal is to develop greater expertise."

"Until now, I haven't mastered my emotional states. My goal is to gain greater mastery."

"Until now, I used to be a fearful wimp. My goal is to develop greater confidence and courage."

"Until now, my self-image wasn't that great. My goal is to keep building my self-image and become the person I always wanted to be."

> *I told someone that he would benefit greatly by adding the word "yet" when saying that he doesn't know something or can't do something.*
>
> *"It will sound strange," he argued. "I will feel funny saying it. I know that I will never know some things and I will never learn how to do others. So who am I fooling by adding a simple little word?"*
>
> *A couple of months later he called me up. "When you first suggested that I would gain by using the word 'yet' more often, I disagreed with you. I didn't think I would do it and I didn't think that it would be helpful to me if I did. But then I found out that someone I had known for a long time used this pattern; he added the word 'yet.' It seems that he had been using it for a long time, but I had never noticed it before hearing about it from you. I heard how natural it sounded. And it is true: His attitude was that he would be able to learn, know, and do many*

more things in the future. I started using the word 'yet,' like you suggested. I realize that every time I do say the word 'yet,' I feel that eventually one day I will be able to know and do a lot more."

"For a Lazy Person, You Do a Lot"

I once met a very intelligent, accomplished person who told me, "I frequently told myself for many years, 'For a lazy person, you do a whole lot. For a lazy person, you work very hard.' Finally," he said, "I realized that I'm not lazy."

"When I was younger, others saw me as lazy," he continued, "and that's how I viewed myself. But for many years I have been highly active throughout the day and into the night. I find it fascinating that it took so long for me to realize that I'm not lazy."

The person who said this has deep insight into human nature and has helped many people build up their self-image. But he still found it challenging to change the way he grew up perceiving himself.

We maintain and repeat our old, outworn perceptions even though on some level we realize that this is not the totality of who we are.

I have heard people say similar things:

"For a shy, introverted person, I am actually very friendly and outgoing."

"For a timid person, I have a lot of courage, even bravery at times."

"For a non-studious person, I spend a lot of time studying."

"For a selfish person, I do a lot of kindness."

Give the matter thought. In what ways are you still viewing yourself the way you did as a child, even though you could now see yourself in a much more positive light?

> "I grew up with a very low self-image," a powerful-looking man told me. "I was told again and again, 'Your inferiority complex will hold you back.'
>
> "When I tried to get a job after graduating, I wasn't surprised that I wasn't hired by anyone. I didn't have very much belief in my own abilities, and with the way I presented myself to a potential employer, it was no wonder that everyone turned me down.
>
> "I bumped into an old acquaintance of mine and told him how rough my life was.
>
> "'You are intelligent and honest,' he said. 'You should be able to find someone who would hire you.'
>
> "I told him, 'It's impossible for me to present myself as someone with confidence. I really don't have confidence and I don't think I am capable of looking like someone with confidence.'
>
> "'I disagree with you,' he said to me. 'I saw you in a Purim play a few years ago. You played the role of an extremely powerful person. Your voice filled the large, crowded auditorium. You looked like one of the most empowered people that I've ever met.'
>
> "'But that wasn't real,' I argued. 'I only acted that way because I was in a play.'
>
> "'Have you ever done that before?' he asked me.
>
> "'Plenty of times,' I told him. 'But it was never real. I did so well in that Purim play because I pretended to play that role many times before. I wish that I could really do that. But it's not who I am.'
>
> "My old acquaintance didn't let me get away with that. 'Since you can act that way when pretending, it means that you also can speak and act this way in real life. You really can do this. Even though you don't identify yourself this way, you actually have confidence in your repertoire. Stop repeating that you have feelings of inferiority, and start speaking and acting this empowered way when you go for your next job interview. Since you can do this, it's real.'"

From that moment on that powerful-looking person realized that he has already acted the way he needs to in order to present himself as being powerful. He got a job, and this new behavior became part of his identity. Years later, when he told people that he really wasn't as powerful as he seemed, no one took him seriously. His earlier, limited identity had prevented him from seeing himself the way he really was.

"I Would Never Have Believed That I Could Accomplish What I Did"

Throughout the years I have heard many accomplished people say, "When I was growing up, I never would have believed that I would accomplish what I have accomplished."

They're really saying, "When I was younger, my self-image would not let me do what I have actually done." The people making this kind of statement prove an important point: Thinking you can't accomplish something doesn't mean that you won't actually accomplish it in the future.

Keep asking yourself each and every day: "What would I like to accomplish today?" What would you like to accomplish but don't yet believe that you will be able to do? List things you have already accomplished that you didn't think possible. Let everything on your list remind yourself that you can accomplish more things than you now imagine.

When you focus on accomplishing, you will accomplish much more than if you don't focus on accomplishing.

Accomplishments come in many forms. Everything you do to connect with the Almighty is an accomplishment. Learning something new is an accomplishment. Developing your character traits is an accomplishment. Doing something that might seem trivial but is difficult for you to do is an accomplishment. Bringing more happiness and joy into someone's life is an accomplishment. Forgiving someone is an accomplishment. Helping another person build his self-image is an accomplishment.

Throughout the day, you can ask yourself, "What can I accomplish right now?" Then your self-image will be, "I am an accomplishment-oriented person." As you view yourself as someone who is accomplishment-oriented, you will find yourself accomplishing more.

> *I found that the person I spoke with didn't want to focus on accomplishing. "What part of focusing on accomplishing isn't to your liking?" I asked him.*
>
> *"I have found that I don't always accomplish what I would like to accomplish," he said. "Then I feel frustrated and much worse about myself. If I don't try to accomplish, I know I won't accomplish that much. But at least I don't suffer from disappointment. When I try to accomplish and don't accomplish as much as I had planned, my self-image goes down."*
>
> *"So you find it challenging to try to accomplish without succeeding to the degree that you wish?"*
>
> *"Yes," he replied.*
>
> *"But you agree that if you tried to accomplish, you would accomplish more than you do now?"*
>
> *"Certainly."*
>
> *"That means that for you to accomplish more, you need the inner courage and strength to try to accomplish, even though you have no guarantee that you will accomplish as much as you want."*
>
> *"That's right."*
>
> *"So it seems to me that just by focusing on trying to accomplish, you are automatically accomplishing. You are building up your courage to think about accomplishing, which is difficult for you to do. This way you will have a guarantee of accomplish-*

ing something. The very act of thinking of accomplishing is an accomplishment for you."

"I never thought of it that way before. This mental breakthrough is a major accomplishment for me right now."

Stop Thinking Thoughts That Lower Your Self-Image

A person creates a low self-image with his thoughts. Someone who constantly repeats demeaning self-talk will build a low self-image. The more he continues thinking and focusing on negative thoughts that lower his self-image, the worse he will feel about himself.

If you wanted to create a low self-image, your *yetzer hara* (evil inclination) would suggest that you consistently think about:

- What is wrong with you and what you have done wrong.
- Your faults, mistakes, and failures.
- Your limitations and what you can't do.
- Your inability to do things right and well.
- Not accomplishing as much as you wished.
- The negative and nasty things that other people, even well-meaning parents and teachers, have said to you throughout your life.
- Other people who are brighter than you and who have accomplished more.
- How you can compare yourself negatively with other people you know, you read about, you heard about, or you imagined.
- How far away you are from being totally perfect.

The *yetzer hara* would also tell you *not* to think about:
- Your virtues and strengths.
- The good you have done.
- Any of your accomplishments and successes.
- What you can do now to become a better person.
- Actual steps to overcome your limitations and prevent mistakes, and how to become the way you want to be.
- Who to consult about developing yourself.

Being around an extremely critical person can be very distressful. But having a very active inner critic frequently criticize what you say and do without letup creates even more distress.

"But it's true. I do have many faults and I don't have too many good points," some highly self-critical people claim.

They would be much better off if they focused on gratitude to the Almighty for all the good in their lives, and all the goodness and kindness that they could do in the world. They should focus on the positive skills and talents that they would like to improve, and on the knowledge that they would like to gain. Instead of complaining about what they don't know, they could review the ideas that they would like to remember.

Some people claim, "I think thoughts that lower my self-image because I have such a low self-image." But the truth is really the opposite. A person who feels that he has a low self-image feels this way because of the thoughts that he chooses to think. Once someone *consistently* thinks thoughts that build his self-image, he will see himself in a much better light.

"But these negative thoughts are already in my mind. How am I supposed to get rid of them?" some ask.

When you consistently think thoughts to build your self-image, these positive statements become stronger and stronger and the old negative ones get weaker and weaker. The neural pathways to the recent life-enhancing thoughts are enlarged and your mind will find it easier to travel this more beneficial path.

Keep in mind that every young child has immature ways of thinking, speaking, and acting. As people grow up the vast majority think, speak, and act in more adult ways. Even though the childish ways of thinking, speaking, and acting are stored in the brains of adults, the more mature behaviors become automatic and spontaneous.

Everyone who attempts to learn a skill and gain new knowledge is just a beginner at the start. Those who reach expert status start to automatically think and act like experts. The earlier limitations are totally overcome by the present expertise.

Some people who habitually think image-defeating statements complain that the negative thoughts are still prevalent, after thinking just a few image-building statements. To overcome a pattern of many repetitions, you need to repeat positive messages many times. Enjoy the process. You are building your mind and your thinking pattern. This will build your entire future. Realize the value of what you are doing.

If you were attached to an EMG, a biofeedback machine that measures the muscle tension you experience when you think distressful thoughts, you would see clear evidence: When you repeat positive statements and feel good about what you are doing, the current positive feelings are what you experience. Even though you might have thought negatively in the past, what you are currently thinking creates your present brain waves, muscle tension, and biochemistry.

Set goals that are reasonable and reachable. One way to create a low self-image is to aspire to goals that are impossible for you to reach. For example, "I want to *always*..." or "I want to *never*..." By focusing on improving and developing yourself in important areas, you're more likely to be successful. This will raise your self-image and motivate you to continue improving and developing.

Be totally committed and resolved to stop thinking unnecessarily negative self-image statements. Keep your focus on the thoughts that will elevate you and enhance your life.

> *"Are you claiming it's easy to stop thinking negative thoughts about oneself when one has been greatly criticized and put down by others in the past and present?" someone wrongly thought I was claiming.*
>
> *"No. I'm not claiming it's easy," I said strongly. "I am saying, however, that it's important, very important. It's certainly not easy. If it were easy, no one would think the negative thoughts*

that prevent them from being all that they could be. But just like people gain other skills and talents because they are motivated to gain them, so, too, the habit of focusing on image-building thoughts instead of the opposite is a skill that those who are motivated to do so can master.

"Ask yourself, 'How important is it for me to build my self-image in order to live a happier and more joyful life, to build my character traits, and to make and reach valuable goals in life?' Would you consider this a top priority?

"Because it's so difficult to stop thinking the image-lowering thoughts, you must be very motivated to start better patterns of thinking. You can't be wishy-washy about it. You need to be strongly committed to gain greater mastery over your thoughts."

"But I've tried to stop the negative thinking, and it hasn't worked," the fellow argued.

"What do you mean 'it hasn't worked'?" I challenged him. "There is no 'it' that is working or not. You actually mean that this is really difficult for you, and you have not yet been as successful as you wish in stopping the negative thoughts. But because it is so important for your entire life that you do stop, you need to keep doing all that you can until you see major progress."

"If I was sure I'd succeed if I kept trying, I'd be motivated to keep trying," the fellow said.

"I am absolutely certain that if you are totally committed to do whatever it takes to stop thinking image-lowering statements and instead fill your mind with more life-enhancing thoughts, you will eventually be successful," I told him.

I've had this conversation with more than one person. What have been the results? Those who were highly motivated and highly committed to stop self-defeating thoughts eventually were successful. When you personally are highly motivated and you keep persevering as long as it takes, you will see in the end that it was worth the effort.

"Next!" To Thoughts That Build Your Self-Image

There are thoughts that build your self-image, and there are thoughts that do the opposite. To build your self-image, you want to increase your image-building thoughts and decrease the thoughts that do the opposite. This sounds quite logical, doesn't it?

Whenever you think an image-building thought, you can add to its effectiveness by giving yourself positive reinforcement. "That was another image-building thought. I'm glad that my mind is doing this for me. Thank you, mind. This is great!"

But what if your mind comes up with thoughts that do not help build your self-image? What is the wisest thing to do then? You can say to yourself, "Next! On to a thought that will build my self-image." For example: "I'm happy that I recognize which thoughts are not helping my self-image. This way, I can choose better and wiser thoughts."

Realize that every moment is a new moment, and you have the ability to choose any thought at any moment. When you remember that you choose your thoughts, you can interrupt a negative thought by purposely thinking something better.

You can choose to think any of these encouraging thoughts:

• "Right now I will strengthen my inner knowledge and awareness that I have tremendous value because I am created in the Almighty's image."

• "Even though I have faults and have made mistakes, I also have many strengths and positive qualities."

• "I will do something to improve myself. Even before I take positive action, I will think about some of the positive things I can do. By planning positive actions, I increase the likelihood that I will actually follow through and take action."

- "Every failure or mistake is feedback telling me that I haven't done what I need to do. From this feedback I will learn to do something that has a better chance of being successful."
- "I will now be grateful to the Creator for all the good in my life. This gratitude will increase my ability to experience more happiness throughout my life."
- "What acts of kindness can I do now?" or "What words of kindness can I say the next time I see these people?"
- "I will now say a prayer and ask for world peace."
- "I have already chosen many positive thoughts, words, and actions throughout my life. Let me keep adding to them."
- "What have been some of the best moments of life so far?"
- "Being able to choose my thoughts is one of the greatest skills I could possibly have. I am grateful that I am becoming more and more aware of the effects of my choices of thought. Every time I willingly choose my thoughts, I build up my skill of being able to choose the best and wisest thoughts."

You can choose to think of inspiring thoughts that you have heard from various people. You can choose to sing a song that raises your spiritual consciousness.

Even if you can't think of an image-building thought after you say, "Next! On to a thought that will build my self-image," the very process of trying to find one will enable you to search for more thoughts to build your self-image in the future.

> *I once spoke to an expert who helps people build their self-image. I asked him what he thought is the biggest challenge people face when they try to build their self-image.*
>
> *He answered, "If someone built up the habit of putting himself down, even after working on building his self-image he is very likely to have put-down sentences running through his mind, at least once in a while.*
>
> *"People who are highly successful at building their self-image realize that the negative thoughts that run through their minds are just thoughts. The thoughts are not who they are.*

They realize that they can choose more positive thoughts at any given moment.

"The pattern of people who find it difficult to think thoughts that build their self-image goes something like this: 'These derogatory thoughts keep coming to my mind because they are absolutely right. I see that I haven't changed and improved. Every depressing thought shows me that I still have a problem with feelings of inferiority and a low self-image. Only if I never, ever have these negative thoughts about myself can I truly say that I have built my self-image.'

"It's almost inevitable that a person who is in the process of building his self-image will have counterproductive thoughts once in a while. That is not a sign of the absolute truth. Rather, it's just a product of habitual thoughts coming to one's mind every once in a while.

"To build one's self-image it's important to notice image-building thoughts. When you look for them, you will find them. And then when a depressing thought comes to one's mind, one can say, 'I appreciate the fact that I am now thinking more image-building thoughts. The more image-building thoughts that I think, the more spontaneous and automatic those thoughts will be.'

"When I meet with someone a number of times about improving his self-image, I start by asking, 'What are some of the self-building thoughts you have thought since the last meeting?' Asking this question has them thinking about the self-building thoughts they can report having. I also ask about their image-building actions since the last meeting. I frequently give people homework to do at least three actions to build their self-image each day. Almost everyone does many actions each day that could be considered image-building. Viewing them in this light adds to their effectiveness."

If you find that you've made a mistake, make an image-building statement. State that next time you plan to improve and do better. The form of these statements uses the "This time" and, "Next time" format:

"This time I didn't make a 'to do' list. Next time, I will."

"This time I forgot to mail an important letter. Next time I will set an alarm to help me remember to take care of it."

"This time I didn't consult anyone before I took action and I made a mistake because I acted impulsively. Next time when I have similar issues, I will discuss it with three different people."

"This time I wasted a lot of time. Next time I will be much more efficient."

"This time I lacked the courage to speak up. Next time I will say what needs to be said. I will visualize myself doing this and I will repeat these mental pictures over and over again so I will be conditioning myself to have the courage that I need."

The Power of Teshuvah

Teshuvah, repentance, has tremendous power to transform a person's entire being. Someone might have done much wrong in his life and rightfully lowered his self-image. But then he can gain an awareness of the severity of what he did wrong and the importance of becoming a new person. Sincere repentance elevates us and builds our self-image.

What are the steps of repentance? 1) We regret what we did wrong. 2) We are totally resolved not to repeat the wrongs that we have done. 3) We say *viduy*, an oral confession to the Almighty for what we have done wrong. 4) And if we have hurt another person or caused him some loss or harm, we must make amends and ask that person's forgiveness.

If a person did something wrong intentionally and then repents out of fear of the Almighty, that transgression is considered an unintentional transgression. When a person repents out of love of the Almighty, then the transgression is retroactively considered a mitzvah, a positive deed.

Why is this so? Because repenting out of love, not fear, changes a person. In this post-repentant state, he would have done positive things and never would have transgressed! This mindset is his reality from now on. This person has improved his mind and outlook, and from now on his status as a person is enhanced greatly.

Making a sincere and authentic change of mind elevates who we are and elevates our self-image. We should no longer look at ourselves from the perspective of what we were like when we did wrong. From now on, we should see with our current, more elevated awareness of who we are and what we want to do and not to do.

We see from the Talmud that one has the ability to make this identity change in one sharp moment. Before, the person was considered evil. Now, this person recognizes this and makes a powerful statement to the Almighty and to himself: "I am no longer the person who did those negative things. From now on I am totally resolved and committed to be a much better person." He might still feel bad about the wrongs that he committed, but that is no longer his identity.

When the Torah is taken out of the ark in the synagogue, there is a prayer that is recited. In this prayer there is a statement, "I am a servant of the Almighty." What does it mean to be a servant of the Almighty? It means that your identity is totally connected with the Master. Your will is to do the Master's will. You do what the Master wants you to do, and refrain from doing what the Master does not want you to do.

After repenting to the Almighty, one makes a greater commitment to increase the amount of good he will be doing. One strengthens the commitment to keep away from saying and doing things that would be against the Almighty's wishes.

Rabbeinu Yonah, author of *Shaarei Teshuvah,* wrote a classic essay on repentance. In it, he said that at times a person might be so overwhelmed with the wrongs that he did that he feels it would be impossible for him to improve. Then Rabbeinu Yonah advises a person to view himself as if he were a newborn baby. He should look at himself as if he were starting life all over again from the beginning. Then he will feel emotionally lighter and will have greater belief in his own ability to live life on a much higher level than ever before.

This advice from Rabbeinu Yonah has been a lifesaver to many people over the years. If you ever feel that you need to make a new start, remember this valuable suggestion. A person might feel, "How can I view myself as a new person? That isn't the reality!" But the authority of Rabbeinu Yonah has the credibility to allow us to use this wise, compassionate, and inspiring suggestion.

> *A person who grew up in a non-religious environment and later became mitzvah observant once told me, "Before I was Torah observant I had much more difficulties with guilt than I do now. I was always a person with a strong sense of values. I grew up in a home where there was a large emphasis on right and wrong. When I did something wrong, I was told, 'You should be ashamed of yourself for acting this way.' I did end up feeling ashamed of myself quite often. But without the formal process of teshuvah, the bad feelings that I felt stayed with me for a long time. I once heard the statement, 'G-d can forgive us for our sins, but our nervous system won't.' This applied to me very strongly. Not only did I feel strong guilt, but my self-image was always very low since I kept my major focus on all the things that I did wrong.*
>
> *"Once I became Torah observant and gained a greater realization of the infinite compassion of the Almighty, I realized that when I sincerely repented for the wrongs that I did, the Almighty would forgive me. Since the Almighty deals with us measure for measure, I made a strong commitment to forgive others each day before I went to sleep. With the merit of forgiving others, even when it is difficult, I pray that the Almighty will forgive me. My self-image is so much better now because I know that I have a deep drive to do the Almighty's will, and I sincerely repent for any wrongs that I do."*

Being in the Presence of People Who Make You Feel Good About Yourself

There are people who consistently make others feel good about themselves. When you are in the presence of someone who has a "good eye" and a "good heart," you see yourself in a more positive light. Such a person treats you with respect and makes it easier for you to increase your own level of self-respect. Such a person says and does things that bring out the best in you.

Remember how you felt about yourself after encounters with such people. Let those experiences build your self-image. Don't just look at it as, "I felt really good about myself when I spoke to this person." Rather, view these encounters as life-enhancing experiences that permanently build your self-image. Even many years later, you can allow these encounters to raise your view of yourself.

Being in the presence of people who make you feel good about yourself sheds light on the positive aspects of who you are. You can mentally relive these experiences on a regular basis. Write a list of the names of some people you respect who made you feel good about yourself. Especially when you feel that your self-image needs a boost, read the list of those names. Recall how you felt in their presence. Remember what you thought about yourself.

Aharon, the older brother of Moshe, was able to make others feel good about themselves. He was the High Priest, an elevated spiritual person. He would go out of his way to befriend people who needed a spiritual lift. Those people would say to themselves, "Since Aharon is treating me with respect it shows that he sees the good in me." They would see the good in themselves and this would permanently elevate those people.

Be a person who makes others feel good about themselves. Speak to people in a way that makes them feel respected. Identify other people by their good qualities and their strengths. When you do, your very interaction can help them gain a greater awareness of their own positive qualities. You will raise their self-image and have a positive influence on them.

To help other people feel better about themselves, some questions you might ask are:
- What are five successes you've had in your life?
- What are five of your favorite memories?
- What are five of the most positive things that people have said to you?
- What are five things that you are good at?

> Years ago, someone told me how a change of schools made a major difference in his entire sense of identity. The principal and teachers were highly critical at the school he attended when he was younger. They had high standards. But they corrected the students by pointing out everything they were doing wrong.
>
> In the presence of those teachers, he felt that he was always making mistakes and always doing things that were wrong, and he always lacked proper respect for his teachers. His self-image was low and in general he felt bad about himself. He had a bleak view of his future.
>
> Then, when he was around eleven years old, his family moved to a different city and he was enrolled in a new school. The first meeting he had with the principal was a liberating experience. The principal had a friendly smile. He said to the new student, "You look to me like a boy who will do wonderfully in our school. Our goal is to help you bring out the best in yourself. If anything isn't going the way you would like, please come to my office and we'll try to work it out together."
>
> The teachers kept pointing out the good things that he was doing. When he answered a question in class, he was highly praised, just like all the other students were. There was a great atmosphere in this school.

Whenever he met other alumni years later, they would all talk about how the approach of the principal and the teachers did wonders for their self-image. He attributes much of his success in life to those wonderful teachers who gave him such a positive sense of his own identity.

Authentic Self-Image Versus Projecting an Image for Others

People with a positive and healthy self-image will be authentic. They want to be who they really are. Their goal is to truly be their ideal type of person. They think, speak, and act in ways that are consistent with the ideals, values, positive traits, and qualities that they wish to live up to.

They realize that everyone has ups and downs. They realize that they are likely to make mistakes and errors. They realize that they might slip and be off balance at times, but they take stock of themselves and strengthen themselves. They reinforce their deep resolve to think, speak, and act according to their ideal selves.

Other people become performers, even though they don't actually perform. They keep their main focus on how other people react to them. They consistently want to impress others. They keep thinking about what others are thinking about them. When others applaud and praise, they feel good about themselves. If this admiration is lacking, they feel bad about themselves. Applause and praise is pleasurable. But there is a major difference between making applause, praise, and admiration a goal in itself, or just using it as a tool to feel better. When a person keeps his main focus on projecting an image for others, his self-image will totally depend on the responses and reactions of others. A self-image built on other people's reactions won't be stable. It will go up and down depending on how the audience reacts. The emotional states of people with this mindset are totally dependent on others.

It is much wiser to create your self-image based on your ideals and values, on your own thoughts and actions, not on the responses of others. Some individuals can totally transcend the reactions of others, but this skill takes much time to develop. Each and every day you think, speak, and act in ways that truly build who you are.

A person who is excessively dependent on the reactions of others will feel strong distress when others disapprove or are critical. Not only will they feel bad, they will feel bad about themselves. They will feel that they are worth less as people because of the way others look at them.

They need to build their self-image in a way that is real and authentic. They need to think, speak, and act in ways that they feel good about. They need to pray and say blessings with a greater connection with the Almighty. They need to do good in this world for their own inner approval. When you approve of your actions, you feel good about yourself. Then the positive thoughts and feelings you have about yourself are a foundation on which you can keep building. It is a foundation that is strong.

> *Someone told me, "I once heard a rabbi speak about not needing the approval and honor of others. He kept saying how those who depend on honor and approval are like robots: Others push their buttons. Others control them. We need to have a greater focus on having the approval of the Almighty. The approval and honor of other people is just a temporary and short-lasting pleasure. It can't possibly last. 'Don't care what others think about you,' the rabbi said emphatically.*
>
> *"That's easy for him to say," my acquaintance had thought. "He's a scholar and a great speaker. Everyone honors him. So he's humble and truly doesn't look for honor. But he gets so*

much honor anyway. I hardly get any honor. Honor is much more important for me than it is for him.

"I don't really want honor for its own sake. I want to feel good about myself. I want the basics of having a positive self-image. Once I do feel good about myself and have a positive self-image, then I too can focus on not needing honor. His talk made me feel bad, even though I know he meant well.

"When I woke up the next day I thought about what the rabbi had said. I realized, 'He really is right. It makes total sense to make my own self-image and happiness in life depend only on my own thoughts and actions. Let me try this out for an entire day. I will treat other people with respect and won't say or do anything to cause distress to others. But I will keep my total focus on appreciating the good I do for its own sake.'

"The results were amazing. At the end of the day, I felt really good. I decided to keep acting this way for an entire week. At the end of the week, I had a much greater realization that deep down I had very high ideals and aspirations. I truly wanted to speak and act in ways that were consistent with high ideals. I felt much better about myself than I had in a long time.

"I have been continuing my experiment, but to tell the truth, I still enjoy the positive feedback of others. I feel good when people tell me, 'Well done,' and similar statements. Hearing praise is still pleasurable, but it's no longer my focus. I feel liberated. My mind feels free. The good feelings that I feel are much more independent of anyone else's reaction. I see that I haven't lost anything by not focusing on the reactions of others. I have only gained spiritually and emotionally."

Self-Mastery Builds Your Self-Image

Every time you have self-mastery in any way, you build up your self-image. You can tell yourself, "I am a person who is gaining more and more control over my emotions and actions all the time." Every time you have the emotional self-control to do something that you find difficult to do, you build up your self-image. Every time you refrain from saying or doing something, you build up your self-image.

There are two basic approaches to gaining a greater amount of self-mastery. One is to recognize the many benefits you gain by controlling your actions and emotions. The other is to gain greater awareness of how you lose out by lacking self-mastery. Use both approaches together to gain greater levels of self-mastery.

Some people fine themselves in order to increase their ability to refrain from doing something. Some people reward themselves in order to increase their ability to have self-mastery. A general rule for fines and rewards: The fine should be something that you strongly want to avoid, and the reward should be something that you greatly want to receive.

Some people keep self-mastery journals. Writing down their successes and victories in exhibiting self-control improves their ability to exhibit a greater amount of self-mastery.

Some people find that even if they don't actually give themselves rewards and punishments, they can add to their ability to have self-mastery by questioning themselves. If they want to do something but find that they need extra willpower, they ask, "What reward would motivate me to actually do the thing that I would want to do?" To stop doing something, they ask, "What pain or fine would increase my motivation to refrain?" Just thinking of the answers to these questions helps people with strong imaginations gain more self-mastery, even without giving themselves the actual reward or fine.

> *Someone who had a great challenge with overeating told me, "For me eating wasn't merely a matter of being healthy, getting energy, and enjoying myself. Instead, eating was a constant challenge to my self-image. I felt good about myself when I controlled what I ate, and I felt awful about myself when I lacked self-discipline. My self-image would go up and down depending on my level of self-control about food.*
>
> *"I have a friend who has a similar issue with smoking cigarettes. When he overcame the urge to take a cigarette, he felt much better about himself. His self-image dropped whenever he gave in to the urge to smoke.*
>
> *"I told him that even though we have issues with different areas of self-mastery, we have a similar challenge. We agreed to be partners in building up our self-mastery. We would encourage each other. We would celebrate our successes together. And if one of us would fail to have self-mastery, the other would encourage him to increase the level of self-control.*
>
> *"One pattern that kept working for both of us was to remind each other, 'You will feel much better about yourself when you have self-mastery. You will feel much worse about yourself when you lack self-mastery.' We found that this constant reminder made it easier for us to forego the pleasure of overeating or smoking. When you know how awful it feels to feel bad about yourself, feeling good about yourself is such a great feeling that nothing else can compare with it."*

Thinking About Self-Image: Self-Centeredness and Beyond

People reading this book will be thinking about their own self-image automatically. Just reading the previous sentence places your focus on the word "self-image." Isn't self-centeredness a serious fault? Isn't thinking about yourself an aspect of being selfish?

Every infant is totally self-centered. Every little child is self-centered. As we grow older and have a broader perspective of life and our mission in the world, we gain greater awareness of other people. We become more aware of and concerned about other people and their needs and wants. The most kindhearted and giving people in the world will think about many other people — but they do this from their own perspective: "What can I say and do to help other people?" The "I" is still there. Let's take an objective look at the human condition. You think about eating each day, don't you? For some people this is just a minor thought in their day, and for others it is a major focus. But *everyone* has to think about their own eating to some degree. Someone who doesn't eat at all for an entire day will spend some thought about not eating.

You think about sleep each day. You think about your activities and plans for the day and you think about what you need to do. You think about other people, but you always think about them from your perspective. You might think about the weather, but you will be thinking about the local weather that will affect you. "Will it rain? Do I need a coat or an umbrella?"

Aren't all these thoughts focused on you? Yes. And as a human being, you must focus on you, your needs, what you are doing, and what you need to do. We live in our own minds and in our own bodies, and therefore our nervous system registers how everything affects us. You can't *not* think about yourself and what's important to you.

A self-centered person thinks mostly about meeting his own needs. The more we think about doing good for others, the more we go beyond our own self-centeredness. Parents view their children as an extension of themselves and therefore give much attention to meeting the needs and wishes of their children. The more elevated and kind and giving people are, the more individuals they consider as extensions of themselves. A person who cares about a vast number of other people identifies with them and considers them to be part of his own life. In a way this care and concern about others becomes an integral part of his own need.

As we build up our kindness-to-others consciousness, we become more elevated. The more we go beyond our own selves, the more meaningful and purposeful our lives become.

> *There was once a person who kept claiming, "I can't stand how selfish most people are. They only think of themselves. I am a person who only cares about others. I do so much for other people, more than many other people do. I live for others. All that I do is to help other people. I only want the things I want so I can help other people. As a matter of fact, other people are my main concern.*
>
> *"I love telling people how much I love to help. I love telling people about what a wonderful person I am because I am so good to others. I love telling the people in the store where I shop about how I am always thinking of other people when I buy things.*
>
> *"I only want to help people who acknowledge my kindness and how good I am. If someone lacks gratitude, it would be wrong of me to do things for them; I would just be making them more ungrateful. It bothers me so much that other people don't think of others as much as I do."*
>
> *This individual had a self-image believing that he was kind and giving and totally selfless. If only he would realize that while others were the topic of his thoughts, he used them as a*

means of building up his own ego. He was strongly self-centered when considering other people. Acknowledging this would have helped him be less selfish in his thoughts and actions.

Many truly unselfish people might even consider themselves to be selfish: "Doing things for other people is really selfish on my part. I love to do kindness. It makes me feel so good that nothing else I could do would give me as much pleasure."

Humility and Arrogance

Torah writings highly praise humility and modesty, and strongly condemn arrogance and conceit. How does having a positive self-image fit with this?

True humility isn't a lack of a positive self-image. It's an awareness of the greatness of the Creator and how tiny we are in comparison. It's an awareness of how much good there is to do and how little we are doing in contrast.

The Steipler, Rabbi Yaakov Yisroel Kaniefsky, was known for his greatness in Torah and his authentic humility. He used to tell the following story to explain his humility:

Imagine someone on a train ride through Europe. He travels through Switzerland, France, Belgium, Germany, and other countries. He sees many cities, many mountains, many lakes, and many people. He visits the train stations in many places.

Although he traveled many miles, you can't say that he really knows those places well. His knowledge of the areas he passed is really superficial. Compared to someone who never visited those places at all, he has seen a tremendous amount; in relation to what there is to know about those places, he knows only a small amount.

"That is my reality when it comes to knowing Torah," the Steipler said. "I have learned many hours and know a lot, only when compared to not knowing it. But compared to what there is to know, I know only a drop in the bucket."

Moshe is praised in the Torah for being "more humble than all other people." Moshe was the leader of the Jewish people in Egypt and the Wilderness. He grew up as a prince in Pharaoh's palace. He confronted Pharaoh and proclaimed that Pharaoh should free the Jewish people from slavery and let them leave Egypt. He was the greatest prophet. He knew the entire Torah and was the ultimate teacher and main judge of the entire nation.

How could he possibly be humble?

Humility is the awareness that all our knowledge, skills, and talents are gifts from the Almighty. Exactly because of Moshe's superior awareness of the greatness of the Creator and Sustainer of the universe, he realized that he was nothing in comparison. All that he had and knew and did were merely because of the Almighty's kind gifts.

Having a positive self-image comes from realizing that because you're a child of the Almighty, created in His image, you have intrinsic worth and value. You have no reason to be arrogant or conceited because of this, just grateful.

Because of your gratitude to the Creator, you have greater awareness of all the assets, skills, and talents He has given you. You appreciate them immensely. But because you're aware that they are Divine gifts, you are free from arrogance and conceit. There is a major difference between knowing that you are competent in some area and having feelings of superiority because of it.

Your respect for other people comes from your deep awareness that they are created in the Almighty's image. Therefore you never treat anyone else condescendingly. You never belittle anyone. You realize that everyone has something you can learn from. You realize that you need to respect everyone you encounter. This way of interacting with others is an expression of humility.

People who are conceited tend to boast a lot. People try to boost their self-image and feel good. It is normal for humans to want others to view them in a positive light. While the ultimate in humility would be to refrain from boasting entirely, a balanced amount of boasting is understandable; one would not be considered conceited for modest boasting. Excessive boasting, however, is a sign of conceit and arrogance. A braggart can be highly annoying to others, especially if he tends to repeat himself. Some boasters will try to minimize their boasting by saying, "I don't want to boast, but…" Of course this person wants to boast! Most people would want to, even if they refrain because they view it as a fault or because they don't want to arouse envy.

It's important to differentiate between boasting and sharing your successes with people who sincerely wish you well and enjoy your success. Children especially have a strong need to show their parents that they have been successful. This is a way they build their self-image. Parents can encourage them to be grateful to Hashem for their success, building gratitude and balanced modesty.

Arrogance leads to anger. "How dare they speak to someone like me like that!" "They should realize how important I am and treat me with the respect that an important person like me should be treated." "How dare they keep me waiting?"

Everyone deserves to be treated with respect. But a modest person with a healthy self-image will be much calmer about slights, especially if unintended.

An arrogant person won't acknowledge mistakes and errors. He might not even acknowledge to himself that he could be making a mistake. "Who, me? I'm never wrong." He certainly won't admit to anyone else that the other person was right and he was wrong. A person with a modest and healthy self-image, however, seeks truth and reality. He is happy to rectify errors and correct mistakes. He has the quality of "acknowledging the truth."

A person who is excessively ego-driven will make many mistakes. He might think that he has a positive self-image, because he is "just being honest with himself about how great he is" and "how much more superior" he is than others. But his arrogance will lead to his saying and doing many things that antagonize others. His arrogance will make him self-centered.

Some people who are arrogant and conceited speak and act as if they have a very positive self-image. But in reality their self-image is fragile. It can be shaken and thrown off balance. As the popular saying goes, "A superiority complex is actually an inferiority complex." Similarly, it has been said, "Rudeness is a weak person's imitation of strength."

When someone has a comprehensive view of life, he will be aware of the limitations and frailties of the human condition. He will be aware that a person might be a president or prime minister of a powerful country, but a single bullet can totally disable or kill him; a heart attack, a stroke, or Alzheimer's can render him helpless. A person might be considered an Iron Man, but a debilitating disease might weaken him to such an extent that he is unable to hold a pen in his hand.

We need to be grateful for our lives and for the abilities that we do have, but knowing that it's all just a gift makes us realize that it's ours temporarily. How can anyone be arrogant when he knows that he doesn't know what will be in just a moment!

A person who has authentic modesty with a healthy self-image has an inner security. He will be more flexible and open to discuss differences. He will be much calmer and will experience much less stress.

A modest person with a healthy self-image will be a happier person. He doesn't have demanding expectations of life. Therefore he has greater satisfaction and appreciation for what he does have and less distress from disappointments.

A person with a modest and healthy self-image will get along more harmoniously with others. He will be much more at ease and he will bring out the best in others. He will be respected and liked. He won't arouse needless envy and antagonism. He will speak and act pleasantly. In general, he will be more balanced in all of his ways.

> *A number of years ago, I spoke to an esteemed Torah scholar who spoke to many students. "In previous generations the emphasis was on developing humility and keeping away from arrogance. Why is it that in recent years the importance of having a positive self-image is considered a high priority?" I asked.*
>
> *He replied, "I personally have been alive only during the years when I was alive, so I can't really tell you very much about the generations before I was around. But I can say with certainty,*

after speaking to a large number of students and doing what I can to influence them to learn Torah with joy and to feel good about themselves, that the issue of having a positive self-image is highly important.

"Arrogance always has been and still is a negative trait. It has been equated to denying the Almighty. It is in itself a major fault and it leads to many other character defects. True humility combined with joy and courage is a highly positive trait in itself and it leads to many virtues and positive qualities.

"There are students who I feel need more humility, and they need to conquer their conceit and arrogance. But the majority of students need to gain a greater awareness of their value and worth. They need to believe in their abilities and know that they will be able to accomplish in important ways. They need to feel proud that they are studying Torah. Building up their level of self-confidence allows them to have a much greater positive influence on others."

Realizing the Complexity of Accurate Self-Knowledge

It's important to differentiate between building your self-image and having detailed self-knowledge. When we refer to building your self-image we are talking about an overall view of yourself, your self-concept as a valuable and important human being, your knowledge that you are in a constant process of developing positive character traits and patterns of thoughts, words, and actions.

We can talk about improving your self-image. But the concept of self-knowledge is much more complex and comprehensive.

Rabbi Yisroel Salanter, founder of the *Mussar* movement, observed, "People can live with themselves for seventy years and still not know themselves."

As I wrote in the Introduction to *Gateway to Self-Knowledge* in 1986,

> *"It has been noted that if we assume a person's personality would contain just twenty characteristics, each of which can be rated on a ten-point scale, over a hundred quadrillion different descriptions of people would be possible. This vividly illustrates the uniqueness of each and every person, especially since there are many more than twenty traits. Each person is born with unique tendencies and potential for development, and grows up in a unique and changing environment. The mixture of the tendencies one is born with and the influences of one's environment shape our personality. When working on self-improvement one must take one's basic personality into consideration. But your own choices of thoughts, words, and behaviors are the key to who you are. You create yourself with your choices."*

Being more aware of the choices that you are already making allows greater awareness of your present self, and greater clarity as to the wisest choices to keep making.

The great *Mussar* teachers have taught that no person ever knows himself totally and perfectly. We all have blind spots and areas of unawareness. It's difficult to obtain self-knowledge for many reasons: It's easy to be unaware of what motivates us; we might fail to remember all our experiences and our choices; we might distort what actually happened in the past; and we are likely to speak and act differently in different situations.

In *Gateway to Self-Knowledge*, p. 36, I wrote:

> *Some people become confused about knowing themselves. Their confusion goes something like this: "I don't know who I am, or what I want. Who is the real me? I have an identity crisis." Often, the problem is the question itself. Human beings are the sum total of all their thoughts, words, and actions. Since this*

includes a multitude of categories and myriad factors in each category, it is impossible to sum up the true identity of a person in a few sentences.

For accurate self-knowledge, people must break down their thoughts and motivations, feelings and emotions, words and sentences, actions and behaviors, into specifics. It is not that a person either has self-knowledge or does not have it. Rather, it is a matter of degree. Everyone has some self-knowledge, but hardly anyone will have total self-knowledge.

Rabbi Avraham Grodzensky (the *Mashgiach* of pre-World War II Slobodka Yeshiva) wrote about self-knowledge: "To know yourself properly it is not sufficient to take a superficial, general look at yourself. Rather, you need to take a close look at each and every detail. You need to try to understand every word that comes out of your mouth. You need to be aware of every minor action and movement, every thought that goes racing through your mind, every change in your emotional state, every passing feeling of happiness and sadness" (*Toras Avraham*, p. 395).

The great *Mussar* personalities excelled in this total process. One major point to keep in mind: These elevated people had a strong appreciation for the greatness of being created in the image of the Almighty and for being children of the Creator and Sustainer of the universe. They were immersed in Torah study, prayer, and kindness. They had exemplary character traits. Therefore they were able to engage in the process described in *Toras Avraham*. The vast majority of people need to first build their self-image before analyzing all the thousands and thousands of tiny details of each thought, word, and action.

Rabbi Shlomo Wolbe wrote in the first volume of *Alei Shur* (p. 151), cited in *Gateway to Self-Knowledge* (p. 32):

> *"One of the major difficulties in obtaining self-knowledge is that in our imagination we might have an illusory picture of ourselves. The picture we might have is without any shortcomings and our positive qualities might be exaggerated a thousand times over. Moreover, it is possible that in our imagination, positive traits we actually have are missing from*

> *our view of ourselves and in their place are other virtues that in reality we are missing. The problem is that we might relate to ourselves from the perspective of our imaginary picture. This picture might be directing our actions and our words. If you sincerely want to know yourself, you will have to be aware of what is illusory and what is reality. You have to try to observe yourself as you actually are."*

There are two extremes in being mistaken about oneself. One pattern is a pattern described in *Madraigas Haadam* (Section: *Cheshbon Hanefesh*):

> *"There are some people who have a tendency to always judge themselves favorably. Whatever such a person does, he always assumes that he has the loftiest of motivations. When he shouts at someone, it is always for the other person's good. He feels sad; it is because of thoughts of repentance. He pursues power; it is only to help others. He refuses to change his opinions; it is because he is consistent. He is abrupt when speaking to others; he wants to speak concisely. He acts impulsively; it is because he acts with the attribute of alacrity. He bears a grudge; it is to teach others a lesson. He lies; it is always for the sake of peace. He does not do others favors; it is because he is afraid that he will have ulterior motives."*

On the other hand, there are people who focus excessively on their own faults. Even when they perform good deeds, they judge themselves unfavorably. They always assume that they have negative motivations and never accomplish enough good. They consider themselves to be much worse than they actually are.

Both extremes are harmful. People who always judge themselves favorably won't correct their faults, because they assume they don't have any. Conversely, people who see everything they do in a negative light are apt to consider themselves failures and might feel despair about ever improving. They might be guilt-ridden and depressed, and won't have the inner strength and energy to improve themselves.

It is most productive to be balanced. We must be aware of our strengths and virtues. Then, when we are aware of what we need to do to improve, we will have the self-confidence and inner strength to do what we need to do.

Even though we will never know ourselves totally and perfectly, thinking about our thoughts, feelings, words, and actions will help us gain more awareness about ourselves than if we wouldn't think about this.

Two stories that appeared in *Gateway to Self-Knowledge* (pp. 34-35) are appropriate to cite here:

> A young man once came to his rabbi and asked him for advice on how to overcome the trait of arrogance.
>
> "You have asked a very important question," replied the rabbi. "Please sit down until I finish some communal matters and then we can discuss your problem."
>
> While the young man was waiting, the first person who came to consult the Rabbi asked him for a loan. He had to marry off his daughter and needed financial assistance. The rabbi turned to the young man and said, "Can you lend this person the money he needs?"
>
> "I'm sorry, but I am poor myself. I don't have any money to lend to someone else," the young man answered softly.
>
> A few minutes later someone else came to the rabbi with a very difficult question in Jewish law. The Rabbi turned to the young man and asked him how he would answer the question. The young man replied, "I'm not a very big scholar and that question is far beyond my knowledge."
>
> A few minutes later a businessman came in and consulted the rabbi in reference to some business difficulties he was having. "What would you suggest that he can to do to solve his problem?" the rabbi once again asked the young man.
>
> "I really don't know anything about business," the man replied.
>
> After the businessman had left, the rabbi turned to the young man and said, "Look, you don't have any money, you lack knowledge in both Torah matters and the business world. Why do you need any suggestions about arrogance? You have nothing to be arrogant about!" (Al Hatorah-Aikev).

> In reference to a statement by Rabbi Eliyahu Dessler who said, "One can study about humility and feel conceited for doing so" (Michtav MaiEliyahu, vol. 3, p. 320), we cited the Baal Shem Tov who related, "False humility can be illustrated by this story: A gifted person who was both learned and charitable was afflicted with the blemish of conceit. He was told that when he learned humility he would become a perfect person. He therefore studied humility until apparently mastering it. Soon afterwards, someone failed to show him respect. The supposedly humble person was enraged and shouted, "How dare you act disrespectfully towards me? Do you not realize that since I have learned humility I am a person of perfect character?" (Keser Shaim Tov, p. 23a).

Accurate self-knowledge demands a large amount of self-discipline and inner strength. Someone with a strong sense of innate self-worth and value who wants to read questions about various character traits to reflect on details of his strengths and weaknesses should read *Gateway to Self-Knowledge.* Please read *Gateway to Happiness* first.

Finding a teacher or coach who recognizes your strengths and potential, who sees you in a positive light, who cares about you and considers it a high priority to continue to help you develop yourself further, will be highly beneficial in the process of gaining a more comprehensive self-knowledge, Such a teacher or coach will help motivate you to make and reach valuable goals.

Be patient. Self-knowledge is a lifetime quest. The more self-knowledge you gain, the greater awareness you will have about what thoughts and actions will enable you to increase your general level of happiness and joy. These are resources you need for the journey.

"Challenges Strengthen Me"

Let challenges strengthen you. Every human being alive faces challenges. Some have more challenges and some fewer.

Once you have become stronger from any challenge you faced, you can have a self-image of: "I am a person who has already been strengthened by a challenge." You probably have been strengthened by more than one challenge already. If this is true for you, you can have a self-image of: "I am a person who has already been strengthened by challenges."

Remember times when you were strengthened by challenges. Each time you recall an incident that both challenged and strengthened you, you can say to yourself, "Here is another example of when I was strengthened by a challenge." This strengthens your positive self-image.

From now on, whenever you find yourself facing any challenge, let it strengthen you in some way. Think of some positive character trait that you can continue to develop because of the challenge. Then you can say to yourself, "Since I have already been strengthened by challenges, this too can add to my inner mental archive of another time that I will be strengthened by a challenge."

Rabbi Moshe Chaim Luzzatto wrote in his classic work *Mesilas Yeshorim* (Ch. 1): "Every life situation is another challenge for a person. Health is a challenge and illness is a challenge. Wealth is a challenge and poverty is a challenge."

Think about how you can grow from health and how you can grow from illness. Think about how you can grow from wealth and how you can grow from poverty. Think about how you can grow when things go the way you want, and how you can grow when things don't go the way you want.

Some people who find it difficult to face challenges with a positive attitude view their reaction as coming from the reality of the situation. But our reaction to any situation is always based on our own subjective way of looking at it. There is a multitude of ways to look at any situation.

Let's give one example: If five people were to witness a bank robbery, you would have five different versions of what happened. This is especially so if one person was the bank teller who was held up. One was a grandmother who was waiting in line with her grandchild. One was a hidden co-conspirator of the bank robber. One was a teenager who loved excitement. One was a victim of a previous violent crime.

And with another five people you could have another five versions. One was a person who had a strong tendency to focus on the good in each and every situation. He would be happy and grateful that no one was hurt. One was a pessimistic, negative thinker who frequently complained that negative things frequently happen to him. One was a person who desperately needed the money he was about to withdraw from his bank account. One was a freelance writer for a magazine who appreciated the opportunity to write about something newsworthy that he witnessed. One was a person with a heart condition who was warned by his physician that he needed to stay calm for the health of his heart.

And the eleventh person there was someone whose attitude was, "Every single challenging situation in my life is sent as an opportunity for me to develop my character." This person had mastered staying calm and seeing the good.

He was able to speak to the bank robber because he approached him from a place of unconditional love and compassion for everyone. He calmed the robber so that the robber wouldn't hurt anyone. And he calmed those who were nervous about the experience, agreeing with the one who focused on what there was to be grateful for.

The negative thinker was highly impressed with the lesson of the eleventh person. He had begun to look at the situation as, "Oh no! Here is another example of a negative thing happening to me." But now he realized, "I see that there is another way to view what happened. I can be grateful that we were safe and unharmed." He then realized that many of the "bad luck" events and occurrences in his life were really much more positive. Moreover, he saw how calm and understanding the eleventh man was, and he became a student of that person's outlook on life. This was the best thing that ever happened to him in his entire life. He was so grateful that each year he would celebrate the day that he gained a wiser understanding of the purpose of life and how he could be consistently calm and happy.

Whenever you come across a story about someone who has grown from a challenge, think, "Since I have read or heard this story of how someone grew from this challenge, I now have this pattern stored in my brain. My brain is always with me. So I can add to my self-image: 'I am a person who has read and heard about patterns of growing from challenges.' This will strengthen my own resolve to grow from challenges. Instead of worrying about potential challenges that I might face, I will keep thinking about how I will grow from any challenge that might come my way."

> "I used to consider myself a worrier," someone told me. "I worried about a long list of things. I was told as a young child, 'You are just like your mother. She is a worrier, and you inherited her worry genes.' Every time I worried, I said to myself, 'There you go worrying again. That's who you are and there is probably little you can do about it.'
>
> "One day in class the teacher said, 'No one is a worrier. Worrying is just a pattern of thinking. One might say, "I tend to think in a worrying pattern. When I do think this way, I feel nervous and full of anxiety." But since you are not a worrier without your worrying thoughts, you can make a profound decision. You can be resolved to change your thoughts. You can say, "Every time I worry about something happening, I will say to myself, 'Every time I think a worrying thought, either it won't actually happen and I will feel relieved. Or it will happen and I will grow from the experience. I will also think about potential solutions. I will think about what I can do to prevent the thing from happening. Every challenge will make me a stronger person, and will add to my expertise in finding potential solutions.'"'"

"Even before I overcame my tendency to worry, I saw that I was improving by thinking in better patterns. After a little improvement, I was able to say to myself, 'I can't honestly define myself as being a worrier. I see that this is a pattern of thought. Little by little I am getting better at thinking in ways that enable me to be and remain much calmer than before.'

"This was enough to change my self-image. I stopped calling myself a worrier. I understood that worrying was just a habit of thought. Being aware that what I was thinking created worry motivated me to think in better ways. That one change in my thinking has been tremendously helpful. Viewing myself as a born worrier added to my tendency to worry. Viewing myself as a person whose thoughts could create worry, but who could learn to think in better ways, gave me the realization that I could keep working on my thoughts and no longer had to view myself as someone condemned to worry his whole life. Every bit of improvement added to my self-image of someone who was developing better patterns of thinking."

Some Benefits of a Low Self-Image

Since there are so many people with low self-images, there must be some benefits. Those who have a low self-image and find it difficult to improve would gain by focusing on some of the positive aspects of having a low self-image. So here goes:

Benefit 1 of having a low self-image: When you presently feel low about who you are and what you have done, you might try harder to be more and accomplish more. You might feel so bad that you have a low self-image that you will try to do a multitude of positive things in order to try to feel better about yourself.

As the saying I might've coined goes, "Many charitable organizations are heavily sponsored by people who would like to feel better about themselves." Please, never tell people who donate to a worthy cause that now they can feel good about themselves; this might scare them away from giving the donation.

Since there are so many negative ways that people can try to feel good about themselves, when someone tries a positive way, he deserves to be commended. As the Sages have taught: "A person should do good even without the highest motivations. When you do something positive without pure motivations, you are likely to elevate your motivations."

Benefit 2 of having a low self-image: When you put yourself down, you save other people the bother of putting you down. They are likely to say, "He puts himself down all the time. I don't have to put in the effort to put him down. He'll do it to himself for me."

Benefit 3 of having a low self-image: If anyone claims that you are arrogant or conceited, you can say, "I might not be modest and humble, but I know that I'm not arrogant, because I don't have anything to be arrogant about."

Benefit 4 of having a low self-image: You will belong to the low-self-image club. When others tell you that they have a low self-image, you can gleefully announce, "It's great to meet a fellow low-self-imager. I also have a low self-image."

Benefit 5 of having a low self-image: You will be free from feeling bad about not accomplishing very much. "Who am I to accomplish anything?" a low-self-imager can say. "I'm surprised that I know the alphabet and can read."

Benefit 6 of having a low self-image: You will save yourself from any tension and stress that someone might have from competing about anything. You will assume from the start that you will probably lose anyway. So while you might not feel the joy of victory, at least you will be saved from the stress and tension of the competition.

Problem caused by having a high self-image because of a trivial victory: When I was about ten years old, I helped my sister win in a neighborhood competition in the park near our house. (It's famous for the cannon left over from the War of 1812. Because it was the United States against England, regardless of who would win the war, I grew up speaking English and this book was originally written in English.)

Back to that early childhood victory: There were multiple category entries in a major doll contest. There were categories such as: The prettiest doll, the biggest doll, the tiniest doll, the cutest dog doll, the nicest Teddy Bear, the fishiest fish doll, etc.

I figured that there would be hundreds of little girls who would want to win in the prettiest-doll category, and my sister wouldn't have too much of a chance of winning. We didn't have a very large doll in the house or a very tiny doll.

The category that I thought wouldn't have too many entries was "the most battered doll" category. I figured that not too many little girls would feel proud about winning in this category. So with a ten-year-old boy's thinking pattern, I took one of my sister's dolls and smashed it with a hammer. I tore the doll and made it look as if it were found in the trashcan in our inner-city neighborhood.

I felt great joy when we went to the area of the large park where the contest was held. There were hundreds of entries in the prettiest doll category; that category had the largest number of entries. The category that we entered had only three entries. I was puzzled how anyone could have considered one of the entries "the most battered." It had only a few scratches. I had done such a good job of destroying our doll that I was absolutely confident that my sister would get a ribbon for being in first place in our category.

I was right. We won! (At least in our category.)

Ever since then I have had a victorious early childhood memory. We came in first place. That raised my self-image. Whenever I would think of competing, I knew that I already had a self-image building experience.

This dubious victory shows one of the problems and down sides of having a positive self-image too early in life. You might be satisfied too easily with something trivial.

I have to mention that many years later, when we were both grandparents, I reminded my sister of that "victory."

"That's why you did that!" she exclaimed. "I always wondered why you ruined that doll of mine. It wasn't like you to break my toys."

I found that fascinating. For me, that was a positive memory. If I had known that it would be distressful to my sister, I wouldn't have damaged the doll. I apologize.

A Purim Parable: A Lesson for the Entire Year

I woke up one Purim morning as a turtle. You might be wondering what kind of turtle I became. Well, it's hard to describe myself objectively since by definition we're all subjective about ourselves. But I can tell you that I wasn't one of those small little midget turtles. I was a relatively large one. Not one of those super giant turtles, just your average "large" size.

To say that I was surprised about this change would be a gross understatement. I had always been a human being when I woke up in the morning. This was my very first time to wake up as a turtle. I used to wake up and express my profound gratitude to the Creator for returning my soul to me once again. As I was about to do the same this morning, I was quite astonished to notice that I had woken up as a turtle.

You must be asking how I felt. Well, how would you feel if you woke up and found yourself transformed into a turtle? Was I frightened? No. I always felt very strongly that one of the highest priorities in life is to accept the Almighty's will. At times this can be difficult. At times this can be highly challenging. But that was my goal. And although this experience was more difficult to accept than most, I still felt an inner joy about being given an opportunity to accept the Almighty's will in ways that I had never planned for.

When you expect to be faced with a specific difficulty, you can train yourself in advance. You can visualize yourself accepting it with inner strength and courage. You can mentally picture yourself handling it in an elevated manner. But in my wildest dreams I had never imagined that I would one day wake up and find myself being a turtle. Well, truth can be stranger than fiction. And since this was my present reality, I immediately focused on accepting the will of my Creator. If this was my test for today, this was the test that I was totally dedicated to pass.

I saw myself moving slowly. I didn't yet have a clear plan about where I was heading, but one must always have a goal. So I figured that my first goal would be to create a meaningful goal for myself. Since this was my first day tasked with being an excellent turtle, I didn't yet have enough information to decide what my goal would be. So I couldn't make a specific goal with all the details planned step by step. I had a general goal of using my potential to its fullest. Those who make this their goal will usually have problems deciding what their potential actually is and what they need to do to utilize this potential. But we must always do the best we can and, so far, this was the best I could do.

Although I was moving slowly, I was making steady progress. When I was a human being, I realized the importance of being grateful for the gifts we were given. This realization stayed with me now that I was a turtle. As a turtle I didn't have as many things to be grateful for as when I was a human being, but I did find something. I was extremely grateful that I had my hard outer shell. This protected me in case a predator tried to take advantage of my lack of speed. If anyone would shout, "HURRY UP!" at me, I would just disappear into my shell. That's what shells are for.

I wanted to make steady progress, but at my own speed. If others weren't satisfied with the rate of that progress, it wouldn't bother me. The depth of gratitude for my hard shell increased as I thought of all its many benefits. I was full of inner joy, and a joyful turtle is a healthy turtle.

For me, the speed I was going was normal. Progress is relative. If others would see things from my perspective, they wouldn't be so judgmental. I didn't choose to become a turtle. It just happened to me. If you were a turtle, you might be one of those speedy ones, but even then you wouldn't be going too much faster than I was.

After my initial surprise about my change in status, I didn't feel bad about being a turtle. If this was what the Creator wanted from me, this was His will and I accepted it with love. On Judgment Day, I won't be asked why I didn't act like a lion. I won't be asked why I wasn't as tall as a giraffe. That's just not the way we turtles are. I won't be asked why I didn't fly as fast as an eagle. We turtles weren't meant to do that. The question I will have to face is, "Were you the very best turtle you could have been?" This question became my mission statement. I kept repeating this question to myself over and over again. I found it intensely inspiring.

Was I envious of any of the other animals in the world? Of course not! I had my mission in the world. I didn't have the mission of anyone else. I knew that the Almighty had given me the innate skills and talents to fulfill my own mission. I wasn't in competition with any other animal, not even the other turtles. I was focused on the wisest thing for me to think, say, and do. Since I wasn't in a race with anyone else, I was able to wish everyone else success in their personal life missions. I blessed others from the bottom of my heart. These thoughts felt very elevating.

I don't know if anyone who saw me realized what was going through my mind. I know that when I was a human being, I had no idea what the inner workings of a turtle's mind were like! I hadn't given the matter any thought. Tell me the truth: How often have you asked yourself, "I wonder what that turtle is thinking right now?" Once you read this, you will become more sensitive to a turtle's feelings. It is worth sharing my story with you, even if this is the sole benefit you gain from it. This will make you more compassionate when you see another turtle. And once you are compassionate towards turtles, I'm certain that this feeling will spread to your being more compassionate towards other animals and even other human beings who seem different from you.

I spent each moment being a good turtle. I put in as much effort as I could. This felt great. I was doing my best and my self-image was soaring. I remained humble and modest. Let's face it, I still was a turtle and, as I would have said when I was a human being, "That's nothing to brag about." But I had self-esteem. I recognized that while I was not created in the image of the Creator as humans were, I still was part of the Creator's creation. And nothing could be a greater accomplishment than that.

My goal was to change from being a good turtle to becoming a great turtle. I was successful beyond my wildest imagination. I reached the first level of greatness by mid-day. The way I understood things, this was quite unusual for a turtle. It was something like being the first human being who ran the four-minute mile. It wasn't as great as being the first human being who ran the three-minute mile, but it was a monumental achievement.

After reaching the first level of turtle greatness, I kept growing with unbelievable speed. Before I knew it, I had reached the fifth level of turtle greatness. I literally zoomed through levels two, three, and four. I had a major advantage over the other turtles in the world. They had been born turtles right from the start of their existence. But I had been a human being. I have to admit that I had not used my full potential as a human being, and if I could do it all over again, I would do a better job. But having had the experience of being a human being who could read and write, who could talk and attend lectures, I knew much more than all the other turtles. So I couldn't say that I was competing with other turtles. I had a head start that put me into a different category since I didn't start out as a turtle right from the beginning.

But besides being an asset, having started out as a human being and suddenly finding that I had become a turtle did have its disadvantages. Those who were born as turtles didn't have anything to compare their present situation to. All they knew was what it was like to be a turtle. But since I had been a human being for so long, I had kind of gotten used to it. I could have complained that it's not fair that I couldn't continue being a human. Why was I chosen to become a turtle and not someone else? As these questions are usually asked, "Why me?" But I had no idea of the answer. I had realized my choice earlier: I could make the best of being a turtle, or I could spend my time whining and complaining about the disadvantages of being a turtle. This would not have been the path of spirituality. This would not have been accepting the will of my Creator. This would not have given me joy. Instead, I would have been totally miserable. I would have felt resentment and frustration.

I would rather choose to be joyous. I was totally dedicated to accepting the Almighty's will with love and joy. And that is why I was making the tremendous progress that I had been making all day.

Then all of a sudden, something strange happened. I felt that I was becoming different. I felt that I had grown from the challenge that I was facing. But the amount that I had developed was beyond my wildest turtle dreams. I had turned into a mighty, majestic lion! I didn't realize this at first. But I happened to see a reflection of myself in a mirror. At first I was startled. I still considered myself a turtle. And when I saw the lion, I didn't immediately realize that it was me. Lions can be highly intimidating to a turtle — and to human beings, too! Especially when they roar.

What had happened? I was soon to learn that I had experienced The Special Purim Law of Turtles. This law is complex and deserves a lengthy and learned discussion. But to make a long story short and to say it concisely: "Any turtle that progresses to a fifth level of greatness on Purim automatically gets an upgrade to become a lion."

I hadn't known this law when I was still a turtle. Perhaps if I had known it, fear of success might have slowed my progress. I was just trying to do my best as a turtle. I had no idea that my hard work, persistence, and total devotion to my goal would have such a positive outcome.

I began experiencing life on an entirely new level. This wasn't just a minor improvement; seeing the world as a lion gave me a magnificent sense of empowerment. Now I was living on a totally different plane. I had actually experienced a metamorphosis from a turtle to a lion! Only if you personally experienced this, could you know the extent of this change.

Previously, I had no idea at all of what was possible. Now I felt totally different than before. I acted differently. Having attained a royal status, my entire behavior pattern was changed. To say that everyone treated me with more respect would be another one of those gross understatements. I was now a regal lion. Others considered me a king, and that's how I felt. When I was a turtle I felt good about myself, but, looking back as a lion, I realize that what I had felt about myself before was nothing compared to the way that I felt about myself now.

Having once experienced life as a turtle, I was a lot more compassionate than the lions born into royalty. Now that I was a lion, I had new opportunities, new privileges, and new obligations. I had more talents, more skills, and more knowledge. My mission statement had to be upgraded, together with everything else about myself.

I would now be asked on Judgment Day, "Were you the very best lion that you could have been?" My life goal is to proudly respond with a roaring, "YES."

To summarize the essence of what we can learn from this story: Regardless of whether you consider yourself to be more of a turtle or more of a lion or somewhere in between, make it your goal to be the best you that you can be. No one can be something he is not. But we all have the ability to keep changing ourselves.

On Becoming a Kinder Person

Kind people live more spiritual and elevated lives. Kind people are much happier. Kind people get along better with others. Kind people have more friends. Kind people have more positive self-images.

The kindness that we are referring to is unconditional kindness. Unconditional kindness comes from the goodness of your heart; it's the kind things you say and do to benefit others. Unconditional kindness comes from understanding other people and their needs, from your compassion and caring.

As Rabbi Eliyahu Dessler explained, "Kindness that comes from being a giver and not a taker." Everyone needs to give and everyone needs to take. A giver has a giving attitude even when he runs a business and charges for his products or services. He takes money to earn a living and to be able to continue giving and doing for others, but his mindset is a giving and helping mindset.

Every kind act you do makes you a kinder person. Kindness is one of the main pillars of the world. Life gives us a tremendous number of opportunities to do kindness. What you focus on, you find. Build up your inner desire to do kindness and you will constantly find ways that you can say kind words and do kind actions.

Each kindness you do adds to your inner happiness and adds to your self-image. Identify yourself as a person who loves to do kindness. This positive self-image will increase your level of doing even more kindness.

We have the authority of the Rambam (*Hilchos Daos*) that in order to acquire any trait, do many acts that are consistent with that positive trait. So even if you personally don't consider yourself to be a kind person, as long as you keep doing many acts of kindness, according to the Rambam, you are involved in the process that will make you a kinder person.

The authority of the Rambam is greater than the authority of anyone who will argue, "Yes, I keep doing acts of kindness, but I am not yet really kind." It could be true that you are not yet "really" kind, but if you keep on doing many acts of kindness over time in order to become a kind person, you are at least on the path of becoming kind. That itself is a worthy goal. And then your self-image could be, "I am doing many acts of kindness to help others, and to develop the trait of kindness."

When you are doing apparently tiny and trivial acts of kindness, you are really doing something that is highly valuable. You are turning yourself into a kind person.

When it comes to being kind, some people focus on all the kindness that they are not doing. Their self-image is: "I am far from doing all the kindness that I can do. I don't always feel like doing acts of kindness. I'm really not a kind person."

This deficient self-image is likely to cause people distress when they think about being kind. "It's awful that I am so far from being a kind person!"

When you realize that each kind act you do gets stored in the tremendous mental library in your brain, you realize that you are storing more words and acts of kindness with each kind act.

Now your self-image about being kind is: "I have already done many acts of kindness. Each new kindness that I do increases the amount of kindness that I have stored in my brain."

Some people might be concerned, "Perhaps if people keep thinking that they are already kind, they might do fewer acts of kindness."

Is this possible? Yes. But the Torah ideal is that we need to keep increasing the acts of kindness that we do. The goal is to have *ahavas chesed*, a love for doing kindness. When someone loves to do kindness, he will feel good about the kindnesses he does. This will increase the quality and quantity of his kindness.

When kindness is part of your self-image, you will find it easier to do more kindness.

We need a balance. We need to realize that once we've done even a few acts of kindness we already can have a self-image of, "I am a person who has already done acts of kindness." At the same time, no matter how much kindness anyone has done, there are many more acts of kindness that we must do to help the many needs of other people.

Some people who have a low self-image might turn into "people pleasers." They are afraid to refuse any requests because they fear that the other person won't like them or will be angry. While we should go out of our way to do as much kindness as we can, we also need to develop the ability to respectfully say, "No," when it is truly too difficult for us to do something for someone. The ability to say "No" raises the value of the kindnesses you do. You are not doing the kindness out of fear of disapproval; the kindnesses you do come from an authentic wish to be kind.

> *Someone once told me, "I was told as a child that I was very selfish. It was frequently pointed out to me that I didn't share enough with others. That I always thought of myself first. That instead of being kind to others, I selfishly focused on my own wants and needs.*

"I felt awful about myself. Every time someone told me, 'That was kind of you,' about something nice I did, an inner voice answered, 'You are really a selfish person, no matter who mistakenly thinks that you are kind.'

"I asked a rabbi, 'What is the real me? Kind or selfish?'"

"'The real you is probably a mixture,' he said. 'I know that you love to do acts of kindness. At the same time, it's natural for the vast majority of people to also be selfish. Keep focusing on your kind thoughts, words, and actions. By focusing on them, you will make yourself more kind. Whenever you think you're being selfish, immediately say to yourself. "I love being kind. I remember many times that I have already been kind in the past. I will keep increasing my kindness in the future."'"

"This was tremendously helpful for me. I saw that it was much more pleasurable for me to speak and act kindly towards others. Each kind sentence and each act enabled me to consider myself less selfish and more kind."

Help People Raise Their Self-Image

The highest level of charity is not giving charity, but helping the person become self-sufficient. When you give someone charity right now, you help only as long as that money lasts. This is a wonderful kindness, but not as much as when you help train someone to get a job or to learn a skill. Then you help this person for many years to come.

When you make someone feel worthwhile and valued, you are doing much more than making him feel good right now. You are helping this person throughout his life.

When you help people raise their self-image by pointing out their strengths and positive qualities, the benefits can last a lifetime. When you raise someone's self-image, that person's children and children's children can be the beneficiaries of your kind words and actions.

It is a crime to lower the self-image of others. Someone who lowers another's self-image causes distress not only for now; this person might lose out for many years to come.

How do you raise the self-image of others?

By making people feel valued.

"Greet people with a friendly facial expression and with joy" (*Pirkei Avos*, Ch. 2 and 3). When you show someone that you are happy to see him, you are giving a message that you value him. When you give someone your undivided attention, you also give him the message that he is important and that you believe in him. When you say things that sincerely demonstrate your high regard for him, he is likely to feel more valued.

Give people positive feedback. Your positive feedback increases a person's awareness that he did something positive, praiseworthy, and especially well.

Each person is unique. At times you might find it helpful to ask someone outright, "What do you think you would need to feel good about yourself?" Sometimes, the answer can point to a direction that will be beneficial. Other times the person might answer in a way that shows he is thinking in a way that needlessly prevents him from having a positive attitude towards himself. By correcting his thinking pattern, you will be able to help him improve his self-image.

Every person has positive traits, qualities, and patterns, and every person has faults, deficiencies, and negative patterns. When someone identifies with his imperfections, he will feel worse about himself. Someone who focuses mainly on his shortcomings will have a lower self-image, which prevents him from being at his best. Help people identify with their positive patterns. When someone's main focus is on what he has done right already, he will continue to keep developing his good points.

Show people that they have strengths and positive qualities that they might not totally realize they have.

I personally am forever grateful to Rabbi Avraham Pinkus, of blessed memory, father of the late Rabbi Shimshon Pinkus, for a conversation he had with me at a bus stop near both of our apartments.

Close to twenty-five years ago we were waiting together for a bus. When he saw me, he said to me, "You are very creative."

At the time, I hadn't viewed myself as creative. "My father, of blessed memory, was very creative," I said. "But I'm not creative."

"But you wrote two books," he argued with me.

I explained why I didn't consider either of those books as really being creative. "My book *Guard Your Tongue* is an English adaptation of the Chofetz Chaim's classic work. I added examples, but I didn't come up with totally new ideas." I also explained why I didn't think of my second book as being creative, either.

Rabbi Pinkus said, "But what you did in both books is really creative."

After his explanation, I agreed that even though what I did wasn't a wholly new creation, there were many aspects of creativity involved.

From then on, I have considered myself creative. This was a helpful mindset while writing the next eighteen books I've written, plus the current book you're reading now.

I am forever grateful for that short conversation I had with Rabbi Pinkus; it had a lifelong positive influence on me.

I recently heard a mother relate, "I used to view a certain son of mine as a very wild child. He had a lot of energy and was highly independent. Going places with him was always a challenge. One day in a busy grocery store, he was acting up. I felt a bit embarrassed and highly frustrated. Then an elderly rabbi came over and said, 'He will grow up to be someone special. He will give you much pleasure when he gets older.' From then on I looked at my son from the positive perspective of that rabbi. This had a very beneficial impact on my son's behavior."

Raising someone's self-image is frequently a long-term project that will take much time and effort. Stories of instant transformations are the exceptions. Be patient when you want to upgrade someone's self-image. When you make it a goal to raise someone's self-image, all the effort you put into your goal is part of a great act of kindness.

> *About five years ago someone said to me, "Fifteen years ago you tried to help me build my self-image. You pointed out to me that I had many strengths. You assured me that many other people have similar faults and similar struggles, and they ended up living very worthwhile and meaningful lives. But I kept arguing with you. I didn't believe what you said was applicable to me. I 'knew' that I was deeply defective. I felt that something was wrong with me on a deep level. What you said to me sounded good, but it didn't move me emotionally. I had a much more complex way of thinking than most people, and I doubted that anything anyone would say to me would make a difference.*
>
> *"You accepted me the way I was. But I didn't accept myself. I couldn't put my finger on what exactly was wrong with me, but I was certain that whatever it was couldn't be overcome with just words. I was stubborn and argued with everything you said to me. Over the next few years I basically wasted a lot of time and didn't do anything constructive.*
>
> *"I was constantly under stress. A major factor in my stress was that I always felt so bad about myself. One day I passed a Jewish bookstore and saw one of your books. I didn't buy it because I still didn't think that what you would say would make a difference in my life. But after seeing your name, I recalled what you said to me when you tried to help me feel better about myself.*
>
> *"I remembered that you told me that every human being has many strengths and can build up more strengths. We need patience and persistence. We need to stop putting ourselves down. And we need to improve our character traits little by little each and every day. Now it made more sense to me than when I first heard you say this.*
>
> *"I want to thank you. It took a long time until your words entered my heart. Since then, I've added your encouragement to other things I've read and heard about building one's sense of self. Thank you."*

This feedback added to my awareness: All we can do is share ideas to try to encourage and inspire someone else. Each person we speak to is unique. We can't know right away what any specific person needs to hear to make a difference in his life. And we can't know how long it will take for what we say to have an effect. Still, we need to keep trying, even if we feel that what we said didn't make any difference at all. At times we will be wrong; what we said actually created a positive seed in someone's mind. Eventually our words could have a positive effect.

Believing in Others Can Help Them Believe in Themselves

"**M**y parents believed in me and my abilities and therefore I believed in myself."

"I had a great teacher who believed in me and therefore I was able to believe in myself."

"I worked for a wonderful boss who believed that I could accomplish greatly. That is when I really started seeing what I could actually do."

"I told a great rabbi that I felt so low and unimportant. He congratulated me on my humility and told me how to elevate myself. He was so respectful towards me that I became much more self-respecting."

"For many years I had a very low self-image. But as my children grew older, I saw how much they believed in me. This greatly built my self-image."

"Everyone I knew saw me as a person with good intentions, as a nice guy, who wasn't really able to accomplish very much. At a wedding I sat next to a stranger from another city. He was very open to new ideas and I felt very comfortable talking to him. I described some ideas I had about a project I had been thinking about. He was highly enthusiastic. He modestly told me about some successful projects he had worked on. I was impressed with him, and because he liked my ideas I believed that the project I was thinking about had merit. Because of his enthusiasm I was motivated to take action that I probably would not have otherwise taken. I am forever grateful to him."

When you listen to people's success stories, you will usually hear that they had someone or a number of people who believed in them. Think about people who believed in you and how you have gained from them.

Maybe there have been people in your life who have believed in you, but their encouragement hasn't yet registered in your mind. You might have created ways to discount the positive things they said to you:

"Of course, all grandparents believe in their grandchildren."

"That rabbi was a kind soul. He probably tells everyone they can do great things."

"This person doesn't really know me well enough."

"That guy is naïve. He can't do very much himself, so he considers everyone else to be smarter and more talented than they actually are."

Remember those encouraging words again, even if it's already many years later. You might say to yourself, "When that person told me I had great intelligence and creativity that I wasn't aware of, he might have been correct," or "That teacher said I was talented, but I didn't take it seriously. I now think it's possible that my teacher was really right."

If you have not yet found someone who believes in you, you have a choice: You can look for someone who will believe in you, or you can begin to believe in yourself. Ultimately, it is your own belief in yourself that makes all the difference.

Whenever you encounter someone who doesn't yet believe in his own potential, think of what you can sincerely say to express your true belief in him.

For many years I wanted to be a teacher. I wanted to spread Torah ideas. When I was younger I had tutored a number of students, and they had gained from the tutoring. However, a Shabbos guest was more helpful than the tutoring experience. The guest increased my belief in my ability to be a teacher.

I was still studying in a yeshiva myself at the time. That Shabbos, I shared a number of my favorite Torah ideas in the name of various Torah scholars. The guest was new to studying about Judaism and enjoyed what I was sharing with him.

"You will make a great teacher," he said to me.

When an actual teaching job became available, his words came back to me and added to my confidence when I went on that job interview.

Reish Lakish: Before and After His Encounter With Rabbi Yochanan

The Talmud describes the amazing transformational encounter that the Sage Rabbi Yochanan had with Reish Lakish.

Rabbi Yochanan, a great scholar and elevated person, was swimming in the Jordan River. In the distance, Reish Lakish, the head of a gang of robbers, saw a great light shining from the handsome Rabbi Yochanan. Reish Lakish dived into the water and swam over to get a closer look. "Use your tremendous energy and inner strength to study Torah," Rabbi Yochanan exclaimed.

This is remarkable! Most people would have seen the leader of a group of robbers. That is how Reish Lakish saw himself; that is how he spoke and acted at that time. But in an action that took just a moment, the elevated Rabbi Yochanan saw a man with tremendous energy and inner strength, someone with the potential to become a great Torah scholar.

Now Rabbi Yochanan had to motivate Reish Lakish to devote himself to Torah study. So when Reish Lakish told Rabbi Yochanan, "Your beauty is fit for a woman," did he get insulted? No. Instead, he immediately understood that beauty was of high value to Reish Lakish.

Rabbi Yochanan thought of a way to use this knowledge to motivate Reish Lakish to change his entire lifestyle. "I have a sister who is beautiful," said Rabbi Yochanan. "Study Torah with me and I will make a match for you with my sister. We will be brothers-in-law, and we will study together."

Reish Lakish immediately agreed.

At the beginning of the day, what was Reish Lakish's self-image? "I am a robber, and the leader of a gang of robbers," is what Reish Lakish would have said.

At the end of that day, what was Reish Lakish's self-image? "I am on the path of becoming a Torah scholar. I will be the brother-in-law of Rabbi Yochanan, and I will be his student."

Even one encounter with a great motivator who sees our tremendous potential can totally change our self-image. No matter how we saw ourselves in the morning, by the evening we will be on a much higher path. We will see ourselves in a totally different light.

While such an encounter is rare, knowing about it can begin to build someone's self-image. "I am someone who will be higher and more elevated if I meet someone who sees my potential and motivates me to become more than I am now."

Our self-image at this moment is only a statement of how we see ourselves now. If we are motivated by a person, a class or lecture, a book, a recording, a seminar, or anything else, we will think, speak, and act differently. Then our self-image will be based on our new pattern of thoughts, words, and actions.

When you encounter other people who could use an emotional or spiritual boost, ask yourself, "What positive statements could I say to positively influence how this person sees himself?"

The Midrash (*Yalkut Shimoni*) relates that Reish Lakish was once traveling with Rabbi Abahu. When they passed a certain town, Rabbi Abahu spoke against the people who lived there. Reish Lakish got down from his donkey and put dirt from the ground into Rabbi Abahu's mouth.

"The Almighty doesn't want us to speak against His children," Reish Lakish told him.

Why did Reish Lakish react so strongly?

It seems to me that Reish Lakish's strong reaction was caused by the influence of Rabbi Yochanan. Rabbi Yochanan was able to have such a positive influence because he viewed Reish Lakish, right now in the present, from the perspective of what he would be like after he was influenced. That is why Reish Lakish felt it was so wrong to focus on what these people were doing wrong now.

When we can see someone, even a person who is doing much wrong, in the way he will be after we influence him, we will find positive ways to bring out the positive potential that is hidden deep inside.

This is a powerful lesson for all of us. See other people as they will be when their inner potential is brought out. Then you will find it easier to think of what to say and do to bring out their best.

> I told someone the above Talmudic story, and how being motivated transforms us. He responded, "I have been motivated many times in my life. After each major time of being inspired and motivated, I did think, speak, and act better for a while. But my new and improved patterns didn't last very long. I felt my self-image rise and then it would fall. Each disappointment brought me back to the sad reality. I keep going back to the way I used to be."
>
> "Come on, you talk about the 'sad reality.' Aren't you a bit better now than you were before all those times you were inspired and motivated?"
>
> "Yes, I am. But I'm not consistently the way I was when I felt the spiritual high of being inspired," he argued.
>
> "Let's try this upgraded self-image statement for a while: 'I am a person who has been inspired and motivated many times. Each time I felt this way, some of the benefits of that inspiration stayed with me.' Right?"

"I have to acknowledge that it is true. But I'm still not consistently the way I would wish I was."

"Realize that you have a choice. You might keep on repeating to yourself, 'I'm not the way I want to be. I keep losing what I've gained.' This will help you focus on all that you aren't doing right and what you are doing wrong. Since this will be your mind's focus, you are strengthening your weaknesses and limitations. You will keep feeling bad about yourself and you will be limiting yourself more and more.

"Now let's look at the entire picture if you keep saying to yourself, 'Every moment of inspiration and motivation has made me a better person. This is how I really want to be. I will keep thinking about how I was when I felt inspired and motivated and I will increase the amount of time I speak and act the way I would like to be.' Can you see that this way of thinking will keep helping you develop yourself in more and better ways? Does this make sense?"

"This definitely makes sense," he agreed. *"I can see how thinking with this pattern will make me a much better person."*

Create Breakthroughs by Transcending Someone's Resistance

There was once a woman whose family owned a farm in the American Midwest. She hadn't learned to read or write as a child. The older she became the more she wanted to learn how, but no one was able to teach her. She and her husband looked for opportunities to have schoolteachers as boarders, hopeful that one might be able to teach her how to read and write. But nothing worked.

One day Dr. Milton Erickson heard about the situation. He immediately thought of an approach he could use to teach her. He went to the farm and didn't make any claims that he would teach her to read and write. He knew that even though she wanted to learn, she believed she wasn't able to and no one could teach her even if they tried.

Dr. Erickson, who had grown up on a farm, knew about the various tasks that had to be done. He asked her if she could draw a straight line, and of course she said she could do that. She often had to draw straight lines on the farm. He asked her if she had ever drawn a circle, and again she had done it many times. He had her draw all the lines that the various letters of the English alphabet are drawn with.

Then he had her draw the three lines that constitute the letter A.

Dr. Erikson told her, "On the farm you have animals. There are dogs and cows and horses and other animals. Each animal has a name. The symbol you just drew also has a name. The name of this symbol is 'A.'" Then he had her draw a B and a C and so forth. Everything she drew was comprised of the lines that she already knew how to draw. And every symbol had a unique name, from A to Z.

After she learned the names of each symbol, Erickson had her draw three letters: C – A – T. "When these three letters come together they have a name: the name CAT.

"Then you have another three symbols. C – O – W. These three symbols together have a different name. Their name is COW."

Erickson kept teaching her what other combinations of symbols stand for. And then she picked up enough words that she could actually read.

The key element here is that Erickson knew that if he just tried to "teach her to read," she would repeat to herself that "this is reading and I don't know how to read." So he bypassed her limiting self-image. She knew that she could draw lines on the farm, and she also knew that she knew the names of many animals and other objects on the farm. Her inner mind was open to learn the way Erickson taught her.

This is a great lesson in helping us and in helping others. You probably have things you currently feel are too difficult for you to learn or to do, just because of the way that you are looking at them. If you find a totally new way to look at what you are going to try to learn, you will find that it's much easier for you to learn than you had ever imagined. The new way of looking at things doesn't go against your limiting self-image.

When you want to help other people gain more knowledge or learn a new skill and they have a mental block against learning it, try to think of alternative ways to look at what you are trying to teach. Find a new way that won't conflict with the way the person is limiting himself.

> *Someone I knew had a self-image that he isn't a fundraiser. "I've never been a fundraiser before and I'll never be one," he would say when asked if he could help any cause.*
>
> *Knowing that he had a very positive influence on others when he was enthusiastic about something, another person said to him, "You don't have to become a fundraiser. But you do feel that this specific cause that I want to help out is a very worthy cause, don't you?"*
>
> *"Yes, I do, and I even gave a nice donation to that cause," he said.*
>
> *"So all I'm asking you to do is come with me to a number of people and tell them why you are so enthusiastic about this cause."*
>
> *"Although I'm not a fundraiser, I think I can do what you asked," the fellow said.*
>
> *And so with his non-fundraiser self-image he was able to present the cause in a way that convinced others to contribute.*

Write Short Image-Building Notes

Written positive feedback notes are more effective than verbal statements. When someone speaks or acts in especially positive ways, write short notes to that person expressing your admiration for what he said or did. This is especially valuable for parents, teachers, spouses, and mentors to do.

People have saved self-image building notes for ten, twenty, and thirty years. Imagine how you would feel if you knew that an image-building note you sent would be a cherished memento even thirty years later. At the very least you will bring a smile to someone's face.

There are teachers who write positive notes to parents when the students have done something exceptionally well. This can greatly improve the way the parents view their child.

Think of some people you know who would benefit from short image-building notes from you.

Every positive note you write to someone helps build that person's self-image. And each time you write such a note to someone, you are building your own self-image, too: "I am a person who writes positive image-building notes for other people."

> "I had tremendous resentment towards my parents," someone told me. "They consistently put me down. They often said, 'You're not meeting our expectations of you,' 'You are a total disappointment,' 'You could be much better than you are. Why do you act so bad?' and 'What did we do to deserve you as a child?'
>
> "It was unbelievable how they kept breaking my ego. I hated talking to them and became more and more defiant.
>
> "Then they consulted a rabbi who had a reputation for bringing out the best in people. The rabbi asked them what their goal was.

> "'We feel that if we keep telling our son how bad he is, he will be motivated to act better,' they said.
>
> "'Maybe on a different planet there are intelligent beings who respond this way,' the rabbi replied, 'but that's not the way humans on Planet Earth react. Refrain from making negative statements. Look for every slightly positive thing your son says and does, and write a positive note that tells him you appreciate and admire what he said and did.'
>
> "This persuaded my parents to focus on what I was doing good and right. It meant so much to me that I was highly motivated to speak and act in ways that brought out the best in me. Deep down I always wanted to be a good person. I needed a positive approach.
>
> "The positive notes made a major transformation in my life."

Rabbi Preida's Student

The Talmud (*Eruvin* 54b) tells the story of a very special Torah teacher named Rabbi Preida. An unnamed student of his needed to hear every lesson 400 times before he understood it, and every day Rabbi Preida would repeat it to him 400 times.

One day during their study session, some people came to Rabbi Preida and asked if he could join them in performing a mitzvah. Rabbi Preida replied, "Right now I'm busy teaching my student. After the lesson, I will be happy to join you."

Rabbi Preida calmly repeated the lesson the usual 400 times. Then he saw that the student still didn't understand that day's lessons.

"Why is today different than every other day?" Rabbi Preida asked his student. "Every other day after you hear the lesson 400 times, you understand it. How come you didn't understand it today?"

"Today I couldn't concentrate as well as I usually do," replied the student. "Since those people asked you to join them, I've been repeating to myself, 'My teacher is soon going to leave. My teacher is soon going to leave.' This prevented me from concentrating on the content of what you were saying to me, and I didn't understand."

"Please relax and be calm," Rabbi Preida kindly said. "I will repeat the lesson over and over again until you understand it. If you need 400 more repetitions, that's fine. I'm willing to repeat it as many times as you need to hear it to understand."

The student was able to relax and be calm. Now he was able to concentrate and, after another 400 repetitions, he understood the lesson. The Talmud praises Rabbi Preida highly for his extreme patience.

Some teachers might become angry with the student and say, "I go out of my way to repeat the lesson to you 400 times. Why don't you have the respect and gratitude to pay attention?"

But will this help the student? No. The student needed reassurance that Rabbi Preida would be willing to calmly repeat the lesson as many times as the student needed. Blaming the student for not paying attention would just create more tension and stress. Calm reassurance helps the student reach the emotional state needed for comprehending the lesson.

Now let us look at the student's self-image. How would the student feel about himself if he had a teacher who was willing to repeat lessons only 100 times? He would say to himself, "I see that it's impossible for me to learn things like the other students. I never understand what the teacher is teaching. I don't have the brainpower to understand anything. I am a total failure. I'll never be able to learn." The student would have the same defeated self-image if the teacher had the patience to repeat each idea only 200 or 300 times.

Since Rabbi Preida was willing to repeat each lesson 400 times, the student had an entirely different self-image. He was able to view himself as, "I am a person who can understand everything that is taught. All I need to do is listen carefully 400 times and then I understand."

If Rabbi Preida's student would attend today's schools, where the students take tests and receive grades, he would receive a zero on each test. This would easily lower his self-image. Having a wonderful teacher like Rabbi Preida changes the student's self-image to, "I love learning Torah. I am so fortunate to have a magnificent teacher like Rabbi Preida. I understand all the lessons that he teaches me. My own patience and diligence are great qualities that enable me to understand every lesson."

Torah learning isn't a race of, "Who can catch on faster?" Rather, the goal is to learn Torah at your own unique pace. If we don't understand something right away but can understand it after reviewing it many times, we would be wise to choose a self-image of, "I have the ability to understand everything, as long as I review the ideas enough times."

> *Thirty-five years ago I heard the following from the late Rabbi Shalom Schwadron, the Maggid of Jerusalem.*
>
> *Rabbi Schwadron would pray in a certain synagogue in Shaarei Chesed. He heard an elderly fellow enthusiastically reading a volume of Talmud. Reb Shalom saw that the man didn't understand even a little bit of what he was reading.*
>
> *"You don't sound like you understand the Gemara," Reb Shalom said in a friendly way.*
>
> *"You're right," the man said. "I don't understand anything that I am reading."*
>
> *"Then why are you sitting here and reading with such enthusiasm?"*
>
> *"A person who is a patriotic citizen might want to know the names of the country's generals," the man explained. "That person might not know a thing about military strategy, but he still feels good about learning the names of the generals who lead the army.*
>
> *"That is how I feel about knowing the names of the great Sages of the Talmud. I want to be familiar with the names of Rava and Abaye, of Rabbi Pappa and Rabbi Huna, of Rabbi Meir and Rabbi Yehudah. Even though I don't understand what they are saying, I feel privileged to know their names."*
>
> *That man didn't think, "I can't understand what I am reading." Instead, his self-image was happy to recognize, "I am a person*

who loves to read the Talmud in order to know the names of all the scholars who are quoted in the Talmud."

There is much to learn from this enthusiastic idealist about leading a joyful life.

Let Every Story About the Positive Patterns of Others Add to Your Self-Image

People love stories. The stories you read and hear about great people are stored in your brain. You become a bit greater yourself with each positive story. Knowing how great people spoke and behaved makes it more likely that you will speak and act with similar patterns. Of course, we won't immediately act exactly like every great person we read and hear about, but we will improve.

The elevating and inspiring stories you read and hear about are part of the process of building your self-image: "I am a person who has added another story about positive thoughts, words, and actions into my brain and mind."

"But how can this add to my self-image?" some people ask me. "I'm still not like this person. I myself haven't acted with the greatness of a great person just because I have read about it."

That's definitely true. Just reading about positive character traits and difficult behavior patterns doesn't automatically transform you into a replica of those people. But it does make it more likely that you will learn from those stories to improve and be better.

Positive stories can influence you for weeks, months, and years after you read them. This story is stored in your brain, and your brain is always with you.

It's said that people who read and hear about violence are more likely to speak and act violently. Conversely, people who read and hear about goodness and kindness are more likely to emulate that goodness and kindness. So positive stories elevate you.

See what happens when you frequently repeat to yourself, "Every positive story I have ever read and heard about great people makes me a better person."

You can suggest to your inner mind, "Let my inner mind apply the lessons I have learned from all the positive stories I have ever heard and read. Each positive story adds to my life-long process of building my character."

Some people have told me that they feel bad about themselves when they read or hear stories about great people. "I'm so far from being like that person," they say to themselves. This pattern of thinking can cause discouragement.

We each have the ability to upgrade our thinking. If people find that positive stories cause negative feelings, they would be wise to tell themselves, "With each positive story I am planting a positive seed in my mind and brain. I need to be patient. Planting seeds doesn't immediately give you a full-grown tree. But without a seed, there won't be a tree. Eventually I will see growth."

Whenever you see that a specific story has a positive influence on you in practical ways, you can say to yourself, "I see from this that positive stories do have a practical impact on me. Let me keep growing from this story and all the other inspiring stories that I have read and heard about in the past."

I used to live near Rabbi Chaim Zaitchyk, author of many Mussar books. On Friday night and Shabbos he used to have a minyan for the prayer services, and after the Kabbalas Shabbos prayers, he would deliver a weekly mussar lecture.

He once spoke about the importance of reading stories about great Torah personalities, in order to learn from them. He had written a book called Meoros Hagdolim, which has stories about great Mussar personalities. Rabbi Moshe Feinstein had told him that before Yom Kippur he had read the book. This great Torah scholar found that reading about elevated people had inspired him.

Life Isn't a Competitive Game

Each human being is unique and one of a kind. We each have a unique purpose in life. We each have our own unique ability to connect with our Creator. We each have our own strengths and weaknesses, virtues and faults. We are not meant to be an exact clone of anyone else. Therefore life isn't a competitive game. We each are meant to serve the Almighty with our unique character, temperament, and personality based on our unique life situations and circumstances in the past and present.

What should someone do if he has been caught up in the competitive trap? What should he do if he feels bad about himself because he is not ahead in his subjective competitive race?

Allow his thoughts to free him.

Your thoughts create that competitive attitude; therefore, your thoughts can free you. Your thoughts can create more happiness and joy each and every day. Your thoughts can enable you to appreciate your Divinely given value and worth. Your thoughts can allow you to experience joy for the good that you do.

The Almighty wants you to do good in this world. Nowhere in the Torah does it praise competition. In fact, in the portion of *Bereishis* (*Genesis*) we read how a competitive attitude caused the first murder in the world. Cain killed his younger brother Abel because he wanted to be the Almighty's favorite. Imagine what would have happened if Cain would have said, "I am happy for my younger brother's spiritual success. I, too, wish to be better than I am now, so I will learn from my brother to improve in my own unique way."

The Torah ideal is to have *ahavas chesed*, love for kindness. It doesn't say that you have to do more kindness than anyone else. The Torah ideal is to study Torah, with your own mind and your own intellectual strengths and challenges. Each time you pray, you have your unique connection with the Almighty; you continue to build your unique relationship with your Creator. Your life is for you to build your unique character traits. You mission in life is to handle your unique life challenges and tests.

Some people would feel basically positive about themselves, but other people get in the way. Not the actual people, but the thoughts that they have about other people: "Other people are smarter than I am." "Other people are better off than I am." "Other people do more good than I do." "Other people are more talented and skilled than I am." "Other people are happier than I am." "Other people are just plain better than I am."

Some people have these thoughts running through their minds in the negative: "I am not as smart as other people." "I am worse off than other people." "I do less good than others and I also do more bad than others." "I am less talented and skilled than others." "I am not as happy as others." "I am just plain worse than others."

Life isn't a competitive game. If it were, then only a few outstanding individuals could feel good about themselves and everyone else would be full of anxiety and unhappiness. In a competitive game, there is one winner and everyone else is a loser. Take, for example, a lottery with one great big prize and millions of people who buy tickets. One person or group of people is the big winner and everyone else is a loser. There is one success and many failures. But that is not the Torah ideal of life.

The Torah (*Devarim* 26:11) tells us to rejoice with all the good that the Almighty has given us. When your mind is full of rejoicing for all the good in your own life, it won't let you think of — or feel bad about — what anyone else has. If you aren't yet as happy and joyful as you could be, the only way to become happier and more joyful is to think the thoughts that will increase your appreciation and gratitude. It's not what anyone else has or has done that prevents you from being happy; your present thoughts create your feelings and emotions. Make it a priority to upgrade your own thoughts, and you will upgrade your life. Let your mind be so full of gratitude and appreciation that there is no room for thoughts that make you feel bad because of envy of someone else.

There are people who have a strong need "to be the best." When a person has this attitude, regardless of what he does, he feels that he needs to be number one, on top, the winner, the greatest, the smartest, the most talented, and better than everyone else.

People with this attitude need others to lose, to be worse than they are, to be less than they are. They feel that they can only have a positive self-image if it is clear that they are "the best."

Many problems are caused by this attitude. A key problem is how to define "being the best." In sports there are scores and rules of winning and losing. In all kinds of games there can be a clear winner and loser. But we need to remember that a game is just a game, nothing more. The whole idea of being a better person because one was won is just an illusion. This illusion actually affects multi-millions of people who rejoice and feel better about themselves when "their" team has won a game. The downside is that they are sad and feel worse about themselves when "their" team has lost. Since this high or low isn't based on reality, for the vast majority of people this is only a temporary feeling.

A person whose goal in life is to be better than others is likely to feel bad when others do well and others have it good. Similarly, he is likely to feel good when others do badly and suffer losses, adversity, and misfortunes. This is the opposite of the Torah commandment to love others as ourselves.

The Torah and Torah writings do not tell us that we have to be the first, the best, the winners, the victors. Instead, the Torah tells us to walk in the ways of the Almighty. The Torah tells us to love the Almighty and to follow His commandments.

The Greeks who tried to destroy the Jewish People's adhering to Torah and the commandments were into competitive sports. Our great ancestors weren't. Abraham, Isaac, and Jacob devoted their lives to connecting with the Almighty. They strived for character excellence. The great Torah scholars throughout the ages didn't try to compete with others. They focused on their own spiritual and character development.

When it comes to spiritual and character development, we each have our life-encompassing mission. It's not like a race down a specific track where individual speed determines the winner, because everyone has the exact same route to run. No two lives are the same, so absolute comparisons are impossible. Read this last phrase again: Absolute comparisons are impossible. We never know the entire picture.

People who have competitive mindsets feel a need to be and do more and better than others. Therefore, their self-image will be based to a great degree with how they compare themselves with others.

I once saw a cutout of a photograph from *The New York Times* in someone's office. The picture showed a wealthy businessman who was quoted as saying, "I used to consider myself wealthy because I had over 800 million dollars. Then I read about some young fellows who are worth between two and three billion dollars and I felt much less of myself."

Of course, the Torah perspective knows that the money you have is the money that was given to you to accomplish good things in this world. Your money is not your worth. The charity you give and the good that you do is your worth.

People who feel a strong need to be "the best" are competitive. They are likely to keep looking over their shoulders to see how they are doing compared to others. Their self-image is likely to go up and down based upon how they think they compare with other people they know or hear about.

The Torah ideal is to be joyful for the joy of others. This was the level of Aharon, Moshe's older brother. When Moshe was chosen to be the leader who would go to Pharaoh to demand that he let the Israelites go free, Aharon felt joy, not envy, for his brother. He felt happy for his brother's success. As a reward for this joy, Aharon became the High Priest, who wore the one-of-a-kind special garments.

If you begin to think worse about your own self-image because of thoughts about another person, elevate your thoughts by blessing that person in your mind. "I wish this person success and everything good." Because you are blessing that person, you can now view that person's success as a source of happiness and joy for yourself. This will add to your self-image: "I am a person who blesses other people and wishes them well."

Do it even if it is difficult for you to bless other people and wish them well, and then your self-image can be, "I am a person who blesses other people and wishes them well even when it is difficult for me to do this."

When we think about other people, remember two main thoughts: "What words and acts of kindness can I say and do for this person?" and "What can I learn from this person?"

"A wise person learns from each and every person" (*Pirkei Avos* 4:1). It is wise to view each person you encounter as someone you can learn from in some way. Think about the questions you can ask anyone you meet, in order to learn from that person. People who consistently think this way aren't competitive. Rather, they view each person as part of their ongoing process of gaining more knowledge and wisdom.

View life as a partnership. You are a spiritual partner with others in the world. Other people are your partners in helping you develop your unique character traits. The success of any of your partners is your own success.

To summarize: Your own thoughts create the quality of your life. When you think about other people, think in ways that enhance your own life and the lives of others.

> *I met a very joyful person who seemed very calm and relaxed about his own accomplishments. I heard someone ask him, "Aren't you a bit distressed when your competitors do better than you?"*
>
> *He laughed and said, "I don't have any competitors. I want to be a joyful person who is consistently happy and joyful. I don't have any competition when it comes to this. My happiness and joy come from my own thoughts. The success and accomplishments of others don't take anything away from me. Even if every single person I knew did much better than I do, I can be happy and joyful with my thoughts, words, and actions. So I don't con-*

sider anyone to be a competitor, since I am not in a contest or race with anyone else.

"My goal in life is to bring out the best in myself. I don't know exactly how to measure what the 'best in myself' would be. I can never be certain that I am doing my best. So when I see what others do well, it gives me more insight into myself. I try to learn how to do better than I am doing now."

International Committee for Self-Worth (ICFSW)

I would like to inform you, the reader, that I have just been elected the CEO (Chief Executive Officer) of the International Committee for Self-Worth. The Committee is often referred to as the ICFSW. There was one person present at the meeting and I have been elected unanimously.

As the CEO, I have the right to choose the rules of the Committee, and then we have a vote. Since I am the only one attending the meetings, there is a good chance that all votes will end up unanimous and unchallenged. At times, the votes might end up one half against one half, when I have mixed thoughts about a rule.

Right now there is a rule up for discussion. The rule is: "Everyone who doesn't yet have a 100% sense of self-worth and wants it just needs to say, 'I would like to have a 100% sense of self-worth.' After saying this, that person immediately has a 100% level of self-worth. This officially takes place even if the person does not yet feel that he has 100% self-worth."

Your subjective feelings at any given moment can't change the nature of reality. Even if you don't feel that you have 100% self-worth, you still do. Knowing and internalizing this is likely to help you be calmer and happier. But even if you feel like a total nervous wreck and are not a bit happy, your temporary distressful feelings can't diminish your real value.

Learning the skill of being able to laugh just because you decide to laugh might help, too. You will feel better since your body will produce the bio-chemicals that make you feel better. But even if you never learn this skill, your intrinsic, infinite worth is still awesome.

Of course a person still needs to develop positive character traits and positive qualities. A person stills need to make and reach positive goals. But they aren't needed for a sense of self-worth.

At this time, I must inform you that the above rule has passed unanimously.

This rule now applies to every human being. The assumption is strong that if someone has a strong feeling of self-worth that person will be kinder and more compassionate. That person will treat others better and will be careful not to cause distress to other human beings.

Since you are reading this now, or at least listening to someone reading this, or at least listening to this on a recording, you can say right now, "I would like to have a 100% sense of self-worth."

If you said it, the new rule applies to you. You now have a 100% sense of worth.

Some people might wonder, "What if I think that this whole idea is funny and ridiculous?"

The answer of the Committee is, "You are entitled to think of it as funny if you wish. But it's definitely not ridiculous. The Committee officially declares it ridiculous for anyone to think he doesn't have high worth! Believing you've got low self-worth is not funny, but it is ridiculous. Since the Committee has given you an official statement of worth, there is nothing you can do to cancel the Committee's decision. You can say that you don't recognize the Committee, but the Committee recognizes the value of all human beings. This was officially accepted at the meeting. And there is nothing you or any other human being can do to cancel the ever-lasting effects of that meeting."

The ICFSW does not have any official property or belongings. It does not have a mailing address, telephone number, or other contact information. It does not collect dues from anyone. It does not have any meetings open to the public. It does not have any special requirements to join. And every human being, who has unconditional worth anyway, is automatically affected by its rule of just needing to say, "I would like to have a 100% sense of self-worth" to have said worth.

If you have read this, you might say to yourself, "I personally do not have 100% sense of self-worth. And I don't care what this International Committee decided." You might not care what the Committee decided, but the Committee is not the source of your worth. The Creator is. And you can't negate the Creator's giving you value. But if you have let any mortal decrease your sense of importance, the Committee is overruling that irrelevant decision on your part. So you have worth, no matter who says you don't. Even you.

Congratulations!

If you want an official-looking certificate to state that you have 100% worth, the Committee hereby gives you permission to type up or print your own certificate.

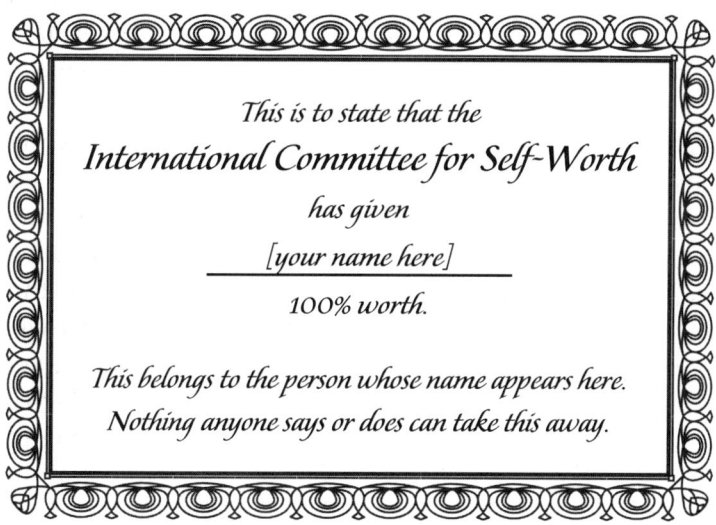

54
"I Am My Choices"

Many people spend much time complaining and whining about who they are. "I'm not all that I want to be," is the essence of these complaints. Most people are probably not all that they want to be.

Contrast this complaint with knowing, "I am my choices."

Throughout the day you make a tremendous number of choices. The details of those choices could fill a book every day. Your choices are in many different areas, moment by moment, but the three key areas are your thoughts, your words, and your actions.

You also choose your feelings. But your feelings are created by your choice of thoughts, words, and actions. The essence of who you are comes from your choices.

When you say, "I am my choices," you are stating a fact. You are stating a truth. You are not being specific about which choices you have already made. You are not describing yourself in particular detail. You are not lowering yourself in any way.

The benefit of realizing, "I am my choices," is that you are setting a foundation for developing your self-image. You are setting a foundation for becoming a better, more advanced person.

"Who am I? I am my choices!"

Every time you repeat this question and answer, you gain a greater awareness that right now, and throughout each and every day, you build your self-image through the choices of your thoughts, words, and action.

"I don't like who I am."

"I'm not satisfied with who I am."

"I don't like myself."

"I have a problem with my self-image."

People who had these negative statements but agreed to change them to the more neutral, "I am my choices," then became more open to thinking, "I will keep building my self-image, by choosing better thoughts, words, and actions."

Realizing the powerful effects of your choice of thoughts, words, and actions automatically leads you to choose better thoughts, words, and actions.

Make it a habit to repeat to yourself many times a day, "I am my choices. I am my choices of thoughts, words, and actions."

> *A few days ago, I bumped into someone on the street who had a very problematic self-image. He was truly different than most "normal" people. He was highly learning disabled. He looked different than the average person. He didn't accomplish very much. He wasn't able to attend regular schools when he was younger, and now he could only handle menial jobs. I told him that he should keep his focus on his thoughts, words, and actions. He smiled and said, "Is that all I need to think about? That sounds possible for me to do."*
>
> *Just a few hours ago I bumped into him again. He wanted to review the principle for life that I had told him. With a smile he said, "I understand now. If I keep thinking about choosing better thoughts, words, and actions, my life will be much better."*
>
> *Instead of thinking, "Something is wrong with me. I'm not as good as others," he realized that this sentence is not beneficial to keep thinking and repeating to others. Now he was resolved to frequently think, "I am my choices. I am the thoughts that I think, the words that I say, and the actions that I do."*

We All Start Out as Newborns

You have something in common with every great Torah scholar, with every billionaire, with the head of every business and organization, with every genius, with everyone who has great character traits, with everyone who has loads of friends, with every person who is successful in life, with every joyful person, with every kind and compassionate person, with every confident and courageous person, and with every great person who ever lived. You and each one of these people started life as a newborn.

People aren't born with self-images. Everyone who has a self-image of any kind acquired it after he was born. Therefore, all negative self-images were acquired, and all positive self-images were acquired. Every self-image is based on what a person currently thinks about when he thinks about who he is.

Every single human being you ever met, heard about, or read about started his life as an newborn. Regardless of how much knowledge anyone has gained, he didn't have it when he was one day old. He needed to learn it piece by piece. Regardless of how much anyone has ever accomplished, he wasn't born with the skills and talents to accomplish anything.

Everyone had to learn everything after birth. Everyone had to gain every skill and talent after birth. Everyone had to develop character traits after birth. Everyone had to develop thoughts and attitudes after birth.

If an infant understood the concept, his self-image would be, "Right now I can't do too much of anything. My knowledge is minimal; I hardly know anything. I haven't read any books on anything. Everyone is taller than I am. I have no idea yet how my life will unfold. If I compared myself to a four- or five-year-old child, I would see myself as inferior. One could even say that I have an inferiority complex. My self-image is very low."

This is not the way most people view newborns. We all realize that this infant will be able to learn a lot. We all realize that this infant will be able to learn many skills and talents. We all realize that this infant is just beginning his life.

Wherever you are in your knowledge, skills, and talents, you are like a one-day-old infant: You still have a future available to keep developing yourself.

How much progress have you already made from the time you were one day old?

There was a time when you weren't able to speak, read, or walk yet. There was a time when you didn't have any knowledge and information or skills and talents. There was a time when you were totally helpless and couldn't do a thing for yourself.

And then you learned how to speak, read, and walk. You learned how to gain much knowledge and information, and developed skills and talents in many areas. And you learned how to do many things for yourself.

How much will you progress in your knowledge, your spirituality, your character traits, your skills and talents, and your accomplishments?

No human being knows yet.

As you focus on your progress since infancy, you will be able to say to yourself, "My self-image realizes that I have progressed immensely from when I was one day old until the present."

Then you will have a right to add, "Since I have already progressed so much, that means the ability to make progress is stored in my brain. Let me keep making more and more progress from now on."

Your progress has made you into what you are now. The progress that you will make from now on will create the rest of your life. May you continue to make more and more progress each day of your life.

> *Someone told me, "For many years I told myself, 'I don't know a fraction of what I should know by now. I don't have very many talents and skills compared to what I could have. I haven't accomplished as much as I wished I would. I lack self-esteem. I*

don't feel very good about myself.' When asked about my self-image, I would say, 'It's so low, it makes me feel bad just thinking about the subject.'

"Then someone asked me, 'How much progress have you made in your life?'

"I answered, 'Not very much. I am still so far from where I wish I would be. I don't have great hope for my future.'

"'You didn't answer the question I asked you,' he said, straight to the point. 'I asked you about the progress you made, not the progress you didn't make. What do you know now and what can you do that you didn't know and couldn't do when you started out in life?'

"'It would take a very long time to give a full report,' I answered truthfully.

"'Exactly my point!' he said. 'Keep focusing on the progress you did make, not the progress you didn't make.'

"This changed my life," he concluded with a big smile.

Consider Yourself a Ten Out of Ten

Mr. Sandler was a highly successful sales-trainer with a strong sense of humor. He used to motivate the salespeople he trained with the following speech.

"Your success at persuading people is not based on your education. Some people who are highly successful at selling were elementary school dropouts. Your success at persuading people is not based on your IQ. There are people with low IQ's who are much more successful at selling than others with genius-level IQ's." Mr. Sandler said.

He continued, "What does it take to be successful at selling, persuading, and convincing? Your subjective view of yourself. From now on, rate yourself a ten out of ten!

"Who chooses your rating? You do. If someone were to consider himself a low number, let's say a two or three, he will speak and act accordingly. He will project a low self-image. He won't speak and act with confidence. And he won't be convincing to others.

"Right now, decide to view yourself as a ten out of ten. This is not based on any external factor about yourself. This is not based on how other people see you. This is not based on how much you have already accomplished. This is not based on your education or your IQ. This is based on one thing only: the way you decide to see yourself from now on.

"Once you do so, you will be successful. Of course, you also have to know your product or service and strongly believe in it. But when you think of yourself as a ten out of ten, you will talk with confidence. Your facial expression and body language will manifest confidence. Your positive sense of self will have a positive influence on other people and you will be successful."

I remember that when I first heard Mr. Sandler say this, I started laughing. This concept is amazing in its simplicity. And it's amazing how powerful and effective this idea can be.

I have shared this idea many times to encourage people who complain of a low self-image, low self-esteem, and feelings of inferiority.

"Right now, without anything new happening in your life, you have a right to consider yourself a ten out of ten. There is no valid reason for not doing this. This doesn't mean that you are perfect or that you know all that there is to know. Of course you still need to keep developing yourself your entire life. You need more knowledge and you need to gain more skills. But as far as your value, you rate a ten out of ten."

Those who have recognized the validity of this simple idea have become much more confident. They realized that they had a right to view themselves as being a ten out of ten. They realized that they are the only ones who could stop them from thinking this way. They understood that just as Sandler's trainees accepted that rating themselves a ten out of ten would be the intelligent thing to do to become more successful, they could and would do the same.

Some people, however, reacted with puzzlement. "How can you do such a thing?" they questioned. "How can you just claim that you are ten out of ten and then consider yourself the best? Nothing has changed. You aren't any different than before. It seems too simple."

The Torah reality is that you always have had great value. You always were a worthwhile human being. You always had a right to consider yourself important. Declaring yourself to be a ten out of ten just gives you an added tool to internalize your value.

"But other people won't accept that I am a ten out of ten just because I say I am," they argue.

"You don't need to tell anyone that you're top-rate. You don't need anyone else's agreement to use this thought," I tell them. "You only need to think this to yourself about yourself."

People who have tried this approach have told me that they were amazed that such a simple idea could have such a fast, positive effect.

> A master at building people's self-image was asked, "If this simple approach to building one's self-image would really work, why don't many psychologists try it out before they try anything else?"
>
> The image-builder replied, "Why was this approach effective for a sales-trainer like Sandler?"
>
> The image-builder elaborated, "First of all, just telling someone who looks down at himself that he is ten out of ten won't be effective if the speaker doesn't really believe it. It is effective for people who are masters at raising people's self-image because they truly view every human being as a ten out of ten.
>
> "A salesperson must truly believe in his product or service to be successful. To convince someone that he is top rate, the person teaching him must believe that the person is truly a ten out of ten. He must speak with the respect and honor due to someone who is valuable.
>
> "When parents and teachers keep telling young children that they are ten out of ten and that this is the right of every single human being, then the children grow up with this awareness. This feeling will come naturally to those children. The children

won't have to overcome feelings of being only a one or two out of ten. The children will have heard that they're valuable so many times that it will be their natural and automatic way of thinking.

"Sales-trainers make larger profits in the opposite way than counselors and psychologists: The faster they help improve the trainees' self-image and get practical results, the more money they will make. When someone attends a sales training class, what is his goal? To learn to sell more. It's easy to understand that when you feel good about yourself, your emotional states will be more positive. This helps you sell more of your product or service. Integrating this idea will help you be more successful. When you are more successful because of a training class, you will share this information with your friends and relatives. They, too, will be more successful and will tell more people about the benefits. Your success with the concept of choosing to view yourself as a ten out of ten does not depend on the statistics of how many people it does or does not work for.

"An authority who tells someone, 'It takes a very long time to change a self-image,' will take longer to improve the person's self-image than an authority who says, 'You are have infinite value and worth. Now let's work together to coach you to speak and act in ways that are consistent with this positive sense of who you are.'

"Even after someone believes he is top rate, he stills needs to build up the qualities of confidence and courage, of joy and happiness, of inner peace and serenity, of interacting with harmony with others, and the ability to make and reach important goals. When people know that even when they have faults and limitations they still rate a ten out of ten, it becomes easier to master the thoughts, words, and actions that will help them become more confident and courageous, more joyful and peaceful, happier and more serene, and so on.

"Try this out for a month. Each and every day repeat to yourself many times, 'I am a ten out of ten. I always really was a ten out of ten and I always will be a ten out of ten. I will consistently speak and act with the confidence and courage of a person who considers himself top rate.' Allow this to work for you and you will see positive results."

On Being Respectfully Assertive

A person with a low self-image might not feel as valuable and important as others, and therefore thinks that his thoughts, feelings, and wants aren't as important as what others think, feel, and want. He might not feel that he has a right to speak up for himself, to ask questions when he doesn't understand, to ask for what he wants, and to express himself when he disagrees, or to negotiate when he wants a fairer deal.

Each person is valuable and important. Therefore, everyone has many rights, including you. You have a right to be respectfully assertive and speak up for yourself. You have a right to ask questions and ask others for what you want. You have a right to express yourself when you disagree and to negotiate when you want a fairer deal. You even have a right to ask someone to stop doing something that annoys or bothers you.

People who find it difficult to be assertive feel intimidated around other people. They give other people imaginary power. The source of these feelings is their fear of how others view them. Since the source of this fear is their own thoughts, they can instead think thoughts that create an attitude of self-respect and respect for others.

Realize that you have a right to be respectfully assertive, like everyone else. Let every time you are respectfully assertive build up your ability to speak up for yourself. You want to build up a state of courage: the courage to ask for what you want, the courage to ask questions, the courage to ask for favors, the courage to negotiate. You build up your courage pattern every time it is difficult for you to be assertive and you are nevertheless assertive.

Imagine that you are just as assertive as the most respectfully assertive people in the world. You might want to think of a specific role model you respect who is well liked and is still able to be assertive. When you want to be assertive, imagine that you're this person for as long as it takes. What would this person say and how would he say it?

You might want to practice being assertive in front of a mirror. Imagine that you feel wonderful about yourself. Imagine that you feel a strong sense of inner empowerment. Imagine that you can say anything to anyone as long as it is self-respecting and respectful to the other person. Every time you practice, you store this pattern in your brain. After enough repetitions, your mind can automatically access this pattern whenever you need to take action.

Let every act of assertiveness on your part build your self-image. "I am a person who has self-respect and respect for others, and therefore I can speak up when it is appropriate for me to do so."

Bob Burg, a friend of mine who knows how to ask respectfully for what he wants, suggests that when we ask someone for something, we say, "I would like to ask you for a favor. If it is too difficult for you to do it, I totally understand."

When you say this to someone, you are not putting pressure on that person. You are saying right at the beginning that you understand if he refuses your request. This makes it much easier to ask for what you want.

Have a friendly attitude: "I will gladly do things to help this person. I hope that this person is willing to help me out also."

Realize that being intimidated when you are not in any real danger is just your own mind and thoughts playing a trick on you. The needless fear is created by your imagination. Let your imagination enable you to overcome it.

Enjoy the process of building your assertiveness. You also build your self-image as you become more assertive. Remember that even if you are never assertive, you have tremendous inner value. Being able to be assertive is just a beneficial state of mind to master. As you master the state of being assertive, you will be able to help many other people throughout your life. There are many acts of kindness that you will be able to do for others by being respectfully assertive.

> *I was told, "I grew up feeling highly uncomfortable about asking other people for things. I was amazed that some people found it*

so easy to ask questions, to ask for favors, to make requests for better service, and to negotiate while I found it so hard to do. I looked at this as a statement about who I was: There are some people who are assertive and some people who aren't, and I'm just one of those people who aren't.

"One day someone I knew came over to me and said, 'I've been observing you for a long time, and I noticed how unassertive you are. I personally find it easy to speak up. I work with the rule, "You never get what you don't ask for." When you do ask, you often get. There is no great loss if you get a refusal. Throughout life you gain a lot by being assertive.'

"He continued, 'I would like you to use my pattern as a role model. There is a lot I can learn from you, but when it comes to assertiveness, you will gain a lot by learning from me.

"'Just observe how I speak to people and listen to the patterns that I use,' he said. 'I am committed to treating every person I talk to with respect and I don't want to put unfair pressure on anyone. But I do speak up. You can use different words when you speak up, but by observing my patterns, you will eventually make some of these patterns your own. You will be doing me a favor by becoming more assertive. I will feel good knowing that I have made your life a little better.'

"Once I observed this person and followed his patterns, it became much easier for me to be assertive. As I asked more questions, asked for more things, negotiated for fairer prices, and asked people to contribute to some worthy causes, I found it much, much easier than I had imagined it would be.

"My self-image changed from viewing myself as a person who just isn't assertive, to being a person who still finds it challenging at times. But I do know that I can be assertive whenever I really want to be."

Money and Self-Image

Money is a challenge for our character traits, according to the Torah attitude. As Rabbi Moshe Chaim Luzzatto writes in *Mesilas Yeshorim*, Ch.1, "All aspects of life are challenges for us to grow from. Wealth on one side and poverty on the other."

We should be grateful for the money we do have. Money is a tool to help us serve the Almighty. Money is for supporting Torah learning. Money is for us to share with others who have financial needs that they are unable to meet themselves. Money is for *tzedakah* (charity) and for *chesed* (kindness). Money is for us to use when being honest in our business dealings with others.

Viewing money as a tool prevents money from being a key issue in one's self-image. If the Almighty wants you to have the tool, you will have it. If you don't have money, realize that this is not a tool that you need to fulfill your life mission. What you do with the money is what counts, not how much you have.

Depending on one's mindset, one's upbringing, and where one now lives, money can easily become an issue of self-image. People with more money might feel superior over those with less. People with less money might have a challenge with feeling inferior and envious. Some people with more money might spend large amounts of money on homes, cars, and expensive luxuries to show off their wealth. Some people without money might just feel bad; others might go deeply into debt to spend money that they don't really have, to show that they are important since they also have a lot of money to spend.

The Torah concept of the value of human beings is totally independent of how much money anyone has. Our value is inherent because we are created in the Almighty's image and are children of the Creator. When your self-image is strong, you can appreciate the money you have. But self-worth is not affected by how much money you do — or do not — have. So your self-image should not depend upon your bank account.

> Two friends worked at the same company for many years. They were both highly skilled at their jobs and earned large salaries. They both had a number of investments and lived well.
>
> Then the company decided to downsize. They were both out of a job. At the same time, their investment values went down greatly.
>
> One was extremely depressed. "I am nothing without my job. I have to cut down on expenses drastically, but I can live with this. I'm now worth much less because I don't have the amount of money that I used to have."
>
> This person felt totally broken. He felt embarrassed around other people. "I can't give as much charity as I used to. I feel totally miserable about myself."
>
> The other fellow, however, took the loss in stride. "I am optimistic that I will be able to find other ways to make money. I will have to cut down expenses now. But I am grateful that I have a house to live in and plenty of money to buy food for my family. I will now have more time to learn Torah. I will find a learning partner and I will make a plan about how to make the best use of my extra time. I will not be able to give as much charity as I am used to giving, but that's not my fault. I look forward to the time when I will earn more money and I will be able to give more charity again. My job was only a means to an end. My value as a person is the same as it always was. Losing the job teaches me a lesson: Not to make my happiness and my sense of self depend on factors that are outside of myself. I will gain new strengths from this challenging experience."

You Don't Need Permission to Declare, "I Will Live the Rest of My Life With a High Self-Image

"Do I have a right to declare that from this moment on I will live my life with a high self-image?" Yes. To the best of my knowledge there is no law in any country in the world against it.

Some people act as if were illegal or unethical to just declare that they are dedicated to live their lives with a high self-image. "But I can't just do that!" they say, either explicitly or implicitly.

Why not? Some responses:

• Don't I need a lot of knowledge and wisdom to declare that I will live the rest of my life with a high self-image?

• Don't I need to accomplish a lot first?

• Don't I need to have a lot of money?

• Don't I need to have a prestigious job?

• Don't I need to have many skills and talents?

• Don't I need to have great sports victories? (Or at least root for winning teams?)

• Don't I need to be famous for something?

• Don't I need to have had a happy and healthy childhood?

• Don't I need to be popular and have lots of friends?

• Don't I need a lot of honor and glory?

• Don't I need to be the best in my class or school?

• Don't I need to look the way I want, and have the right height and weight?

• Don't I need to be number one in every area I want to be number one?

The answer to this kind of question is a loud and unequivocal: NO!

To have a high self-image you need one thing only: You need to think the thought: "I choose a high self-image because I am a human being and I exist."

You can choose this thought even if you haven't accomplished yet all that you wish to accomplish, don't have a lot of money, don't have a prestigious job, don't have many skills and talents, don't have great sports victories, aren't world famous, didn't have a happy childhood, aren't popular and don't have a lot of friends, haven't received great honor and glory, weren't the best in your school, don't look the way you wish, and aren't number one in important areas.

What is the only prerequisite for being a joyful and serene person with a high self-image just because you exist? Be able to sincerely believe that human beings have intrinsic value and worth.

Even a human being who is in a coma and can't speak, go anyplace, and do anything constructive has innate value and worth.

If you are reading this and understand what you are reading, it means that you are conscious and can think. This is all that you need to realize that you have tremendous value and worth. Then you are thinking your way to a high self-image as having value and worth.

But isn't it much better if a person uses his time wisely, works on developing positive character traits, had a happy childhood, and accomplishes positive things? The answer, of course, is, "Yes, it's much better." Nevertheless, you have a right to decide that you have a high self-image right now.

When people who are basically rational and sensible declare that they have a positive self-image, it is very likely that they will speak and act in many positive ways. They will usually accomplish more than they would with a low self-image.

If someone thinks that he can't have a high self-image just because he wants to, he has valid reasons for thinking this way. Many people have the general attitude that you need a special reason to think your way to a high self-image. But this chapter argues that you don't need anything else besides the right thoughts. Each individual has a right to choose for himself what he will think for himself. I suggest that my readers try out the "high self-image" thinking for at least three months before deciding if this is beneficial for you.

> *Someone once told me: "I grew up considering myself to be a very valuable human being. My parents loved me and kept giving me positive messages about myself. As I got older, I would say things that modestly gave over the message that, while I recognized that I had faults that needed to be corrected and that I didn't accomplish yet as much as I would have liked to accomplish, I considered myself as having a high self-image.*
>
> *"But I frequently heard comments that made it hard to sincerely consider myself as having a high self-image. There were a number of ways that these challenges were worded, but the general message was that one needs to be especially successful or knowledgeable or wealthy to have a high self-image. I would argue, but I was told, 'The more you argue, the more you are just proving that you don't really have a high self-image.'*
>
> *"I thought about this and saw that there was some truth to this statement. Yes, if I really had an independently high self-image, I didn't anyone else's agreement that I had a right to think this way.*
>
> *"So I made a decision: I wasn't going to tell anyone else that I had a high self-image. They could think what they wanted. This decision gave me happy feelings. I had a positive self-image because I chose to think this way. I didn't need anyone else to agree that I could think this way."*

The Two Patterns: "The Sword Way" Versus "The Healing Way"

When other people have tried to correct you, they probably used one of two patterns. King Solomon calls one the way of the sword and the other the healing pattern of the wise. The verse states: "There is one who speaks [harshly] like the piercing of a sword, but the tongue of the wise heals," (*Mishlei* 12:18).

The Vilna Gaon explains the two patterns of speaking when correcting people. One pattern is just telling them what they are doing wrong. You harshly censure them for their errors. As the expression today goes, "You let them have it!" There's a problem with this pattern: You are not telling them how they should have behaved and how to correct what they did wrong.

The wise pattern shows people how they can correct what they did wrong. This is a healing approach, and the only words said are conducive to healing.

The harsh pattern tends to lower the self-image of the wrongdoer. The speaker might have wonderful intentions and might really want his victim to become a better person. But, unwittingly, he is verbally stabbing that person. He tells him how awful he is and how badly he is speaking and acting. He is right that the person did do something wrong, but if he sincerely wants that person to improve, he should use the approach that King Solomon calls the wise approach — the healing approach.

The healing approach expresses sincere care for the welfare of the beneficiary of these words. Both the tone of voice and the content of what is said are healing and beneficial. When you show a person how to grow and improve by following your suggestions, you build his self-image. You express your belief in his ability to improve.

The Talmudic Sages (*Tamid* 32a) define a wise person as someone who sees the outcome. Before you speak, think about the outcome; will it meet your goal? Ask yourself, "What do I want to accomplish with what I am about to say?"

Your goal is to motivate the wrongdoer to improve his behavior, by speaking in a way that builds his self-image.

An important word of caution: If you are used to other people "correcting" you in ways that put you down, you might repeat that familiar pattern, even if you didn't like it.

If you have memories of being put down by those who tried to motivate you to improve, mentally edit what they said. What would they have said and how would they have said it using the healing approach?

Right now you can try to gain greater understanding of what they tried to do. Imagine hearing them say to you, "I feel that it's important for you to speak and act better than you are doing now. Please follow through on what I am suggesting. I'm speaking strongly because I want you to hear my message. I don't mean to cause you harm. My goal is to motivate you."

Be determined to master the healing approach toward motivating and influencing others. Be determined to speak to yourself in a healing way when you try to motivate and influence yourself, too. At times you might find that you need to speak to yourself in tougher ways, when speaking too lightly doesn't move you. But even then keep the major focus on how much better it will be when you speak and act in positive ways.

> *Many years ago there was a person who traveled from town to town, giving talks about how people need to improve. His lectures were fiery and some people were influenced positively. However, most of his audience went away feeling totally awful about themselves but didn't make any positive changes. He would say, "Even if people didn't improve, at least I made them feel bad."*
>
> *Another Torah scholar, who had a positive influence on the lives of a tremendously large number of people, spoke to the*

fiery speaker about his pattern of speaking. "The goal of correcting someone is causing the person to make positive changes. The Sages tell us that even when we correct someone we should be careful not to embarrass him."

The other speaker argued that he had an obligation to let people know that they were doing wrong.

The scholar replied, "King Solomon was the wisest of people. If in his wisdom he tells us to use a healing approach to point out the right way to do things, who are we to argue with him? If our own way of thinking goes against King Solomon's wisdom, it's more likely our limitations that cause us to think the way we do. If you want to be considered wise by King Solomon, you would be wise to follow the pattern that he recommends."

Speaking Against Others Does Not Build You

Some people try to build themselves up by speaking against others. They believe that talking about the faults and limitations of others makes themselves seem better and more elevated than those people.

It is a total illusion to think that you are actually building yourself up when you put others down. Speaking against other people is a violation of the Torah commandment to refrain from speaking *lashon hara* (negative speech). Someone who speaks against others without a practical and constructive purpose is lowering himself by doing so.

The Chazon Ish wrote, "When you study character traits and good behavior, your focus should be on improving yourself. If that is not your goal, you are likely to use what you study as a sword against others. Whatever you study, you will integrate into your arsenal to enable you to find more and more faults in others. The more faults you notice in them, the more elevated you will consider yourself" (*Emunah Ubitachon* 4:12).

Speaking against others is a sign of having a low self-image. Frequently talking about others announces, "I feel bad about myself. I want to divert attention away from my own faults and limitations by consistently talking about the faults and limitations of others. Also, the more I put others down, the less badly I feel about having similar faults myself. Many people are in the same boat I am, and therefore it's easier for me to tolerate my own failings."

The type of person who wants to build himself up by putting others down would definitely not want to spread a negative message about himself. Realizing the outcome of his words should give him the incentive to be more careful about not speaking negatively against others.

Having the self-discipline not to speak against others despite an urge do so is a character-raising act. This silence isn't passive. It is a conscious action of remaining silent or changing the topic in order to protect the dignity and honor of another human being.

Refraining from negative speech has the power to raise your self-image. "I am a person who considers it important not to cause verbal harm, loss, pain, or distress to someone else."

Every time you control what you say and don't speak against others, you become a higher and more elevated person.

> *Someone once told me of his reaction when he first learned the importance of being careful about not speaking against others. He felt that this was a value that he wanted to apply regularly. He felt good about not speaking against others, so this wasn't too difficult for him.*
>
> *But he found it very difficult to tell people that he didn't want to listen to them speaking against others. He wanted them to be more careful even if he wasn't with them, but he was concerned that they would make fun of him for trying to act so pious.*

"Who do you think you are, telling us what we can and can't say?" they would say. "Why are you acting so holier-than-thou?"

He knew his self-image would drop when others made fun of him, so he spoke to an older friend of his who was very careful with his speech and asked him about his thoughts on the matter.

"Imagine what it would be like to speak to the Chofetz Chaim about your challenge. What do you think the Chofetz Chaim would say to you?" the friend suggested.

"The Chofetz Chaim would encourage me to overcome any fears and hesitations that I have about asking others to stop speaking lashon hora," the fellow said. "I'm sure that the Chofetz Chaim would be proud of me for observing the Almighty's commandments. He would tell me that I was courageous to protect the children of the Almighty from verbal harm. Even though the speakers of lashon hora don't appreciate it now, I am doing them a tremendous kindness by influencing them to be more careful with what they say."

"How does this make you feel?" the older friend asked him.

"This thought helps me gain a wiser and more spiritual perspective. In fact, I will raise my self-image by overcoming the fear of being mocked. I am a person who is able to withstand the put-downs and mocking of others in order to do what I know is right."

How a Donkey Sees a Tzaddik

I was struck by the deep insight of Rabbi Shimshon Pinkus. He said that when a wise person sees a true *tzaddik*, he realizes that he is looking at an elevated, righteous person. He feels a sense of deep respect. However, when a donkey sees that elevated person, all he sees is a human body that weighs a certain amount.

How anyone sees you is a reflection of this person's knowledge, wisdom, insight, spiritual understanding, and awareness of potential.

Some arrogant and conceited people enjoy putting down other people. They like to break the egos of other people to attain an illusion of personal power and one-upmanship. They enjoy doing this even when they aren't especially angry, but all the more so when they are. They try hard to build their own frail egos by getting pleasure out of belittling another person.

On a certain level, those who act this way have a donkey's view of others, because they lack a spiritual view of who the other person really is. When a donkey doesn't realize your true value, it's easy to realize that the donkey is lacking, not you. So, too, when someone puts you down in order to belittle you, that person is lacking a spiritual view of the real you. Don't belittle yourself because of that person's limitation.

> *I met a concentration camp survivor who had lived in the concentration camp for a long time. This person had a tremendous sense of inner confidence and courage.*
>
> *"The Nazis systematically did everything they could to belittle Jews. Did their verbal abuse make you feel bad about yourself?" I asked him.*
>
> *"Not one bit," he replied. "Those so-called human beings acted like wild beasts. I wouldn't expect a pig to realize the value of a diamond. The more they tried to belittle me, the more grateful I was for having Torah values. The more they tried to insult and belittle me, the lower I saw them, and the higher I saw myself for having the Torah viewpoint on the infinite worth of the children of the Almighty."*

Do Things Daily That Are Difficult for You to Do

Each and every day, say or do at least one thing that you find difficult to say or do.

Every time you say something that is difficult for you to say, you build up your self-image: "I am a person who can speak up and say things even though I find them difficult to say."

Every time you do something difficult, you build up your self-image: "I am a person who can do things even though they are difficult for me to do."

This is a highly empowering self-image booster. This way you will keep saying and doing things that you need to say and do, and you won't be stopped by the thoughts of, "I find it difficult to say or do, so I won't say or do it."

You will be able to say and do difficult (but not impossible) things once you have mastered the attitude of: "If it's possible for me to say and do, I will say and do it. The more difficult it is for me to say or do something, the more I develop my self-image by saying and doing it."

Visualize yourself saying and doing those difficult things to make it easier. Mentally picture yourself saying and doing them. See these mental pictures over and over again. Regardless of whether or not you see these pictures clearly, imagining yourself seeing these mental pictures will condition your mind to say and do the hard things you imagine yourself saying and doing. The more times you run the image through your mind, the easier it will be to actually do it.

Feel tremendous joy and pleasure every time you break through an imaginary limitation. You are expanding yourself and your abilities. The better you feel about doing what used to be hard for you to say and do, the more good feelings and breakthroughs you will have.

The emotional blocks created by your negative thoughts and feelings can seem like actual physical blocks. But they aren't real. They just exist in your imagination. And since they only exist in your imagination, your imagination can help melt those imaginary blocks. See the blocks melting away. Feel the great feelings of knowing that you won't needlessly stop yourself from saying and doing the positive things.

Before you go to sleep at night is a good time to run through mental pictures of yourself acting the way you want. Review these pictures a number of times. You can repeat to yourself, "As I sleep, my inner mind will see pictures of me saying and doing the positive things I wish to say and do. My inner mind will repeat these pictures many, many times as I sleep. So even while asleep, I will be improving what I can say and do."

When you wake up in the morning, think about the positive things that you wish to be able to say and do that day. Don't let memories of difficulties stop you. When you were younger, you found many things difficult to say and do that you now find relatively easy. As you continue to say and do difficult things, even more things will become easier for you to say and do.

How many difficult things do you need to say and do until you feel totally confident that you have the attitude of: "I am a person who is not stopped by difficulties"?

You don't need to guess what the answer to this question will be. You will know by constantly saying and doing more things that you previously found difficult. And then eventually you will be able to experience the joy of knowing: "If it's possible for me to say and do something positive, I will be able to say and do it. The thought that something is difficult will not stop me from saying and doing the things that I truly wish to say and do."

I interviewed someone who was able to say and do many things that others found too difficult. I asked him, "How did you develop an attitude that you won't be stopped by thinking that something is too difficult?"

He answered, "When I grew up and I would say, 'That's too hard for me to do,' I was greeted with a big smile and warm words of encouragement. I was told over and over again, 'That's great that this is difficult for you to do. When you do something that is easy to do, that's not a real challenge. You don't develop yourself very much by doing what is easy. You become a greater person by saying and doing what is hard. Don't worry. If you really can't do it, you won't be able to do it. But if you really can do it, it's not too hard. It's just difficult, but not too difficult. You can only know the difference between "hard" and "too hard" by trying. So always keep trying.'

"I smile when I hear people giving excuses like, 'I can't do that; it's too difficult.' My mind has been trained to picture myself saying and doing anything that I might consider too hard to do. There are still many things that I can't do. But I don't want to fool myself into thinking that I can't say and do the things that I really can do."

Intensity of Will

When you strengthen your determination, you will be able to do and accomplish things that otherwise you would not be able to do. Put your heart and soul into accomplishing important things.

When you have people with fairly equal intelligence and skill competing in some way, the person with the most willpower usually comes out ahead.

Let's say that ten people are taking interviews for the same job. They all have a similar background, with similar amounts of experience and talent. But one person has a calm intensity of will. He strongly wants the job. He might think to himself, "This is my ideal job. The other people will probably be able to find other jobs. But for me, this job is one of a kind. I want this job with all my heart and soul. I feel that I absolutely must get it. I want this as much as I have wanted anything in my life."

The way that this person powerfully presents himself will make it much more likely that he will get the job.

Someone who is extremely intense might be too intense for a lot of people. They might feel too much pressure and tension in his presence. He might even be too intense for his own health. This passion might be problematic for his heart and blood pressure. Such a person would be wise to balance his enthusiasm.

But when something is especially important to you, intensify your will. You will do much better that you would otherwise. Your strong motivation will result in accomplishments that build your self-image.

Someone who has a strong need to build his self-image could benefit greatly by intensifying his will to do so. His increased determination can motivate him to do what needs to be done to succeed.

> *Many years ago I spoke to someone who was able to powerfully influence others. He had the ability to build people into being much more than they were. I asked him what he considered the key to his success.*
>
> *"I strengthen my will; it should be stronger than the limiting will of the person I am trying to influence. I need to motivate people to overcome their tendency to be lazy. I need to prove to the people I talk to that they can be much more than they think they can. I don't just say ideas and concepts. Rather, I want to impart those ideas and concepts in a way that convinces them that my words are in their best interest. I want them to feel the strength of my conviction about how they can enhance their lives.*
>
> *"If I ever speak to someone and my heart isn't in it, I usually don't succeed. I know that for me to transfer my awareness to others, I have to increase my level of intensity. When I was younger, at times I was way too strong with some people, and*

then they eventually resented what I was trying to do for them. As I have gained more experience, I have learned how to modify what I do and the states that I am in. But I've found that most people have too little intensity of will rather than too much. They and others would gain from what they have to offer by intensifying their will when it's appropriate."

Resilience: the Art of Bouncing Back

Build up your ability to be resilient, your ability to bounce back after a fall. As it states in *Mishlei* 24:25, "A righteous person will fall seven times and rise up." Everyone can fall; the main thing is to get up again.

When you think in terms of building your self-image, you will focus on the fact that you rose up after you fell. Of course, it would be best never to fall at all. But since falling is part of life, build your self-image by keeping your focus on what you are doing right. And when you fall, keep your focus on what you need to do to bounce back.

A person with a low self-image will be more likely to deny that he has fallen. It's too painful to acknowledge. Therefore, he finds it easier to deny the fall than to acknowledge it and correct it and prevent further falls.

A person with a truly positive self-image is interested in reality. Denying a fall doesn't erase it. A person who truly wants to be his best must try to be as objective as possible.

It takes humility to acknowledge that one can fall and has fallen. A basic aspect of this humility is to be a truth seeker. One seeks the truth, not merely what feels good and gives a positive impression to others.

When we need to bounce back, we might find it difficult to do it alone. Look for teachers, coaches, and mentors who can help you build upon your strengths. Read and listen to inspiring material that can help you make a major positive decision about what to do now.

Every young child who learns how to walk has learned to stand up again after a fall. Young children are able to do this because they don't repeat negative and self-defeating thoughts. Always have hope. Keep repeating positive thoughts of your current options and possibilities.

When you bounce back, you will have greater belief in the human spirit's ability to bounce back. Eventually you might be able to serve as an inspiration to many others. This knowledge should give you more inner strength.

Every time you bounce back, you build up your self-image: "I am a person who can bounce back after falling. Each experience gives me more inner awareness and self-knowledge."

> Be on the lookout for stories of people who have bounced back after major failures and setbacks. Look for stories of people who have hit rock bottom and have risen high. Every story that contains this message can serve as a personal inspiration.
>
> Regardless of the setbacks that one has suffered, know that there have been many people throughout history who have made comebacks in similar situations. If one person could do it, his example teaches everyone else that it's possible to suffer a serious reversal but then make wiser choices of thoughts, words, and actions.
>
> What if you are the first person in the world to fall the way you specifically have fallen? Then you will be a pioneer for others. You will be the first human being on the planet who has risen from your fall. Building up your inner strengths and bouncing back aren't just for you; you are a representative of all the people that you will be able to help by showing that it's possible to bounce back.

Make Health-Oriented Choices

When Hillel went to a bathhouse, he told a student that he was going to do a mitzvah, a good deed. When he came out, the student asked, "With all due respect, Rabbi, how could you say that you were going to do a mitzvah when you went to a bathhouse for personal reasons?"

"That is exactly the mitzvah I was referring to," said Hillel. "A statue of an emperor is washed and cleaned. When I wash myself, I am washing a human being who was created in the image of the Creator. That is an aspect of expressing respect for the Creator."

Making health-oriented choices in your life builds your self-image by enhancing the health of a being created in the Creator's image.

Build your self-image by making these health-oriented choices:
- Choose to eat food that is good for your health.
- Choose not to eat food that is not good for your health.
- Choose to eat food in moderation.
- Choose to exercise in order to enhance your health.
- Choose to get a proper amount of rest.
- Give up bad habits that are harmful to your health.

> "I decided to give up smoking," someone said to me, "because I felt that it was a choice that would make me feel much better about myself in the long run.
>
> "This was a very difficult decision for me. I had tried to give up smoking many times, but it was a great struggle. I would stop for a while, but then I would take another cigarette. I felt awful every time I began smoking again. But I felt so tremendously deprived after refraining from smoking that I decided it was just way too hard for me.

"I finally quit smoking because I realized that not smoking made a tremendously valuable statement: That I truly value myself, my life, and my health.

"Whenever I began to feel the urge to smoke, I would tell myself, 'I am way too valuable to ruin my health and well-being because of the good feelings I get from smoking.' The emotional and spiritual feelings of doing something difficult out of profound self-respect finally enabled me to make the commitment not to smoke again. I still find it challenging from time to time. But I feel so much better about myself for not smoking that the healthy choice wins, and I can joyfully say that I am now a non-smoker."

A Well-Rested and Well-Nourished Mind Thinks More Clearly

As you know by now, your self-image consists of your thoughts about yourself. A tired and undernourished mind won't think as clearly as a well-rested and well-nourished mind. When you're at your best, you will find it easier to think in ways that build your self-image.

It's possible to be tired and hungry and still have a positive self-image. When your self-image is based on the Torah reality that you're created in the image of the Almighty, that you're a child of the Creator, and that the world was created for you, your self-image is high regardless of how you feel.

When you realize that you are valuable and important, that you have already done many positive things in life, and that you plan to do many more positive things, your self-image will be positive, too, regardless of how rested or nourished you are.

But for people who have a strong need to build their self-image it is very important to get enough sleep. A tired mind and body can cause poeple to feel weaker and not think at their best. Many people regard themselves differently when they are well rested rather than chronically tired or currently exhausted.

When you have a problem to solve, it is easier to think of potential solutions when you are rested. Your thinking then will be more efficient and effective. Many people advise those who are tired and struggling with a problem to go to sleep and think about finding solutions after they feel sufficiently rested: "Sleep on it, and in the morning you will find it easier to think of a solution."

Eat nourishing, healthy food. When you feed your body properly, you will be able to think more clearly. The very act of eating for optimal health is an act of self-respect.

> "I kept changing how I viewed myself," someone said to me. "Sometimes I felt on top of the world. I felt great about how I was doing in life. I realized that I had faults and made mistakes, but this knowledge just motivated me to focus on continuous improvement. It didn't break me.
>
> "At other times, I felt drained and didn't have much energy. I felt pessimistic about my life. I belittled any accomplishments. I felt that I was far from the way I wished I were.
>
> "I wondered how I could feel almost like two different people. One person was a dynamic go-getter, a cheerful, friendly sort of fellow who did a lot and had many friends. The other person lacked energy and was tired and lethargic. This person hadn't accomplished even a small fraction of what he should have.
>
> "I went to discuss this feeling with an insightful person. The questions he asked me were helpful in finding out the underlying cause of the fluctuations. When I was tired and hungry, my thoughts about myself were negative. I lacked energy and this took away the color from my picture of myself.
>
> "Just realizing the positive effects of proper rest and nourishing food helped me understand something: I shouldn't take the

negative thinking caused by my lack of energy as objective reality. I was resolved to sleep more and eat better. It then became easier to dismiss the negative thoughts when I was tired and hungry."

Alert Mind, Relaxed Body

Your mind-body state is a key element to how you feel and how you think. When your mind and body are in their optimal state for thinking clearly, you will be able to remember more of what you know, concentrate better, study better, and function at your best in all areas.

Those who have studied the entire process of studying and remembering describe the optimal state as "having an alert mind and a relaxed body." Describing any state in words is challenging because states are experiential, not concepts. So to understand what it means to have an alert mind and relaxed body, you need to remember experiencing this state.

You can have an alert mind and relaxed body when you are well rested and totally calm and relaxed. Your mind is clear, free from internal and external distractions, and you find it easy to be totally focused.

Your brain and mind will be able to function even when you aren't in this optimal state. But the greater your ability to access this state at will, the better your mind will work.

Since you think at your best when your body is relaxed and your mind is alert, this state is conducive to a more positive self-image.

Does this mean that when people are anxious and nervous, tired and exhausted, feel strong pressure, and are a bit overwhelmed, they won't think at their best? Yes. And that is why one's self-image will tend to be lower when one is anxious and nervous, tired and exhausted, and feeling overwhelmed.

Because the state of "alert mind and relaxed body" is so valuable for thinking, studying, and functioning in all areas, it's worth making it a high priority to master your ability to be in this state. You can do this by sleeping enough, eating nourishing foods, being in a peaceful environment, and using positive self-talk.

Our thoughts are the factor that is most under our potential control. Thinking the thoughts that are conducive for this mind-body state will enable you to experience it more often, even if there are factors that are not optimal.

To help create this valuable state, breathe slowly and deeply and repeat to yourself, "With each and every breath, my mind is becoming more and more alert, and all my muscles are becoming more and more relaxed."

Be patient and keep this up for at least twenty minutes. In the beginning you might need a much longer time. After you have been in this optimal state enough times, you will find it easier to reach it in shorter amounts of time.

Associate slow and deep breathing with your muscles becoming relaxed and your mind becoming clearer; this exercise will benefit your mind, your muscles, and your self-image.

Make a mental note when you experience a state of alert mind and relaxed muscles. Become aware of how you feel. Then tell yourself, "This is my state of 'alert mind and relaxed body.'" When you want to reach this state, say to yourself, "Now I will allow myself to have an alert mind and relaxed body." Repeat a number of times, "Alert mind, relaxed body," until you experience it.

As you gain the benefits of frequently being in a state of "alert mind and relaxed body" you will think and feel better, and this will be beneficial for your self-image.

> *My son-in-law's father, Rabbi Avraham Baharan, of blessed memory, was a master teacher and principal in a high school. He studied the effects of tension and nervousness on his students. When students were calm and relaxed, their ability to remember*

was enhanced and their minds were able to think more clearly. He found that when students laughed right before taking a test, they became calmer and earned higher grades. He had a great sense of humor and it was very easy for him to say things that were funny. He made it a rule in his school that teachers were to say things that were humorous before each test. The test marks in the entire school went up.

If you need to take a test and you don't have a teacher who will make you laugh, make yourself laugh. Word of caution: If you have a teacher who will get upset if you laugh out loud, keep your inner humorous state to yourself.

As you breathe, you can tell yourself, "With each and every breath, my mind is becoming more and more alert and my muscles are becoming more and more relaxed. I will think clearly and remember better and better." It would be beneficial to repeat this to yourself every now and then when you study.

"What Is the Wisest Thing I Can Do Now?"

Life has many disappointments. When we make plans, some work out the way we wish and some don't. We try to accomplish, but not everything we were hoping to do is accomplished. We might want to attend a certain school, but aren't accepted. We might want a certain job, but don't get it. We might have worked at a certain job for a long time, but then that business, school, or organization has to downsize and we lose the job. We might have wanted our manuscript to be published as a book, but the publisher didn't accept it. We might have published a book, but it didn't sell as many copies as we were hoping it would. We might have planned to go on a trip or vacation, but in the end we weren't able to go. We might have wanted to win a certain prize, but didn't win it.

Some people suffered health problems or injuries that prevented them from doing many of the things that they were hoping to do. Natural disasters might destroy property, possessions, and many other things.

When our plans don't work out, we not only lose out on what we hoped to gain, but our self-image might take a hit, too. Someone's self-image could have been raised if his hopes and aspirations actually came about. The accomplishments would have raised his self-image. Getting the job or the school acceptance letter would have raised his self-image.

When we are disappointed, we should think of the following question: "What is the wisest thing to do right now?" No one wants to think of the stupidest thing to think. No one purposely wants to spend a lot of time on thoughts that would increase his distress.

But this question might be difficult to think when we are suffering the distress of disappointment. To make it easier, we should also ask ourselves this question when it is relatively easy to ask it.

Those who keep asking themselves, "What is the wisest thing to do right now?" throughout a regular day will find it easier to ask this question even when they are feeling the distress of disappointment.

When we think about the wisest thing to do right now, we must think more resourceful thoughts and less self-pitying thoughts, such as, "Isn't it awful that this happened?"

Those who ask, "What is the wisest thing to do right now?" will think about the present in a more constructive way.

At times it's wisest to consult someone who can encourage us. The wisest thing might be to brainstorm with kind and creative people who might suggest ideas that we might not have thought of ourselves.

The wisest thing might be to develop ourselves spiritually so we can grow spiritually from the disappointment.

I have spoken to various people who are experts at handling disappointments. Those who do the best follow in the footsteps of

Rabbi Akiva. "All that the Almighty causes to happen in our lives is for the best," Rabbi Akiva used to say.

The spiritual disciples of Rabbi Akiva realize that people are limited in their awareness of the entire situation. A mortal might think that a certain job, school, place to live, or situation would be best, but the Almighty's wisdom guarantees that what happens is the ultimate best.

Whether or not we have integrated the full impact of living life with this spiritual awareness, we would be wise to keep asking, "What is the wisest thing for me to do now?"

After I typed the first draft of this section, my fingers pressed the wrong buttons on my computer. My first reaction was, "I feel disappointed for losing what I have written." My second reaction was, "How perfect this is! Here I am, writing about dealing with disappointment. I could possibly waste time feeling distress about the waste of time and energy and some good ideas that might be lost because of the 'accidental' occurrence. Or I can follow the suggestion of this section, and ask myself, 'What is the wisest use of my time right now?' The wisest use of my time is to rewrite this section. I am better off now than I was when I first wrote it. The first time around I didn't know yet exactly how I would write it. Now I have all that I have written stored in my mind, if not on the computer. So even though I don't consciously know it by heart, I am more aware of the essence of my message. Writing this second draft is an act of fulfilling the message of asking myself, 'What is the wisest thing to do right now?' And if I write a little differently in this draft and it's helpful to someone, I can feel good now that someone might benefit from this story."

How we react to disappointments is part of our self-image. By frequently asking yourself, "What is the wisest thing to do now?" after experiencing a disappointment, you can build your self-image to: "I am a person who tries to think of the wisest thing to do whenever I experience a disappointment." And each time you actually apply this and think of the wisest thing to do, all the positive things you've done will be added to your mental database of your answers to the question of, "What is the wisest thing I can do now?"

"I used to be very late for things, not accomplishing a fraction of what I was hoping to accomplish," a person who considered himself a poor time-manager told me. "I was frequently frustrated by missing deadlines, and always felt that I was running late," he said. "I tried to improve my time-management skills, but I wasn't very successful. How could I succeed when I viewed myself as a person who couldn't manage time?

"Finally I spoke to a number of people who were experts at managing their time efficiently. Some had elaborate time management notebooks and systems. This wasn't for me. One person who accomplished a lot told me that one tool was his key to success: He frequently asked himself the question, 'What is my best option for now?'

"I was surprised by the benefits when I tried his system. I hadn't fully realized how much time I wasted on low-priority activities. Once I realized that I needed to spend much more time on high-priority activities, I was able to make and reach many more goals."

Searching for the best options became a part of this person's self-image. He started seeing himself as a person who is great at thinking about and finding the best options for his time.

Become Part of Worthwhile Organizations

When you become part of a worthwhile organization, you can consider the good that this organization does as a positive part of your self-image.

There are many ways to become part of an organization that does important work. You can find a full- or part-time job with them. You can take part in their fund-raising or publicity functions. You can volunteer to help that organization.

When people first start an organization that plans to do good, they often need encouragement. Even if you are not able to assist in a major way, words of encouragement can be tremendously helpful.

Which organizations do you want to consider yourself part of? Ask yourself, "What do I think I can do for this organization?" Ask people who are already involved in that organization, "What can I possibly do to help you?"

This section isn't complex in its basic concept. But it might take a lot of time, energy, and financial resources to actually put its basic premise into action.

The merit of helping important organizations is great. In addition, your self-image will gain tremendously when you extend yourself to help a number of worthwhile organizations.

> Someone shared with me, "I am limited financially so I'm not able to give major amounts of money to help yeshivas and charitable groups right now. But when I realized that I would be encouraging the people who do much good in the world by giving what I could, this motivated me to give many small donations to more causes.
>
> "I didn't realize this at first, but I saw that after I donated to some causes that I greatly admired, I identified more with the good that they were doing. This built my self-image.
>
> "I came to realize that when I prayed for the welfare of those organizations, I identified with the good that they do even more. While I myself am far from doing all that I would like to do, my asking the Almighty to help them has added an additional sense of meaning in my own life.
>
> "'Who am I?' I ask myself. 'I am a individual who does my small part to do much good in the world.'"

Store the Entire Book of Psalms in Your Mind's Database

Read the entire book of *Tehillim* (Psalms) with the intention of storing the entire book in your brain's mental database. Then you will have all the verses stored in your mind, and you will have the self-image: "I am a person with the entire Book of Psalms stored in my brain."

We are not referring to remembering the verses by heart. Rather, just the process of storing the verses in your mind can be a highly elevating experience. Even if you have already read the Book of Psalms many times throughout your life, it is worth rereading with the intention of knowing that all the verses are stored in your brain.

Once you have read the entire *Tehillim*, every single verse is stored in your subconscious mind. Realizing this will have a positive spiritual effect on you for the rest of your life.

From now on you can have a self-image of: "I am a person who has read the entire *Tehillim* and stored it in my brain. Wherever I go, my brain is with me. So I always take the entire Psalms with me wherever I go."

Every single person who has ever read Psalms can already have this as a self-image. But reading it with the specific intention of storing the verses in your mind is likely to increase the spiritual and emotional power of this awareness.

> Someone I told this to asked, "But can't I do that with the entire Torah? I can do that with Pirkei Avos. I can do that with Mishlei. I can do that with every aspect of Torah that I learn."
>
> And the answer is, "Yes, of course you can. And it's worth doing."

Improving Your Courage

As you raise your level of courage, you also build your self-image. People who realize that they are courageous will also realize that they can go after their goals. They will have the courage to take action even when the outcome is not certain.

No one wants to fail and no one wants to make mistakes. A courageous person doesn't fear failure and is not afraid of mistakes. A person with courage knows that mistakes are learning experiences.

A person with courage will have the inner strength to speak up and be assertive. A person with courage will have the courage to ask questions and will be open to learning new things.

Courage doesn't necessarily mean that a person doesn't experience fear or anxiety. Rather, every potentially fearful experience is another opportunity to raise your level of courage. You are able to speak up and act even though you might feel nervous about it.

Imagine what you'd be like with a high level of courage. Imagine that you were given high levels of courage as a Divine gift. Think about how this would enable you to make better choices of thoughts, words, and actions.

It takes courage to speak and act with more courage than you already have. But when you think, speak, and act like a courageous person, you become more courageous.

What would you do if you actually had more courage? In your mind, watch yourself doing something courageous that you think is important for you to do. Allow yourself to feel the courageous feelings you would be feeling if you were able to create those feelings whenever you wanted them.

Think of some courageous people you have met or read about. Imagine the feelings of inner strength that they have. Imagine being able to transfer their inner feelings of courage to yourself.

Remember that no one is born with courage. This is a quality that one develops. Yes, some young children have this automatically without doing anything special to create it. Everyone else has the ability to learn and develop this quality.

Think of all the ways you are more courageous today than you were when you were three years old. What forms of courage do you already have? Take that courage, which you already have stored in your brain, and apply it in more and more situations.

This is where self-image comes into the picture. Some people aren't as courageous as they could be because their self-image says that they aren't courageous. But you only need one experience of courage in your entire life to teach your inner mind that you already have courage stored in your brain. Your brain is always with you. So as long as you have had courage in any way, in any situation, it means that you have courage.

If you can't remember even one instance of past courage, right now say or do something that takes courage for you to say or do. Then realize that whenever you need to access a state of courage, you have it stored in your brain.

As a young child you certainly had to do things that you were frightened to do. Since you actually said or did something that was scary for you to say or do, that was courage in action. You might have viewed that as a lack of courage because you felt afraid. From now on, view it as having had the courage to say or do what you did even though you were scared. When you have the self-image that being frightened won't stop you when you are not in real danger, you will have the courage to do many things that you previously hesitated to do.

There are many imagery techniques that can enable you to experience more courage. Some examples are: Drink an imaginary "courage drink," or eat a "magic grape." When you imagine drinking this drink or eating the grape, allow yourself to feel courage spreading from head to toe. You can now talk and act courageously.

You can imagine that you have been given calm inner courage as a gift from the most courageous person who ever was. You can now talk and act like him.

Imagine a special computer programmed with every positive inner resource. All you have to do is decide which inner resource you want and then push a button. Push the courage button to experience tremendous courage.

Allow yourself to have a self-image: "I already have spoken and acted when I needed courage to do so. Therefore I have already been courageous. I will keep building my level of courage throughout my life."

> *I spoke to someone who repeated frequently, "I totally lack courage. I am very fearful. I consider myself wimpy. If it takes courage to say or do something, I won't do it.*
>
> *"My father was super-courageous," the fellow continued. "He wasn't afraid of anything. He kept challenging me to say and do things that I was too frightened to say and do. 'You are acting like a baby,' he often said to me. 'You will grow up to be someone who is frightened of his own shadow. You won't be able to manage in life if you are so afraid of everything. What's there to be scared of?'*
>
> *"I know that my father meant well," he said. "But each time my father was upset at me for being fearful, he increased my self-image of being someone who lacks courage. This low self-image prevented me from taking the type of relatively safe risks that most people take. I guess that I'm stuck with being this way the rest of my life. Do you really think that there is hope for me to change?"*
>
> *"Courage is based on your thoughts," I told him. "Regardless of how you have thought until now, at any given moment in your life you can make a strong resolution to begin to think in ways that build your level of courage. When you think, speak, and act with courage, you will see yourself having more inner confidence. Even before you develop your level of courage as much as possible, you will see immediate progress.*
>
> *"Your brain is always with you. You can encourage yourself to continue to gain more and more courage. You can visualize yourself speaking and acting with more courage than ever before," I concluded.*

"Do you really mean it?" he asked. But I could tell as he asked this question that he was already viewing courage as a quality he could develop, rather than as a gift he didn't have.

The feedback I received a few days later from a rabbi who knew him was that he seemed almost like a different person. Once the fellow understood that courage was in his thoughts, it changed his entire view of himself. He was no longer a fearful and frightened person. He was a person who had been conditioned to be fearful, but he could learn to think, speak, and act with courage. Speaking and acting this new and improved way showed him that this way of being was already stored in his brain, which would always be with him.

I told him that he should expect his old patterns to return every once in a while. When that happens, he should repeat to himself, "This, too, will upgrade my level of courage. When I see that I am not courageous and can still access a courageous state with my mind, it means I never have to be afraid of not being courageous. I can always come back to this state."

Building Your Feelings of Confidence Builds Your Self-Image

By building your feelings of confidence, you build your self-image. Confidence isn't just a quality that you are either born with or not. No one-day-old infant is confident. No confident person at any time during history was born with confidence. They all had to learn to be confident. For some people this came naturally and automatically, but throughout history there have been a multitude of people who lacked confidence in their youth. As they gained more knowledge and learned more skills, they became tremendously confident.

What does it mean to be confident? It means that you feel certain that you know or can do something. It could also mean that you feel certain that you can learn whatever you want to know, whether it is knowledge, skills, or talents. It could also mean that you know that you don't have the knowledge or skills you would like, but you feel confident that you can find people to teach you the knowledge and skills you need.

The term self-confidence, as in "I have self-confidence," is usually used when someone exudes a sense of feeling good about himself. A person's manner of talking and body language can reflect self-confidence or a lack of it. Those who say they have self-confidence are likely to have a more positive self-image than people who keep saying that they don't have self-confidence.

Regardless of one's way of talking and one's body language, real self-confidence is an inner attitude.

Is it possible for a person to lack confidence and still have a positive self-image? In principle, the answer is: Yes, it is possible.

A person might say, "There are a multitude of topics and subjects that I'm not confident about. There are many skills and talents that I am missing, and I'm not confident that I can learn them. There is much that I don't know, and I'm not confident that I can learn even a small fraction of it. I'm not an expert in anything special, and I'm not confident that I can become an expert. I don't have business knowledge, and I'm not confident that I can gain it. I'm not good at negotiating, and I'm not confident that I can learn how to do it well. There is a long list of what I don't know and can't do. But when it comes to self-image, I am valuable and have tremendous worth. I have a right to speak with a loud and clear tone of voice, and I do. I have a right to stand and walk with the same body language as any other person in the world, without arrogance and conceit. I know how to live a joyful and happy life because I am grateful for all the good in my life, and I know how to choose joyful and happy states."

This pattern isn't typical, but any individual could decide to experience strong self-confidence in his intrinsic value and in his ability to feel good about himself in all situations and contexts.

I am not asking anyone to stop having confidence in his ability to gain knowledge and master skills. I am just saying that it's possible for anyone to have a generally positive self-image, even if he lacks confidence.

But since it is more usual that a lack of confidence leads to a lower self-image and having confidence leads to a higher self-image, I vote for people to gain more confidence in their abilities.

Some people claim, "I don't have confidence." While I think it is true that people might not feel as much confidence as they would like to have, it is not true that they don't have confidence. Every single normal person has a tremendous amount of confidence.

If you are reading this, it means that you are confident that you know how to read. If you know how to count to twenty and you know that you can, it means that you are confident that you know how to count to twenty. If you know that you know the alphabet, it means that you are confident that you know the alphabet. The same could be said about thousands and thousands of facts.

And as long as you are open to learning new ideas and new skills, even if you are not confident about something right this moment, in a week, month, and year, you will be able to be confident about more and more things.

As you keep becoming increasingly more confident, you will be able to have a self-image of, "I am a person who consistently becomes more and more confident about more and more things."

To add to your inner feelings of confidence, think of a person you met or saw who you consider to be a highly confident person. In your own way, act and speak more like this person. You don't need to choose just one person as a role model; you can collect a composite of many behaviors of many people. Put it all together in a way that you feel comfortable with.

You might practice speaking into a tape recorder to hear how you sound. Keep practicing talking with confidence, and listen to how you sound. You might benefit from speaking to a coach who can give you beneficial feedback.

Similarly, you might want to practice standing and talking the way a highly confident person would stand and walk. Again, a coach can give you beneficial feedback.

The easiest method to gain confidence that I've ever witnessed is to find someone who exudes confidence, and then mirror his way of talking, sitting, standing, and walking. If you find a super-confident person who allows you to do this for a number of hours, great! If you are too intimidated to ask a super-confident person to allow you to copy his actions in his presence, realize that you don't need anyone's permission to copy him when you're alone. Imagine that this person is in the same room as you are, and practice speaking, sitting, standing, and walking the way he does.

Be patient. For some people this works relatively quickly. Others find they need to keep this up for a long time before they find themselves integrating this pattern into their automatic behavior.

After you know how you think and feel when you feel tremendously confident, stand the way you would stand when you would feel this awesome level of confidence. Feel your confidence level getting stronger and stronger. Now double that feeling. Now double it again. Note your facial expression and body language. You can give this pattern a label such as, "My total and absolute confident state."

Now allow yourself to stand the way you would stand if you had absolutely no confidence. Next, say with a totally confident tone of voice, "I will now access my state of total and absolute confidence!" Either have someone give you feedback or look in a mirror and feel this total and absolute confidence. Keep practicing going from the body language of "lack of confidence" to the body language of "total and absolute confidence." Every time you repeat this, you will be training your inner mind to go spontaneously from the unresourceful state to your total and absolute confidence state.

This is a powerful self-image booster. This is great for overcoming shyness and the fear of public speaking. If you ever feel needlessly intimidated by someone, you will be able to melt those fears by mastering the ability to access the state of "total and absolute confidence" at will.

To summarize how to learn to be more confident: Think, speak, and act the way confident people speak, think, and act, and you too will be a confident person. This will improve your self-image and the way others will see you.

Since you are becoming more confident in yourself, if you feel that you think, speak, and act confidently, you won't really care what another person thinks. However, you will be open to feedback. After others express why they think what they do about you, you will either agree or disagree with them. You will be grateful for their feedback, and if you do agree with them, you will continue to upgrade your thinking, speaking, and acting to become more and more confident all the time.

> *Not that long ago I met someone who radiated tremendous confidence. He believed strongly in his G-d-given abilities. He believed that he could constantly learn new knowledge and gain new skills.*
>
> *"There are many things that I don't know how to do and there is much knowledge that I am missing. I realize that regardless of how long I live, I will only be able to learn a small fraction of what is possible to know. But I know what I know. And if I forget something, which I am certain I will, I have the ability to learn it again."*
>
> *"Were you always this confident?" I asked.*
>
> *"Very far from it," he replied. "I used to worry about the future a lot. My first assumption was that I would not be able to cope well. I assumed that I just didn't have many skills and talents that would be helpful in life. I didn't know what I would do in the future to support myself.*
>
> *"My mother meant well, she loved me dearly, but she herself was a worrier and she would often say to me, 'It's too bad that you don't have your father's head.' My father was a child prodigy, so I didn't feel bad emotionally when she said this to me. She was just stating a fact. Even though I have accomplished a lot over the years, I still agree with my mother; I don't have the intellectual ability of my father. But I am grateful for the knowledge I do have and what I have accomplished. I now realize that while*

my father's IQ was much higher than mine, I have applied myself and live a wonderful life.

"Even when I lacked confidence in many areas, I still was confident in some specific areas, and I was a generally happy person.

"I used to view confidence as an inborn trait: Either you had it or you didn't. As I got older, I realized that confidence is a quality that anyone and everyone can gain. It doesn't mean that everyone will actually learn all the knowledge that exists or learn every valuable skill. It does mean that people can be confident in their general attitude and mannerisms.

"I saw a fellow whose tone of voice and mannerisms gave off a clear impression that he was not a bit confident. But the funny thing is that his inner attitude was that he was open to do something that intimidated most people. He believed in his ability to take action. After just one session with a powerful coach who pointed out how to carry himself, how to talk with a tone of voice that expressed empowerment, and how to walk, he began following the coach's lesson, and this strongly upgraded his total sense of confidence.

"All we need is one role model who learned how to be much more confident by thinking, speaking, and acting the way a confident person thinks, speaks, and acts, and we too can learn to be confident.

"Because I see how much I gained from increasing my level of confidence, I consider it one of my life missions to help other people increase their level of confidence."

Excessive Confidence Can Cause Many Mistakes

Lacking confidence can prevent people from reaching their potential. Excessive confidence leads to arrogance and conceit. This attitude is intrinsically problematic and also creates resentment and ill will.

Excessive confidence also leads to many mistakes and errors. If a person feels confident that he is right when he is actually wrong, he could easily make serious mistakes. Someone who is certain that he knows something won't do the necessary research to find out that he is mistaken.

A doctor who feels that his diagnosis and treatment plan are correct when both the diagnosis and the treatment are wrong might assume that a seriously ill person is healthy, and the patient will suffer. At times a patient might want a second opinion that might correct the mistake, but the first doctor's excessive confidence might prevent a second opinion from being sought.

People who refuse to ask for directions waste a lot of time assuming that they know the way. Sometimes this is a minor problem, but in emergency situations it can be a major problem.

Many people who were excessively confident that they knew stock market trends or real estate trends have lost large amounts of money that they couldn't really afford to lose.

People with excessive confidence are often afraid to say the scary words, "I don't know."

At times, excessive confidence is caused when a person didn't realize that he needed to ask others or do more research. He was so confident that he remembered correctly that he didn't feel for even a fraction of a second that he needed to confirm the matter with other people, reference books, or his own notes.

At other times excessive confidence is caused by a lack of a positive self-image. Someone might have felt that questioning himself showed that he's less of a person because he wasn't totally confident. To save himself from these distressful feelings, he assumed that he was certainly right. The more one is open to constructive feedback, the more one will be saved from the pitfalls caused by excessive confidence.

Be aware of mistakes you might have made because of excessive confidence. Also become more aware of mistakes made by highly competent professionals who are both intelligent and experienced, and learn that anyone can make honest mistakes.

> A person who realized that he had excessive confidence consulted his rabbi for advice.
>
> "When I think that I know how to do something or that I have the necessary knowledge, I feel stupid asking other people about the matter," the man explained.
>
> The rabbi replied, "It takes strong self-confidence to consult someone when you feel stupid about asking. Since every single human being makes mistakes, you are intelligent for trying to avoid mistakes that you can possibly avoid. Let this build your self-image. You are a person who does what is difficult in order to avoid mistakes."

Staying Calm Under Pressure

People who stay calm and clear-thinking under pressure can be at their best even when facing challenges, obstacles, and difficulties. They probably have a positive self-image; they know that they have intrinsic value, whether or not things work out the way they had hoped.

People who are not able to stay calm under pressure become frustrated and angry when faced with tense situations. They worry more and experience more anxiety and tension.

Every time you are able to stay calm under pressure, you build your self-image. You will know that regardless of the external situation, your reaction is up to you.

People who are able to stay calm under pressure are sometimes said to have nerves of steel. But staying calm under pressure is really staying in a calm and serene state during challenging situations.

Even if someone is never calm under pressure and worries easily and gets thrown off balance frequently, that person is still valuable and precious. That person is still created in the Almighty's image and is still a child of the Creator, and can still have a high self-image. But being able to stay calm under pressure gives you more self-respect and gains more respect from others.

Build up your ability to stay calm under pressure. Visualize yourself being in challenging situations, and see yourself remaining calm and alert.

If people are trying to pressure you during a negotiation or discussion and you don't feel that your mind is clear enough to answer properly, you have a right to say, "I would like to think this over for a while before I reply."

One of the world's top negotiators was sent by American presidents to handle difficult negotiations. I heard him speak about the art of negotiation. He said, "I only negotiate when I am not biased at all in the results. When I need to negotiate for myself, I always ask an outside expert to negotiate for me. He will be much calmer and more relaxed than I am."

When your goal is to stay calm in situations that might overwhelm you or cause you to experience stress, fear, or anxiety, realize that these are all unpleasant emotional states. Your goal is to be able to handle these situations while remaining in a calm state. You want to master the skill of remaining in a calm state.

In all situations when you feel pressure, realize that your thoughts and your imagination are the only things causing that pressure. Therefore, your thoughts and your imagination can enable you to become calm.

Think of the following imaginary scenarios to help you stay calm under pressure:

- Imagine being in the calm and serene places you've calmly visited.
- Imagine that you have a calming drink that composes you any time you imagine sipping it.
- Imagine that you are a powerful giant and you can say anything to anyone in any situation and feel empowered.
- Imagine that snapping your fingers calms your entire emotional state.

I asked a person I once met how he became so skilled at staying calm under pressure. He said, "I pretend that everything that happens is on a large video screen. Every person I interact with is part of the scenery. I'm the only person that is alive and real; everyone and everything else is just what I see on the screen of my mind.

"My choices of thoughts, words, and actions are like a game I am playing on the screen. I always maintain self-respect and respect for others, but nothing anyone says or does will intimidate me.

"If someone raises his voice and yells at me, I imagine the clown on the screen acting like he has lost his temper. I don't have to worry as long as I'm not in physical danger.

"I keep asking myself, 'What would be the wisest thing for me to think, say, and do now?' Because I keep calm, I am able to think more objectively."

> Someone once said, "I am a person who easily gets angry. I've lost my temper millions of times. Well, not really millions, but very many. I get nervous when facing challenges and my nervousness leads to mistakes. This is just who I am. Can I really learn to be calm and collected under pressure?"
>
> "So you have many memories stored in your memory bank of not being calm under pressure, is that it?" I clarified.
>
> "That's it," he said.
>
> "Would you like to build up your ability to stay calm and clear-thinking when facing pressure?" I asked.
>
> "That would be absolutely wonderful," he replied.
>
> I suggested, "Review the challenging situations when you didn't stay calm, but now see yourself remaining calm and clear-thinking in those same scenes. After you run this through your mind feeling calm in the present, you will be building up your belief in your ability to stay calm in those situations. It is in your mind that you experience these feelings and you are conditioning your mind to be in a calm state.
>
> "Then imagine having to deal with similar situations in the future and see and feel yourself staying calm and clear-minded. Review it again and again, even hundreds of times. As you run this through in your mind, you will be building up your self-image that you are a person who can stay calm under pressure. When you actually do stay calm under pressure, you will know that you have developed a valuable skill."

Having High Expectations

People with very high expectations of themselves might consider themselves to be much lower and inferior than they actually are. They are not in competition with others, but they want to reach higher than they possibly can. In religious and spiritual matters they have ideals that are great to strive for, but they don't meet their own high standards. Therefore, they consider themselves to be less than they are and consistently feel bad about themselves.

If expectations are really impossible, one can't possibly reach them. It is rational and sensible to give up impossible expectations. Some high expectations might be possible, but it may take a long time, even years, to meet them. Some people might be impatient. They want to improve themselves right away.

In order to have more joy in life and to maintain a healthy self-image, keep your eye on high goals but take pleasure in striving to reach them. As my teacher Rabbi Gavriel Ginsburg used to repeat very often, "When you reach for the stars, you might not catch any, but at least you won't get your hands caught in the mud." Feel good that you are striving high. Enjoy the entire process of developing yourself.

Having a balanced attitude towards having high expectations and living a happy life enables you to maintain a positive self-image during the lifetime journey of reaching high levels. You realize that it's not all or nothing. It's not that either you meet your high expectations or else you are a total failure. Rather, each and every day you strive high. And each and every day you take pleasure in what you are doing to reach those high expectations.

Stop judging yourself. Stop giving yourself marks. View it as someone might view his mountain climbing — he does it for sheer pleasure, for the adventure of enjoying the climb. You want to climb high, but the goal is not just to reach the top of the mountain. The goal is to enjoy the entire process of what you are doing.

Those who have high expectations of themselves and try to reach them in a modest and humble manner have one goal: to live a full and meaningful life. Their goals don't include showing off to others, boasting, or considering themselves better than anyone else. This way of thinking enables a person to have a positive self-image that is not being measured in terms of success and failure. Instead, it is a life lived with an eye on doing worthwhile activities and being the type of person that one wishes to be. One learns from each experience and continues trying to improve and grow.

> *A person with a positive self-image had very low expectations of himself. He used to say, "I feel good about myself now. Why should I strive to accomplish more and be better than I am? If I have higher expectations of myself, then I might go around feeling bad that I didn't reach my potential. I feel that I'm much better off now, with my limited view of myself. I save myself a lot of frustration this way."*
>
> *Someone who wanted him to strive higher replied, "Yes, it's true that you are basically happy now. But when you strive to accomplish more in your life, you don't need to give up your happiness. It's a mistaken way of thinking to assume that you will need to be more frustrated if you raise your sights to improve yourself. You probably have some role models of people who did strive high and consistently felt bad that they didn't reach their expectations. You, however, can develop a joyful attitude towards life and towards striving to reach your goals.*
>
> *"Those who experience high levels of frustration feel this way because of their patterns of thinking. They have their sights set only on the final results. They keep repeating that they are far from reaching their goals. They keep telling themselves that it's so difficult to do what what's necessary to reach their high expectations. It's understandable that this way of thinking causes much stress and frustration.*
>
> *"You should enjoy each step of the way. This is a new way of thinking for you, so it can take some time before it becomes your*

automatic way of thinking. But you will add greatly to your life by adopting this pattern of thinking. You will accomplish much more and feel more joy in your life."

The person who heard this advice reported that after developing this way of thinking, he saw that he was able to have much higher expectations than ever before and still experience even better feelings than before. While he was limiting himself, deep down he knew that he could and should be doing more with his life. Now he was taking action in ways that he had always wished he would.

It's Not Over Until It's Over

There is a rule in competitive games: It's not over until it's over. As long as the game is still going, there is a chance that someone who started out not doing so well can "make a comeback" and do much better.

The same applies to living life: It's not over until it's over. As long as you are alive, you have the opportunity to do more and be more.

You might complain about your self-image because you view your current self-image as a final reality. It isn't. We human beings are works in progress as long as we are alive. If you aren't satisfied with your self-image right now, say and do things that will raise your self-image. You can even raise your self-image with just your thoughts.

Whenever you read this, your life is still going on and you can raise your self-image with just one sentence. Take, for example, the sentence: "I would like to do some great things in my life."

Say this sentence out loud to yourself right now. If you don't want anyone else to hear your aspirations, whisper the sentence. Or you can just think it. Once you say or think this sentence, then your self-image can be: "I am a person who is talking or thinking about doing great things."

That's a lot different than having a self-image of being a person who doesn't think and speak about doing great things.

Some people will argue, "But just thinking or talking about doing great things isn't the same as actually doing them." This is certainly a true statement. Few would argue with it. But just thinking about wanting to do something great is much better than not thinking about doing some great things.

Since you are alive and you are thinking about doing something great, an opportunity might arise that you hadn't anticipated. Maybe you'll see someone throw a hand grenade into a large crowd of people and you'll risk harm to yourself to save those people. You'll run over and throw the hand grenade to a safe place. You'll have done a heroic act that took just a few moments but changed you forever. You'll be a person who saved the lives of others with an act of heroism. I have spoken to people who have done similar things. It was just one moment that changed them forever.

In just a short time, you can make a commitment to become a much better person. In just a moment, you can make a resolution to stop a negative pattern, to start a positive pattern, to help other people, and to become a more elevated human being.

It's not over until it's over. Someone might be feeling really awful about himself, but then he'll think of someone to positively influence. In a short time he can make a major difference in someone's life. His self-image will grow.

In just a short time a person might realize that he has done many good things that he has taken for granted. Now he can gain a greater realization of what he has already accomplished. Since life is still being lived and it's not over, the person realizes that he can still add to the good that he has already done. His self-image immediately becomes higher than before.

An elderly person during his last moments of life might say or do something that is awesomely elevated. The final chapter of his life is awesome. During his last few seconds he'll realize that those last moments have changed his self-image.

Realizing how we all can keep changing who we are, we will never look at our current self-image as final. It is always just how we see ourselves until now. Our next actions can shed more light on our lives and who we are.

So if you ever feel down or discouraged, hear an inner voice saying to you, "It's not over until it's over. Let me intensify my will to do and become more right now."

> *There was an elderly person in an old age home who was usually sad. When people who tried to cheer him up would ask him what they could do for him that would make him happier, he would reply, "I can't think of anything. I am an old man and I'm not able to do very much. When I was younger I would work hard and earn money to support myself and my wife. Now I can't do very much. My wife passed away a couple of years ago. I still enjoy music and that makes me feel a bit better, but I consider my life to be almost over. I see myself as someone who is just waiting for the Angel of Death to come."*
>
> *People came to visit him and sing for him. This would make him smile. But it didn't cheer him up for long.*
>
> *A man who played music for the elderly man asked his out-of-town guest to visit the old man to cheer him up.*
>
> *"What have been some of the highlights of your life?" the visitor asked the elderly man.*
>
> *"I've had a number of special moments in my life, but now my life is almost over. When I think about who I am, I feel bad. I'm just a plain ordinary old man who can't do very much," the elderly man sighed.*
>
> *"I would like to make a suggestion," said the visitor. "I would like you to do five things each day and then you can view yourself as a person who does these five things daily."*
>
> *"I can't do very much in this place. But if what you suggest isn't too hard for me, I might try," the elderly man agreed.*
>
> *His visitor said, "The first thing is: Each and every day say a short prayer for the welfare of everyone who works in this home.*

You can say, 'I wish everyone who works here good health and joy.' Then you can view your self-image as, 'I am a person who wishes everyone who works here good health and joy.'

"The second thing is: Each and every day say a short prayer for the welfare of everyone who lives in this home. 'I wish everyone who lives in this home everything wonderful and good.' Then you can add to your self-image: 'I am a person who wishes everyone who lives here everything wonderful and good.'

"The third thing is: Each and every day say a short prayer for the welfare of everyone you have ever met. You can say, 'I pray that everyone I have ever met during my entire life should be blessed.' Then you can view your self-image as: 'I am a person who prays that everyone I ever met during my entire life should be blessed.'

"The fourth thing is: Each and every day say a short prayer for everyone in the world. You can say, 'May there be peace in the world. May there be much happiness in the world. May there be much joy in the world.' Then you can view your self-image as, 'I am a person who prays that there should be peace in the world and that everyone should be happy and joyful.'

"The fifth thing is: Each and every day say, 'I am grateful for all the good things that I've ever experienced in my life. I am grateful for all the positive memories that I have. I am grateful for anyone who does anything for me. I am grateful for anyone who visits me.' Then you can view your self-image as, 'I am a person who is grateful for all the good things that I've ever experienced in my life. I am a person who is grateful for all my positive memories. I am a person who is grateful for anyone who does anything for me.'

"Your friend who plays music for you can have this list typed up. That way, when people come to visit you, you can ask them to read this list of statements together with you. As they read it, you can repeat it with them."

You can guess how beneficial it was for this elderly man to repeat a number of times a day:

"I wish everyone who works here good health and joy. I wish everyone who lives here everything wonderful and good. I pray *that everyone I have ever met during my entire life should be blessed. May there be peace in the world. May there be much happiness in the world. May there be much joy in the world. I am grateful for all the good things that I've ever experienced in my life. I am grateful for all the positive memories that I have. I am grateful for anyone who does anything for me. I am grateful for anyone who visits me."*

Does Saying "I Can" Mean That I Can?

I promote the ideas that our thoughts are the key to the essence of who we are and that our self-image is created by our thoughts. This sometimes causes people to ask: "Does a person automatically have knowledge, skills, and talents just because he says he does? Are you claiming that a person just needs to say that he has accomplished a great deal and he now has that self-image, regardless of whether or not he actually accomplished?"

The answer is a strong and emphatic: Nope!

Gaining knowledge takes a lot of studying and reviewing. Developing skills and talents takes time and practice. Developing character traits takes a lot of time and effort; it is a lifetime process. Accomplishing and achieving require much time and planning.

Just saying that you have knowledge doesn't add to the knowledge you actually have. Just saying that you have skills, talents, and positive character traits doesn't automatically enable you to have them. Just saying that you want to accomplish and achieve doesn't automatically create accomplishments and achievements.

When I say that your thoughts create you, you can't just make up a story about who you are and have an authentic self-image. But I am saying that as soon as you think of yourself as valuable and worthwhile, that is your true self. Since this is your true self, as soon as you think of yourself as having value and worth, that is your authentic self-image.

I am saying that when you truly decide to develop your character traits, you are on the path to developing your traits. Your thoughts are thoughts of: "What is the next step I need to take?"

When you think of gaining knowledge as a lifetime process that you are starting immediately, right away you can have the self-image of: "I am a person on a lifetime quest to continue to gain more knowledge."

Every valuable idea has a proper context to understanding it. When an idea is taken out of context and applied in ways in which it was never meant to be applied, it will be misunderstood and the idea won't be valid.

When a valuable idea is used appropriately, it will be highly beneficial. Just saying an idea isn't the same as integrating and internalizing it. But even before you integrate a positive idea and make it automatic and spontaneous, talking about the ideas you want to integrate is an important step forward.

> "If someone says negative things to me about myself, I feel very bad about it. My self-image immediately goes down. This happens so quickly that I feel there is nothing I can do about it. Do I have to suffer so much every time that someone puts me down?" I was asked by a person with a sensitive nature.
>
> "If someone is five-and-a-half feet tall and someone says to him that he is four-and-a-half feet tall, does he become any shorter?"
>
> "Of course not," the fellow responded.
>
> "And if you studied something and know it well, and someone spitefully says that you don't know it, does this person's attempt to have you feel bad about yourself really make you know it any less than before?"

"Again, of course not."

"If someone tells you that you have a great amount of knowledge that you don't yet have, you don't automatically have that knowledge. And someone saying that you achieved great achievements that you have not yet achieved doesn't make those achievements real. So, too, if someone says that you don't have virtues and positive qualities that you really do have, you still have them even if this person claims you don't.

"And the same with your immense value as a person. It is only your own thoughts that can cause your self-image to go down. Those who have a Torah consciousness towards the value of people will speak to you with respect. Even if someone does have good intentions, it's very important for that person to speak to you with respect, in a way that will motivate and inspire you to be and become more.

"Increase your awareness that it is only your own thoughts about yourself that can lower your self-image. Make an association in your mind: If anyone ever tries to put you down, hear your own inner voice repeating, 'My value is immense, as someone who is created in the Almighty's image and as a child of the Almighty. Only my own thoughts have the power to lower my self-image, and my own thoughts are becoming more and more positive all the time.'"

The fellow who used to feel lowered because of the put-downs reported that he gained a greater realization that only his own thoughts could lower his self-image. He was highly motivated to think the thoughts that gave him a true awareness of his greatness as a human being. He no longer feared the negative statements of anyone else.

"I Feel Bad About Myself"

There are people who frequently say, "I feel bad about myself." This is a core issue for some people, and they struggle with feeling good or bad about themselves.

If someone basically has a positive self-image he can temporarily feel bad about himself for a specific wrong he did, or for not acting as kindly or generously as he should have. He might be able to bounce back in a relatively short time. He might be able to do something positive that he feels good about, and then he'll feel, "Now I feel good about myself."

Someone with this pattern might overeat and then say, "I feel bad about myself for overeating." Then at the next opportunity to overeat he'll have self-discipline and then say, "Now I feel good about myself again."

Someone with this pattern might waste time and then say, "I feel bad about myself for wasting this time." Then he can accomplish something positive and say, "Now I feel good about myself again."

But for people with intense negative feelings about themselves, this can be a constant battle. It's not just that they feel happy or unhappy, calm or anxious. Instead, they often negatively judge themselves and their feelings about who they are.

Some people who frequently feel bad about themselves might be idealists with high values. Others may see them in positive ways, but they themselves are constantly critical of themselves. It would be wise for them to consult a Torah scholar for a more balanced view.

Some people who consistently feel bad about themselves might have had highly critical childhoods. Some might have suffered traumas whose effects have been strongly distressful. Some might have acted wrongly in the past and now deeply regret their previous mistakes.

Someone who feels bad about himself might try counterproductive ways to drown and disown these feelings. But this creates new problems. It's important for him to acknowledge his distressful thoughts and feelings to himself so that he can work on building his self-image.

People who basically feel bad about themselves often have strong feelings of insecurity. They feel insecure about how good they really are and how well they are doing in important areas of their lives. People who feel this way can feel devastated by criticism and insults. They feel that what was said about them is valid. Their total sense of self can be thrown off balance when they experience challenges that others can take in stride.

Some marriage counselors view feelings of insecurity as the source of most problems in marriage. People might have disagreements, but if both parties feel good about themselves, they will be able to discuss the issues over which they disagree and work them out in a way that is satisfactory to both parties. But when people are insecure they become offended more easily. They become angry more frequently and it lasts longer. They both feel that it's important to prove to the other party that it's all their fault, or at least mostly their fault. Feelings of insecurity can lead to bitter arguments and nasty words. When either or both parties feel more secure about themselves, they will find it much easier to work out solutions.

Telling people who frequently feel bad about themselves, "You need to feel good about yourself," is telling them the truth, but it's usually highly insufficient.

People who frequently feel bad about themselves should make it a high priority to build themselves from the inside out. They should clarify the main reasons that they feel so bad, and what qualities they need to develop to begin to feel better about themselves. What do they need to stop doing? What do they need to start doing? What worthwhile accomplishments and achievements might help them build their self-image?

When our negative feelings about ourselves are very strong, we might need an experienced counselor to gain a greater understanding about why these thoughts and feelings persist and what can be done to improve.

It could be beneficial if an authority figure says, "You have many reasons to feel good about yourself. If you have valid reasons to feel bad about yourself, let's see how we can work it out and improve yourself and your view of yourself."

After listening to someone's story, the mentor or counselor might conclude, "You do have valid reasons for feeling bad about yourself. But now you are in the present. Let's see how you can make amends for the wrongs you have done. And let's see what you can do from now on so that you will feel good about yourself."

> Someone complained to a rabbi, "I feel bad about myself much too often. What can I do to feel good about myself?"
>
> "I don't necessarily feel good about myself," said the rabbi. "But I don't feel bad about myself either. This whole idea of feeling good or bad about myself isn't in my frame of reference. Realize your value as a person since you are created in the Almighty's image and are His child. Then focus on the joy of learning Torah, focus on the joy of praying, focus on the joy of kindness and other good deeds. Be grateful for all the good in your life. When you increase your level of joy and master the ability to be grateful for all that you can appreciate, you will be a very happy person. Then you won't really need to feel good about yourself. You will just feel good as your general way of experiencing life."
>
> The fellow accepted it and no longer had to worry about feeling bad about himself. He built up his self-image with the good he was doing, and he increased his general level of being more joyful.

Rejection and Self-Image

Rejection can be extremely distressful. Rejection can greatly lower one's self-image. Even a person who is naturally confident and secure might be greatly pained by rejection. Rejection can lead to worrisome thoughts about the future. Rejection might cause discouragement, even despair.

A child who grows up in a loving atmosphere where he is consistently cherished and respected will have a solid foundation for his self-image. Therefore, he will probably handle rejection with more equanimity. In contrast, a child who was frequently rejected will probably have to work hard to build his self-image, even as an adult. Once we are old enough to think for ourselves, rejection does not automatically lead to a low self-image. Even though rejection can be very painful, the only way that it can cause a lowered self-image is if it leads to *thoughts* that create a low self-image.

When people are successfully chosen for something that is important to them, their self-image is raised. They feel more valuable. Conversely, being rejected can easily but not automatically lower someone's self-image.

Adopting any of these attitudes can prevent rejection from lowering your self-image:

- "Every rejection brings me closer to having something really wonderful happen to me."
- "I would have preferred to have my request answered positively, but I can never totally know what is truly in my best interest."
- "This rejection is a challenge that will motivate me to grow and become a better person."
- "Someone else's rejection of me is just that person's choice. It is not a reflection of who I am and of my innate infinite value."

- "The more anyone else rejects me, the more I realize that I need to make my own sense of value dependent on my choices of thoughts, words, and actions. This is up to me. I won't allow something so important as my self-image to depend on someone else's choices."
- "I have heard many stories of people being rejected over and over again, and eventually they achieved success beyond their wildest imagination. I can't wait until my own story plays out and I find myself rejoicing with the final results."
- "This rejection is highly distressful. But it's ultimately because of the way I think about it. I am now going to be totally motivated to master being happy and joyful because I will master a more spiritual sense of who I am and what my mission is in this world."
- "This rejection is making me more humble than ever before. I am grateful for this opportunity to develop a greater sense of humility."
- "I do not need to label 'no' as rejection. A 'no' is just a delay in getting what I want. Ultimately I wanted what I wanted because I thought it would enhance my life. I see that the direction that I wanted to go isn't the direction that the Almighty has chosen for me. I gladly accept the Almighty's direction."
- "My goal in life is to help other people feel better about themselves. This rejection makes me feel bad. But the good news is that now I can use this to help other people feel better. When people tell me that they feel bad because they have been rejected, I will be able to respond that I understand how they feel since I, too, have been rejected. My self-image in knowing that my priority is to help others gives me a higher self-image than if I wouldn't have been rejected."
- The following attitude is very rare, and anyone who has it can actually raise his self-image: "My own rejection prevents someone else from being rejected. I feel happy that I can save someone else the distress of being rejected."
- "This rejection is highly distressful. I need to master the ability to laugh just because I decide to laugh. I've wanted to master this ability after hearing about medical clowns who laugh with sick patients in order to cheer them up. If I can laugh now even though I feel so bad, I will know that I have really mastered the ability to laugh at will. I can imagine the smiling faces of the children and the elderly whom I will be able to cheer up."

- "My thoughts about the rejection make me feel awful. I need to master the skill of interrupting my pattern of thinking when it causes me pain. I will use this rejection as an opportunity to build up greater mastery to change the direction of my thinking pattern."
- "I have always wanted to be a master of reframing (the ability to find positive evaluations and perspectives for events and situations). This rejection is an opportunity for me to find at least ten positive ways of looking at this situation."
- "This rejection has truly lowered my self-image. But it's more important for me to do good in this world than to have a higher self-image. I wish those who rejected me all the best in the world. Wishing others well is a higher priority than having a positive self-image. I wanted to have a positive self-image in order to be a happier person. I now choose to be a more joyful person, regardless of what my self-image is." The person with this attitude will be happier and more joyful than if his self-image were still high but he wasn't as happy.

> *I spoke to a very wealthy entrepreneur. "What is the secret of your success?" I asked him.*
>
> *"Rejection," he replied.*
>
> *"Rejection?" I echoed.*
>
> *"Yes, rejection," he repeated. "When I finished school, I went looking for a job. Somehow I wasn't very good at being interviewed for a job. I was so afraid of rejection that I was nervous. My nervousness was easily apparent. I didn't make a very good impression. My fear of rejection caused me to be rejected over and over again. I needed to make money so I looked for something I could sell without a formal job. At first, people turned me down much more often than they would buy what I was selling.*
>
> *"Because I felt desperate to make more sales, I took a course on selling and was told that confidence is the key ingredient that you need for selling. Part of confidence is not worrying at all whether people will buy from you or not. I heard the principle: 'You can get everything you want in life if you give enough people what they want.' When you focus on how the other person will benefit from what you are offering him, you can feel much*

calmer about the entire interaction. I began to close many more sales. After a while I made much more money than I would have made if I had been hired straight out of school. Now I have many investments. I am able to do a lot of good things for others with the money that I make.

"Looking back, I see how fortunate I was that I was rejected rather than hired. I now smile and feel great when I remember being turned down. If I had known then what I know now, it would have saved me a lot of distress.

"I share my story with others hoping that they will be able to take rejection better than I did."

Perfectionism

Perfectionism is an attitude that believes everything that one does needs to be perfect; if it's not perfect it's awful and close to being a total failure.

What is called perfectionism really is a mental focus on mistakes and errors. What you focus on is noticed and also reinforced. If someone searches for mistakes and errors, then that is what he will notice.

A perfectionist attitude mistakenly believes that everything is "all or nothing." Perfectionism prevents true excellence. When a person tries to be perfect, he tends to focus on every minor mistake and error. This focus on what's not yet perfect often prevents positive action. Instead, focus on excellence, on what is already right, and on what you can do now to keep improving.

It's easy for a perfectionist to have a low self-image. Since the focus is on the wrong, the mistake, the error, negativity fills his mind and thoughts.

We need to develop a more balanced attitude. We need to strive for excellence. We need to aim high. We need to strive to do things correctly. We need to be aware of potential mistakes and errors in order to prevent them, or, if they're already made, to correct and improve them.

We need to realize that mistakes and errors are part of growing and accomplishing. Anyone who strives to do positive things will certainly make mistakes. The only way not to make mistakes is to do nothing. But that would be the biggest mistake of all!

We need to learn from each mistake we make. We need to be honest with ourselves to be aware of our mistakes. It's important not to be afraid to make mistakes in order to do more and to keep improving.

A strong perfectionist is excessively afraid of making a mistake. People who accomplish a lot must learn that mistakes are usually not as awful as they fear. Yes, there are areas of life and death where a mistake could be tragic, but we need a sense of perspective. We need to know when a mistake might be relatively easy to correct. We need to know when a mistake might cost us something, but not as much as we might fear.

Develop the self-image, "I am a person who will keep improving throughout my entire life. Of course I make mistakes; I am a human being and all humans make mistakes. I have the inner courage to acknowledge my mistakes and to learn from them. I am a person who constantly strives to become better. I experience joy when I improve."

> *A super successful entrepreneur related, "The biggest turning point in my life was when I overcame my fear of making mistakes. I was terrified of taking risks, even relatively minor ones. Every risk includes the chance to make a mistake. But I came to realize that if I wouldn't take any risks at all, I would not be able to accomplish very much. I had heard many stories of people losing a lot because of the risks that they took. I grew up hearing many warnings to 'never take stupid risks.' I was so afraid of stupid risks that I kept away from calculated risks of all types. This did*

protect me from making mistakes, but it also prevented me from accomplishing. Once I decided to face the possibility of making mistakes in order to accomplish more, I developed a more balanced attitude towards taking risks and making mistakes.

"Before taking a big risk, I would consult at least three different people who were knowledgeable in the field. After hearing the pros and cons of the potential risks that I was about to take, I would make a more informed decision on whether a specific risk was worth taking. I was careful enough not to take a risk where I wasn't able to handle the downside. My willingness to make relatively small mistakes enabled me to benefit from many more accomplishments that I would have otherwise had. My self-image became positive enough that when I made a mistake, I considered it a learning experience that I gained from rather than a devastating failure. I kept my major focus on my successes and this gave me the strength to weigh my actions carefully."

What Are the Positive Aspects of Your "Deficiency"?

Very often a person's biggest deficiency has aspects that can turn it into a great asset.

Some people might be slow when they do things, but being slow enables them to be more thorough! They might have much more patience than the average person, and their patience will enhance their lives in many ways.

Some people who are labeled as having an attention deficit disorder are really mentally much faster than most people. Their attention isn't really deficient; their mind goes quickly from one thing to another. They can't sit quietly in one place to concentrate on something they find boring.

I heard from someone with this pattern that a very high percentage of entrepreneurs have this "disorder." When they are bored they don't focus well. But when they are interested in something, they can easily concentrate for long periods of time. To succeed, they need to find constructive activities that they already find especially interesting, or create interesting ways to do what they have to do.

One person with this attention pattern has made a living out of it. He teaches others with this pattern how to divide their various project tasks into five-minute segments. They should set an alarm for five minutes as a deadline for each task. This will motivate them to be much faster during those five minutes. They won't get bored since they are enjoying the race against the clock. After five minutes they work on another aspect of the task. This way they accomplish much more than they (and others) would have without this method.

Another person with this pattern told me that when he studies by himself he studies each subject for just ten minutes at a time. Then he studies something else for ten minutes. By changing his focus every ten minutes, his mind is alive and alert. He reads and understands faster, and eventually can accomplish the same thing as others who concentrate for much longer periods.

While this pattern of short bursts of focus and concentration would be counterproductive for most people, this new behavior pattern builds the self-image and abilities of some people with ADD who had thought of themselves in limited ways.

Having the attribute of chutzpah can be highly negative. People with chutzpah can easily antagonize others. Someone with this "deficiency" should find constructive ways to utilize this trait to benefit himself and others. Of course, he will need to make a special effort to be respectful to parents, teachers, and anyone who would be offended by his chutzpah, but there are many times when "respectful chutzpah" can lead to positive accomplishments.

Think about your main deficiencies. What positive aspects can be the opposite of those deficiencies? If possible, find role models who have already turned those deficiencies into advantages and benefits.

Some deficiencies are pure shortcomings and you will need to make it a high priority to overcome them. After you have overcome them, however, you can find beneficial ways to utilize the skills and talents that enabled you to overcome those flaws. Many people make a livelihood out of helping others overcome the same things that they had to overcome.

> *I met a retired man who had been a master teacher for many years. His classes were exciting and dramatic. The students loved the way he taught and remembered the material exceptionally well. I asked him how he had developed such mastery of teaching.*
>
> *"I didn't do well as a student when I was younger. I was frequently bored in class and my mind would wander. Because I didn't pay attention the way the teachers wanted me to, I was reprimanded quite frequently. I developed a dislike for school and a low self-image.*
>
> *"After I graduated, I thought over my educational career. I recalled a few teachers whom I did enjoy listening to. I spoke to a number of people who went through similar experiences. I was aware of what I would have needed when I was younger. I found a substitute teaching position for a class that traditionally gave their teachers, and especially substitutes, a rough time. I was determined to enjoy teaching these students in ways that they too would enjoy. I was a success. That began my career. I saw my younger self in each student. I talked to each student with strong respect. I didn't view any of them as troublemakers, but as lively kids who wanted to have a good time. I was determined to educate them in a way that enabled them to have fun when they learned. Fortunately for my students and myself, what I did worked very well."*

If You Knew That in Ten Years From Now…?

Imagine that you could know great things about yourself.

If you knew that within ten years you would:
- gain tremendous knowledge, much more than you can imagine now,
- accomplish way beyond your wildest dreams,
- perform a number of heroic actions that would greatly impress everyone (and most of all yourself),
- positively affect many people's lives,

that would make you feel better about yourself, wouldn't it?

And even if it took twenty years for all this to happen, it would still make you feel better about yourself now, wouldn't it?

"But how can I be certain that this will actually happen?" some people ask.

My response: "You can't be certain that this won't happen, can you?"

A person might have children or grandchildren who will make him extremely proud. A person might positively influence someone who later will have children and students who will do great things.

When you see yourself as someone who eventually will develop himself in great ways, you realize that your current steps to build yourself are an integral part of your personal greatness. This way of thinking makes the entire journey from the here and now to the future a much more enjoyable trip.

> I once visited an elderly person who was greatly respected for his knowledge, his character traits, his wonderful family, and for his many acts of kindness over the years.

"If only I knew sixty years ago what I know now," he lamented. "I used to look down at myself. I was far from being the scholar that I wished I were. I realized that I had many faults. I didn't have any especially outstanding accomplishments.

"I regret not having done more and been more. My negative thoughts at the time prevented me from being as happy as I could have been.

"Looking back at my life, I see that things turned out much better than I had imagined. I have mixed feelings when I think about my life. I have much to be grateful for. But I feel bad that I thought about myself in a needlessly distressful way. I kept comparing myself with the way I see others.

"I outlived many people I knew. From my present vantage point, I realize that I could have been much happier and could have felt better about myself. The more I realize this, the more aware I am that I should be totally resolved to create more joy for myself from now on."

What Might Have Been

Some people spend a lot of time complaining about "what might have been" had they experienced different life situations. These sentences often begin with the words, "If only...."

"If only my father had encouraged me more, I would have done so much more."

"If only my mother wasn't such a negative thinker, I would be a much happier person."

"If only my teachers would have inspired me more, I would have accomplished much more."

"If only people would have praised me more, I would have a much better self-image now."

"If only my boss would have tried to motivate me in more positive ways, my self-image wouldn't be as bad as it is."

There is only one major problem with all "If only..." thinking. There is nothing we can do about what happened already. We can, however, choose this very moment to think and speak and act in ways that will enhance our lives.

If you currently need more encouragement, either find ways to encourage yourself or look for other people to encourage you now. Maybe someone's father did try to encourage him, but when he was younger he didn't listen to what his father had to say. Then again, maybe his father didn't try to encourage him enough. But what can you do now to become more encouraged? Asking this question is the only way to begin to accomplish more and develop who you are.

Even if his mother was a negative thinker, he can now choose to become a much more positive thinker. That person can stop blaming his mother for being a negative thinker and begin to gain more appreciation and gratitude for what was good in his life. He can choose to become happier from now on.

If someone's teachers didn't inspire him, he needs to find his own inspiration. He can search for people who will inspire him. He can look for books, speakers, and recordings to inspire him now.

Even if someone wasn't praised before, he can find ways to praise himself to motivate and inspire himself. Or he can look for people who will give him positive feedback for the good he does and for what he does right.

Even if your boss does not motivate you in positive ways, you should to try to think of ways to motivate yourself to accomplish more and maintain a positive self-image.

You can choose to develop yourself however you want. It would have been better to start earlier, but now the question isn't about what could have been. It's about what you will do now with your mind and your choices of words and actions.

As you think about "what might have been," see what you can do now to change yourself the way you wish.

> *Someone who got off to a late start in life was asked how he had managed to learn and accomplish so very much.*
>
> *He replied, "I don't waste time just wishing I was different and better than I am. Rather, I keep thinking about what I can do now. I found that when I bemoaned the fact that I'm not what I wished, it sent a defeatist attitude to my mind. It gave me the message, 'It's too late. You missed the boat.'*
>
> *"Now, I keep focusing on what I can do now. I am totally focused on how I can learn more and do more. Of course, I do wish that I had had an earlier start. But I started when I did, and I want to utilize my time the best way I can from now on."*

Sometimes a Tough Coach is Better

Some tough teachers, coaches, counselors, and mentors are experts at bringing out the best in their students. Their underlying message brings out the best — or causes resentment.

A person is likely to feel resentment if he feels that a teacher or coach is just being mean or tough because of ego issues. However, when the person on the receiving end knows with total clarity that his teacher, coach, counselor, or mentor is totally focused on the ultimate welfare and benefit of his student, the tough message will result in respect and gratitude. Even though the teacher or coach puts on a lot of pressure, he does it wisely. He knows how much is just the right amount. He knows when to push more and when to ease off. He knows the individual he is talking to. He knows that one size doesn't fit all. He knows when his student is experiencing more stress than usual. He knows when to praise and when to criticize.

Not every teacher has the insight and wisdom to apply just the right amount of pressure. A good teacher knows that not every student will be able to tolerate a tough approach; for some students, the pressure will be highly counterproductive and do more harm than good.

But if you need someone tougher than average to bring out the best in you, find someone who won't let you get away with doing just a minimal amount of work and effort. Find someone who has high aspirations for you.

Sometimes you don't have a choice. You might really benefit more from a softer and gentler teacher or mentor, but you have to interact with the teacher you have. In that case, instead of allowing the tougher approach to overwhelm you, learn from it. Learn how to bring out the best in you. Learn how to handle it with an attitude of being centered, focused, and flowing.

> *"I've always felt that I need someone who is patient with me so I can think more clearly and act better," someone once told me. "But for a number of years I had to deal with a boss who was extremely demanding and impatient. There was a very high turnover rate in the office. Most people didn't last too long. Some people actually told the boss to be more patient and less highstrung. It would be healthier for him, and others would like him more. But the boss just said that he's not trying to compete in a popularity contest. Whoever could deal with his approach would be paid well. Whoever couldn't handle it could leave. As he used to say, 'If you can't stand the heat, get out of the kitchen.'*
>
> *"I needed to keep the job, but in the beginning I felt a lot of stress. I realized that I would have to leave the job or else find a better way to handle it with a calmer attitude.*
>
> *"I noticed that those who had worked for the boss for a long time excelled. By speaking to them, I found out the boss knew the field and knew what he was doing. By ignoring the boss's*

tough style and some insults now and then, I was able to keep learning much more than I would have learned otherwise.

"I experienced pleasure in knowing that I could view the situation with a sense of humor. I pretended I was an outsider watching the situation on a screen. I considered the boss an actor in a show.

"With the new way I viewed it, I no longer experienced much stress. Inwardly I was calm. I didn't feel a need to answer back. I came to see that when the boss would seem to be asking a question like, 'Why didn't you…?' or 'How come you did that stupid thing…?' I didn't really need to answer him. That was just the way he released his own frustration.

"Ultimately, I gained tremendously by learning how to stay calm and clear-minded when I faced tough people. The way I would interact with them won me the respect of those people and the respect of others. My own self-respect and self-image grew greatly. I gained a greater realization that my inner value and worth was based on my own thoughts. This freed me from being overly concerned with the manner of the people I spoke to."

Overcoming Discouragement

Sometimes in daily life someone might feel discouraged. One might have invested a tremendous amount of time and effort in something, and now all the time and effort appear to be wasted. One might have had great plans and dreams, but the end result is nowhere near what one had hoped for. One might have repeatedly tried to improve, but it just isn't going well.

Discouragement comes from one thing, and one thing only: Thinking discouraging thoughts. Changing the content of one's thoughts changes the entire picture!

Discouragement often comes from one's limited self-image. It is possible for a person to have a great self-image, and the discouragement comes from thinking that the situation is hopeless. But usually one's limited self-image plays a major role in discouragement.

When you view yourself in a positive light and see what you've done as valuable and important, even though things didn't work out the way you were hoping, you still feel positive about the effort you put into doing something worthwhile. You know that effort is up to you; results are up to the Almighty. You realize that your own value and worth are constant, and then think about your new wisest course of action for now. Sometimes it might be to put more effort into what you were doing before, and at other times it might be to become involved in something different. But either way, you feel good about yourself.

If you ever feel discouraged, you can say to yourself, "Right now I am feeling discouraged because of the thoughts that I am thinking. What are some wiser thoughts that I can think right now?"

Discuss the problem with some wise and insightful people who have a comprehensive view of the entire situation. Let's say that you all conclude that you should be involved with something else. Now you should put your entire focus into doing your best in the new situation. What is over is gone and done. Learn from it. Think about what you have gained in various ways, and keep moving forward in your life.

Realize that you are in the present right now. In the present, what is the best and wisest use of your time? Obsessing about what is over and done with is not a wise use of time. The emotional feelings may be distressful. A person sometimes needs to feel upset over what was and what could have been. But the more mastery one has over one's thoughts, the less time will be spent on this.

It brings more happiness to your life, more accomplishments and achievements, and a better self-image to keep asking yourself, "What is the wisest thing for now?"

It's certainly easier to keep your focus if you're sure that your current activities will result in satisfaction, achievement, and inner joy. Although you can't be sure of success, you can be sure of one thing: Obsessing about what you can't change isn't going to give you real satisfaction, and it won't lead to achievement. Inner joy isn't what you will feel. When you focus on the positive and constructive things you can do now, you have a much greater possibility of doing something that will be meaningful and emotionally fulfilling.

"I can't believe that this is happening to me," a fifty-year-old accomplished man told an acquaintance. *"I always thought that I would be able to handle whatever came up. Instead, the crisis I am facing now shows me that I'm not as capable and strong as I always thought I was. This failure is hitting me harder than I would ever have imagined. I am in shock. All the work I've put into building my career has been for nothing. My life seems almost over. I feel totally discouraged. At my age it will be difficult to find a new job. I don't have the energy to start something new on my own. I am devastated. I don't know what I can do."*

"But didn't you experience many ups and downs during your years of successful achievements?" the acquaintance asked him.

"Yes, I did. But I always knew that the downs were just temporary setbacks. I believed in my ability to turn things around. I believed that I could handle whatever I was faced with. I believed that I had the inner strength to find solutions for any challenge that might arise. But with the latest setbacks, I no longer believe that I have what it takes to keep afloat. I feel like a drowning person who has no more energy left to swim. I feel like totally giving up," he replied.

"But all the strengths that you have had before in your life are still stored in your brain," the acquaintance reminded him.

"It feels like they are totally gone. I see myself as a total failure. I think that I was just lucky before. The real me is the discouraged person you are talking to now."

"Actually, all the inner strengths that you've experienced at any time in your life are stored in your brain. Because you are viewing yourself as a failure now, these thoughts create

your feelings of discouragement. Because you don't feel your strengths now, you think that they are gone. But they really exist in the archives of your brain. Allow yourself to think this way since this is the actual reality. As soon as you truly get in touch with your strengths, and you know that you have them, you will be able to overcome discouragement."

On Developing the Attribute of Happiness

As you continue to develop your attribute of happiness, you will also be building your self-image. Someone who is happy and joyful will find it much easier to have a positive self-image.

Many people are happy and joyful once in a while. Some are happy much more frequently. Those who know how to use their minds wisely will be able to live a life that is compared in *Mishlei* (15:15) to "a life of constant parties." This is the opposite of those who are masters at focusing on what is wrong and what they don't like, for whom every day will be problematic (according to the first half of the same verse).

Life has many ups and downs. Everything in life is meant as Divinely sent challenges to help us grow and develop our unique emotional natures. We each have unique life histories. We've each been uniquely conditioned and programmed by a wide range of people — parents, siblings, teachers, friends, neighbors, and other people we've met — and the mass media and books we've read. We each have had unique trials and tribulations. And we each have had much to be grateful for and to appreciate.

We each have many ideas and thoughts already stored in our brains. Some of those ideas and thoughts enhance our lives, and some do the opposite.

Maybe there are some individuals fortunate enough to have grown up in perfect environments, with perfect parents, perfect teachers, perfect friends and neighbors, perfect life situations and occurrences, perfect intellect and memory, perfect natural character traits, and perfect and consistent good fortune. Perhaps they've had nothing to worry about or to cause anxiety or unhappiness, and they've had natural happiness and joy from infancy on.

Since I didn't grow up in this unrealistic utopia, I personally had to work on building my level of happiness. I have made a comprehensive study of the subject for many years and have spoken to many people about it. I consider the following points to be a summary of the topic.

You create happiness by:
- regularly thinking thoughts of appreciation and gratitude.
- mastering the ability to evaluate life events and situations in positive ways.
- devoting your life to making and reaching meaningful goals.
- interacting in harmony with other people.
- frequently doing acts of kindness for others.
- serving the Almighty with joy.
- dealing with the challenges the Almighty sends you with trust in His ultimate goodness.

The patterns of thinking that create happiness are consistent with the patterns of thinking that create a positive self-image.

We function at our best when we are happy. Our minds work best and remember better when we are happy. We feel healthier when we are happy. We are more motivated to take action and accomplish when we are happy. We interact better with other people when we are happy. We connect to our Creator better when we are happy and grateful for all He has bestowed upon us.

Your happiness has a positive effect on your breathing, brain waves, blood pressure, energy level, heartbeat, hormones and biochemistry, immune system, muscle tension, posture and facial expression, and tone of voice. The greater your mastery of happiness, the more all these systems work at their optimal levels.

The first step in becoming a happier person is to make a strong decision: "I am going to live a happy life. Happiness is mainly dependent on my thoughts, and I will consistently think thoughts that create happiness."

Here is a detailed list of Nine Happiness-Creating Formulas. I suggest that you frequently read this list.

1. Keep your main focus on thoughts of appreciation and gratitude.

You think many thousands of thoughts each and every day. Your mind is constantly active, thinking one thought after another. "Rejoice with all the good that the Almighty bestows upon you" (*Devorim* 26:11). Many times a day think about what you appreciate and are grateful for. A mind that is full of gratitude is a mind that is free from much negativity.

The blessings you make thanking the Almighty for His kindnesses to you add to your happiness. Shabbos is a weekly celebration for all the good in the world and all the good in your life. Each time you breathe, you can thank the Almighty for that breath (*Midrash* on the last verse of Psalms). When you wake up in the morning, start off the day with *Modeh Ani*, thanking the Almighty for another day of life. Throughout the day you can experience gratitude for being alive.

Develop the habit of regularly starting sentences with the words, "I appreciate…," "I am grateful for…," "I am thankful that…," "It's wonderful that…," "Thank you, Hashem, for…,"

Your mind will find what you focus on and search for. Search for reasons to be appreciative and grateful, and you will constantly be able to find them. May your list of things to be grateful for be long and continue to grow.

Your mind will sometimes think many thoughts that are not conducive to happiness. This is natural for everyone. As a general rule, don't resist and it won't persist. Solve what can be solved. Change what can be changed. But don't unnecessarily dwell on thoughts that are not in your best interest.

Master the habit of coming back to thoughts of appreciation and gratitude, spirituality and character development, wisdom and insight, accomplishment and achievement, joy and kindness.

2. Focus on the positive aspects of situations and occurrences. See how you can benefit.

The way any situation affects you emotionally is caused by the thoughts that you think about that situation. It is your personal evaluation of what happened that creates your feelings about it. Master the skill of always finding positive ways to look at things. Turn potential problems into opportunities.

If water is dripping and you can't turn it off, you have a choice about what thoughts go through your mind. Some people get aggravated and create needless stress and distress for themselves. You can use the sound of the drops to remind you of something good. When you want to fall asleep you can repeat softly and gently, "The dripping water is making me tired and sleepy. The dripping water will help me fall asleep and rest well." When you wake up in the morning and wish to be wide awake, you can repeat enthusiastically, "The dripping water reminds me that I am alive and I can hear. I feel enthusiastic about the day." Of course, hire a plumber if you can't fix the leak by yourself.

Keep thinking about what is good and positive about what occurs in your life. Keep asking yourself, "What is good about this?" "How can I benefit from what happened?" "What might turn out positive about this?"

At times it will be easy to see what is good and positive. At other times you will need to think creatively to find the good. Have patience. With time, you will see that many situations that can cause immediate distress really turn out all right. And with even more patience, you get a much wiser perspective with time.

Start off with the assumption, "This too is for the good." When you search for what is good about something, your mind will come up with ways to gain and benefit. When you do this regularly, you will become an expert. You will also be more aware of how other wise thinkers view things.

All stress and distress comes from the way that one is thinking about an occurrence or situation. A master of positive thinking will be able to master happiness and joy. Use your mind wisely to avoid unnecessary problems. Change what can be changed. And if something can't be changed, let your inner wisdom find a wise way to view the situation.

3. Strive for meaningful goals and achievements.

Life is for accomplishing and achieving. Using your talents and skills to accomplish gives you a sense of satisfaction and purpose. In general, people who strive for challenging goals and achievements are happier than those who are on a perpetual vacation.

Keep building up your skills and talents. Continue to gain more knowledge and wisdom. Accomplishing worthwhile goals builds your self-image. When you make it a lifetime project to enjoy the entire process of making and reaching goals, you will accomplish much more than you might have imagined.

Doing many acts of kindness each day is one of the greatest accomplishments you can achieve. It is also highly conducive to creating inner happiness and a positive self-image.

4. Focus on solutions, not problems.

In everyone's life there are many events that could be labeled "problems." It is wise to focus on solutions. This points your mind in the right direction.

People who consistently focus on problems and not on finding solutions experience much unnecessary anxiety, worry, and unhappy feelings. Focus on finding solutions. You will save yourself much unnecessary stress and distress. Even before you actually find a solution, you will be much happier. And the more solutions you find, the more easily you'll find solutions to new challenges that arise.

Transform "problems" into "goals." When faced with something that might be viewed as a problem, let your mind think of potential goals to improve the situation. Instead of saying, "My problem is that I have a low self-image," one would be wiser to say, "My goal is to constantly build my self-image." Instead of saying, "My problem is that I have so many problems," one would be wiser to say, "My goal is to consistently find positive ways to enhance my life."

Instead of saying, "My problem is that I lack happiness," one would be wiser to say, "My goal is to master becoming happy and joyful."

When you seek solutions, even if a total solution doesn't seem easy to find, partial solutions will still give you a much happier life.

5. Develop your character when facing challenges and adversity.

Each and every day think about the character traits you can develop from the life tests that you face. Keep asking yourself, "What positive traits and qualities can I develop now?"

A quarterback from my hometown of Baltimore was interviewed after he won the Super Bowl. He was asked about the level of his happiness. "I'm very happy now," he said with tremendous joy. "But this is nothing compared to waking up every morning and thanking G-d for adversity. Through adversity G-d allows you to develop your character."

Imagine having a joyful attitude towards developing your character traits when you face life's challenges. Imagine waking up every morning with extreme joy, knowing that you are resolved to live a meaningful and purposeful life.

6. Think joyful and upbeat self-talk.

The way you talk to yourself, both in the content and the tone of voice that you choose, creates your inner feelings of happiness.

If you could have a computer print out all your self-talk at the end of a standard day, what patterns of inner dialogue would you read? If it's not yet mostly positive self-talk, consider it a high priority to make it so.

Choose self-talk that creates happiness and joy. You talk to yourself throughout the day, so make your self-talk contribute to your happiness. When you talk to other people, they decide what they will say. You are the only person who chooses your own self-talk. It makes sense to choose wisely.

7. Speak and act joyfully.

When you speak to others, you have a chance to choose the topics to discuss. You choose what you will say about those topics. You choose whether or not to talk about the good and the positive. You choose whether or not to talk about what you are happy about and pleased with.

When you talk, you choose the tone of voice that you will use. Just as certain musical tones make one feel better or worse, so too, one's tone of voice can create happiness, or not.

Become more aware of how you feel better or worse when others speak to you. Emulate those who make you feel better.

8. Visualize positive and life-enhancing scenes, and remember inspiring words and music.

You have many scenes stored in your mind. Visualize the scenes that create a positive mental environment. After you visit beautiful scenery, that image is always stored in your brain. Flip through your mental photo album to review your favorite scenes and times. Make it a habit to remember celebrations and joyful scenes. See the trees and flowers, the mountains and waterfalls, the sunrises and sunsets. See your moments of inspiration and motivation.

Every inspiring talk you've ever heard is stored in your brain. Even when you don't remember the exact words, remembering various excerpts will lift your spirits.

9. Practice accessing positive emotional states at will.

Every positive emotional state that you have ever experienced is stored in your brain, and your brain is always with you for easy reference. I strongly advise people to give unique names to the various positive emotional states that they experience. By giving unique names to your positive states, you can quickly access them from your magnificent brain. In the beginning some people find this easy, but others don't. With patience, everyone can learn to do this without difficulty.

You can create new positive states at any time by visualizing scenes that you create with the power of your imagination.

Unfortunately, some people are experts at creating stressful and distressful states. Some people remember their least favorite memories over and over again. Worrying needlessly creates a distressful state about something that hasn't happened, and may never happen.

Every special moment of your life can be considered a unique state. May you have many positive moments to review in order to continue to gain the benefits of your most positive experiences.

To gain the most of this entire section, read it again, imagining that you are reading it with a personal joy coach. Hear the coach asking you, "In what ways do you already apply this point? What can you do to apply this even more?"

1. Read this list frequently. Write or type the following nine formulas on a sheet of paper that can be easily read. Those who have gained the most from the list said that they have attached it to a mirror and regularly smile at their reflection when they read it. This makes it easier to access a happy state. Focus on appreciation and gratitude.

2. Focus on the positive and potential benefits of situations and occurrences.

3. Strive for meaningful goals and achievements.

4. Focus on solutions, not problems.

5. Develop your character when facing challenges and adversity.

6. Think joyful and upbeat self-talk.

7. Speak and act joyfully.

8. Visualize great scenes and remember inspiring words and music.

9. Access positive emotional states at will.

> *"'I intend to enjoy today,' I say to myself each and every day," said a person who has mastered the attribute of living a happy life. "I know that some things will go the way I wish today and other things won't. This is beyond my control. What is under my control is the emotional quality of my life. Yes, there are times when being happy would be inappropriate. But I am resolved to have my default state be happy and joyful. I am the one who chooses what I will think about and how I will view things. I have found that the more I practiced gaining greater control over my own thoughts and evaluations of events and situations, the more I was able to experience happiness as my regular way of being."*
>
> *"How have other people reacted to your being consistently happy?" I asked him.*

"Some people appreciate it. They tell me that when they are in my presence, they feel happier also. Others have told me that they think I am not really as happy as I seem. 'Nobody can be always happy in a troubled world such as ours.' I listen to them and try to understand where they are coming from. But I avoid needless arguments. They are entitled to think what they want.

"It's different when people approach me and say, 'I wish I was able to be as happy as you are.' When people are sincerely interested in increasing their own level of happiness, I am very happy for the opportunity to enhance their lives. I consider this a high obligation on my part to spread as much happiness as I can. My biggest pleasure in life is when people tell me that my words have helped them create a happier life."

Smile at Mirrors

When you smile and wave at mirrors, mirror images wave and smile back to you. Research has shown that when you smile, your mind creates positive feelings. Smiling and waving at yourself creates the biochemistry and brainwaves that put you in a positive emotional state.

When you look at yourself in a mirror, you can speak to yourself in ways that build your self-image. Looking in a mirror enables you to see your reactions to your words. It's almost like you are speaking to another person. This is much more powerful than if you merely think positive thoughts about yourself.

When you tell yourself positive statements about yourself while looking in a mirror, you are giving yourself an important message. You are stating that you are feeling positive about yourself.

This isn't vanity if you are doing it purely as a technique to create positive emotions. You are not making an arrogant or conceited statement. You are just creating a natural, healthy way of boosting your emotional state. This is an easy way to put yourself in a good mood. I have enough experience to know that it's a highly effective tool that really works.

One of the happiest people I've ever met regularly uses a mirror as a biofeedback machine. He has mastered the ability to see a natural smile in any mirror he happens to look at. Every so often he laughs to stimulate his biochemistry, and, as research has shown, laughter is good for the heart.

Only you will be able to tell if this will work for you. It will depend on your thoughts when you apply this tool. If your self-talk is, "This won't work. This whole idea seems ridiculous to me," it probably won't work. The thoughts that run through your mind have the power to override the effectiveness of this tool.

This tool will work for you, however, if you say to yourself, "Every time I smile and wave to myself, I will feel better and better. This is an amazing feedback tool. The look on my face gives a valuable message to my inner mind. Every time I smile and wave to myself joyfully, I am storing more joy in my brain. I am becoming a more joyful person every time I do this."

You can chant to yourself as you look in a mirror, "I feel wonderful and terrific, good and great! I feel wonderful and terrific, good and great! I feel wonderful and terrific, good and great!"

Think of the messages about yourself that you want to establish as your automatic way of thinking. What qualities do you want to enhance?

For example, you might say to your image in the mirror: "I am becoming a more confident and courageous person all the time. I am becoming more and more empowered each and every day. Every time I speak and act with confidence and courage, I become a more confident and courageous person. I see the look of confidence and courage on my face. These qualities become stronger and stronger every time I speak to myself this way. I gain greater awareness that I'm able to access confident and courageous thoughts and feelings every time I need them."

Or you can use a mirror as a feedback tool when you feel stress or distress. "Right now I will begin to feel calmer and more relaxed. I will allow myself to breathe as if I were totally calm and relaxed. With each and every breath I am becoming even calmer and more relaxed. I will allow my face to look the way it does when I am totally calm and relaxed. I see the look of serenity on my face. Every time I do this, it becomes easier and easier for me to become more and more calm and relaxed whenever I wish to be calm and relaxed."

If you have a potentially difficult encounter coming up with another person, you can practice speaking to yourself in a mirror. Imagine that the person in the mirror is the person you will need to interact with. What emotional state would you like to access in your discussion or negotiation or request? Look in the mirror to see how you'll come across when you speak.

As you use mirrors as feedback machines to help you master greater happiness, joy, and other positive inner resources, you will be building your self-image as a happier and more joyful person.

> "You suggested that I use a mirror as a biofeedback machine, but it doesn't work," someone complained to me. "Every time I see myself in a mirror all I see is a worried and distressed look on my face. I feel it's silly, even stupid, to smile and wave to myself for no reason."
>
> "I'm afraid that the mirror you used wasn't a magic mirror. You can't see the look of happiness and joy on your face when your thoughts are full of worrisome and distressful content. A mirror can't force you to look happy when you aren't. But a mirror gives you immediate feedback as to the state you are in when you look at it. The very same moment that you start thinking happier and more joyful thoughts, you will notice a happier look on your face.
>
> "If you find it to difficult to change your thoughts right now, you can still smile and wave to yourself. When you realize the great emotional benefits of doing this, you won't feel silly or

stupid. You will realize that it's more stupid not to do something that is good for your health and general feeling of well-being. You might even begin to laugh to create more positive biochemistry and brainwaves. Laugh in a mirror like a young child would laugh. Like any skill, at first this might take a lot of effort and you probably won't be satisfied. But as you practice, you will find it becomes easier to laugh at will. Don't be overly concerned with how you look. Realize that most people look much better when they are happy and smiling. Enjoy yourself when you do this. It's a tool that even benefits your health."

Negative Anchors to Positive Anchors

The term "anchors" in the system known as Neuro Linguistic Programming, or NLP, refers to associations we have stored in our brains that bring out positive or negative emotional reactions.

Some anchors are visual: You see something and it brings out positive or negative feelings. Some anchors are auditory: You hear something and it brings out positive or negative feelings. Some anchors are kinesthetic: You touch something and it brings out positive or negative feelings.

For example, just looking at a picture postcard of a waterfall that you once had a great time visiting will bring out pleasant feelings. Your brain associates this postcard with that enjoyable trip. The postcard makes you feel good now. It is a positive anchor. That is why people enjoy looking at photos of weddings and other celebrations. They once again feel some of that celebration.

Now let's say that a person was once chased by a dog. He wasn't bitten by the dog, just scared by it. Now when he sees a picture of that dog, if his brain immediately goes back to that memory, he will feel a bit nervous. There is no dog in the room. But the picture of that dog is associated with the unpleasant feeling. That picture is a negative anchor.

Someone was frightened by a dog many years ago and now his brain has created a negative association with all dogs. All dogs are now negative anchors for him, even if a specific dog is small and harmless.

Negative anchors can be associated with a low self-image. For example, let's say that Joe didn't do very well in his Algebra class. He had a tough teacher who was humorless and spoke too fast. Whenever Joe didn't get the answer right, the teacher commented, "You're not very bright, Joe." When Joe sees an algebra formula years later, he is likely to feel the same distress as when he saw the algebra formulas on the board in class.

If Joe was the type of student who said to himself, "I am going to become an expert at math in general and algebra in particular. I will show that teacher that I am brighter than he thinks," he would hire a private tutor and work hard. Joe might even find a teacher who believes in Joe's ability to master Algebra. The teacher might make Algebra and math fun. Joe might begin to enjoy studying these subjects that he previously found difficult. Joe might even go on to get a doctorate in math. Joe might even become one of the foremost professors of math in the world. And Joe might even get a Nobel Prize in mathematics for his brilliant and creative work in the field. When Joe sees algebra formulas after winning the Nobel Prize, he might remember the glory and honor he experienced when he received that prize. Algebra formulas are now positive anchors to him.

That is the hard way to make formulas become a positive anchor. And let's face it, this is a great story, but it doesn't happen to most failures in Algebra.

The easier way to make formulas become a positive anchor is to look at an algebra formula and laugh. Yes, laugh like it's the funniest thing in the world. And then proclaim, "I love algebra formulas! Algebra formulas make me feel wonderful, terrific, and great!" You can play joyful music in the background or just in your mind. You might ask a few friends to join you and keep celebrating as you look at algebra formulas.

How often do you have to do this until it works? For some people this will work after just one session. Some people might need a number of sessions. But if a person is really motivated, he will eventually be able to make a positive anchor out of something that was once a negative anchor.

What is the principle here? Your brain has an amazing ability to make negative anchors that last a lifetime. Your brain also has an amazing ability to make positive anchors that last a lifetime. Your brain also has an amazing ability to transform a negative anchor into a positive anchor.

If you have already done anything similar to this, you already know that your brain has the power to do it. If you haven't yet done anything similar, scan your memory's magnificent library. Calmly and gently try to recall something that you once felt bad feelings about and now you feel good about. It might be a certain food that made you feel bad just from looking at it, and now you enjoy eating and seeing that food. It might be a certain picture that scared you when you were a young child and now you laugh when you think of that memory. It might be a person with whom you didn't get along well when you were a young child, and now that person is a close friend. It might be some music that at one time you had a negative association with but now you have a positive association with that music.

People who are not yet skilled at transforming negative anchors into positive anchors might claim, "As long as something still bothers you, it shows that you didn't yet change your self-image."

But, knowing the tremendous power of anchors, one can say, "As long as something still bothers you, it means that this is still a negative anchor for you. You have the ability to transform negative anchors to positive anchors whenever appropriate. The fact that a negative hasn't yet been changed to a positive anchor doesn't necessarily reflect on your entire self-image. It just shows that you haven't yet mastered the ability to transform this specific negative anchor into a positive one."

There are many advantages to being able to create positive anchors. Many minor irritations will no longer bother you, and may actually become positive anchors.

Anger, for example, is frequently aroused by negative anchors. If someone says an expression or makes a face or moves his hands in a way that your brain considers a negative anchor, you will benefit by transforming that anchor into one that brings out good feelings. For example, you might want to associate that expression or face or hand movement with something that you find very funny and humorous. Instead of getting angry, you will smile or laugh.

Many fears are just negative anchors. You really aren't in any practical danger, but your brain has associated that sound or sight with fearful feelings. When you are able to associate that sound or sight with courage and empowerment, you will feel stronger and more empowered when you hear that sound or see that sight.

Many people think of speaking in public as a negative anchor. When they imagine standing up in front of other people and having to speak, they react with distress. But you can imagine great crowds of people listening to you, and you will enjoy the experience. You can start off by visualizing yourself speaking to a few people and feeling wonderful about it. You might even feel a bit of fear, but you raise your self-image to, "I am a person who doesn't allow fear to stop him from doing what he wishes to do." Then speaking in front of others will be an anchor to build your self-image.

Be patient with the process. This way you add to your self-image: you're open to learning new skills and being patient mastering the skill.

Enjoy the process of creating positive anchors that will enhance your life. When you become skilled at this, your self-image can be, "I have the ability to create positive anchors at will." As soon as you start working on being able to do this, your self-image can be, "I am a person who is enthusiastic about the idea of being able to transform negative anchors into positive anchors. I will enjoy seeing how I can benefit from this and help others as well."

I was giving a class in an area where many cars would pass and honk their horns. A few of the students would get annoyed at every beep. I suggested that we all say together, "Every time any driver honks his car's horn, I will be grateful that I can hear and that I am alive!" Everyone in the room repeated this together. A few students started laughing, and their laughter was a positive anchor to cause the other students to laugh. From then on the students weren't bothered by the impatience of the drivers who feel frustrated by having to wait a few more seconds. Those drivers would have gained if they had utilized their waiting time as opportunities to develop their patience.

One of my favorite positive anchors is hearing telephones ringing and saying, "Baruch Hashem I am alive, and baruch Hashem I can hear." Everyone who repeats this enthusiastically a number of times will eventually find that telephones ringing will put them into an emotional state of gratitude.

A Joyful Pessimist

I once met someone who had a self-image of being a highly joyful pessimist. When I tell this to some people, they wonder, "But isn't an optimist supposed to be happier?"

Some are and some aren't.

Let's enter the thinking process of this highly joyful pessimist.

He would wake up in the morning and express his gratitude for being alive, just the way a joyful optimist would. But this joyful pessimist would say at the beginning of the day, "I'm assuming that everything that could possibly go wrong will go wrong today. Nothing will go the way I would wish. Today's weather will be just awful. If I go to the store, they won't have what I want. What I do buy, will be spoiled. Everything I try to use will be broken. No one will greet me today. Every person I need to interact with will be in a lousy mood and I will find it difficult to interact with everyone. I will have only financial losses and no profits. When I try to drive, I will be stuck in traffic jams. Everything will take much too long. My mind and brain will not work too well today. Things that I haven't imagined will go wrong. Nothing at all will go right."

When asked about how he felt when he thought this way, the joyful pessimist would say, "I accept whatever happens with joy. As Rabbi Mordechai Lechovitch used to say, 'If things don't go the way you wish, wish them to go the way they are.' So if everything goes as badly as I think it might, I feel great that I was right. This adds to my self-image of making correct assumptions.

"And if things turn out better, which they always do, I feel happy that things turned out well. I enjoy all that everyone else enjoys, and I'm saved from the disappointment of things not being the way I would like. So I gain either way. With a self-image of being a joyful pessimist I assure myself that I will live a very happy life."

But can't a person be a joyful optimist? Certainly! And I would assume that there are more joyful optimists than joyful pessimists.

A joyful optimist will always assume that things will work out the way he wishes. He feels good before anything happens, because he imagines that things will be great. If things don't work out the way he wishes, he will now assume that things will get better and this makes him feel good now.

While both pessimists and optimists can be joyful, there is a third possibility. A person might have a mindset of: "I'm not a pessimist or an optimist. I have no idea what will happen. I plan for the future, but I know that I don't know exactly how things will turn out. I keep my major focus on the present. I experience joy now because I am grateful for all the good in the present. When the future becomes the present, I will always find things to be grateful for. So since I always find happiness in the present, I know that I will always be able to be a happy person."

Pessimists, optimists, and those who are not committed to either pattern can all choose a joyful self-image. Being joyful is a much better goal than being a pessimist or an optimist.

A word of warning to joyful pessimists: Most people don't get as much pleasure as you do from being pessimistic. Many people feel distress just imagining what might go wrong. They hate it when pessimists elaborate on their negative themes of what might go wrong. So kindhearted, joyful pessimists need to have the self-mastery not to distress others needlessly by elaborating on a theme that they enjoy but others don't. This will add "considerate and kind" to their self-image.

A Positive Self-Image Prevents Much Anger

A positive self-image prevents much potential anger.

Imagine that you made a suggestion that was ignored. If you have a positive self-image, you'll take it less personally than you would if you had a negative self-image. A person with a negative self-image is likely to think, "I am less of a person if he doesn't listen to what I have to say."

A person with a negative self-image will become much more distressed if he feels slighted or not respected. Even minor disrespect will cause him much pain that can easily lead to anger.

A person with a positive self-image will be able to accept the behaviors of other people as just an expression of their thought patterns. They won't keep saying, "How could this person have said that to me?" or "Why isn't this person treating me better?"

A person with a positive self-image will be able to speak to others with mutual respect and work out differences more peacefully and harmoniously.

Since increased happiness and a positive self-image go together, a joyful, cheerful person with a positive self-image will be in better emotional states. This will enable him to transcend potential frustration and anger.

A person with a high self-image can find humor in situations and events that those with lower self-images won't find funny. Humor helps people be in positive emotional states and enables them to put other people in better states.

Parents with a low self-image will get more frustrated and angrier with their children. If their children misbehave they will think, "If my children misbehave, it reflects negatively on who I am." This creates angrier reactions.

Parents must realize that they have tremendous worth and value, whether or not their children listen to them. Their egos aren't involved. Then they will be much calmer and more relaxed. They will focus on the values they want their children to integrate. They will speak and act as positive role models for their children.

As the Rambam states in *Hilchos Daos* (Ch. 1), some people get angry easily and some people rarely get angry. The Rambam adds that regardless of a person's present character traits, he can and is obligated to develop positive traits and also overcome negative traits.

If a person gets angry only once in a long time, it is usually because of the special issue at hand that gets him angry. But if a person gets angry frequently, self-image issues might be a root cause of the anger. In *Anger: The Inner Teacher*, I have elaborated on nine steps to conquer anger. By consistently building one's self-image, the core of frequent anger, one will find it easier to master the emotional states and traits that are antidotes to anger.

Conquering anger is difficult and is a great achievement. Every time a person is able to remain in a calm state in challenging situations, he builds his self-image. Once someone is already angry but masters what he says and does, that, too, is an image-building achievement.

Visualize yourself having a Torah consciousness of your self-worth. See yourself remaining calm in challenging situations because you realize that you are created in the Almighty's image and you are a child of the Creator and Sustainer of the universe. Nothing that anyone says or does can take away this immense value. Remembering this will help you find it easier to view potentially frustrating situations as opportunities to develop your character traits.

> *I know someone who used to get angry frequently but eventually mastered his ability to stay calm and serene even when facing challenging people. He told me, "I used to get angry easily. I felt I had a right, even an obligation, to stick up for my right to be treated the way a self-respecting person should be treated. Therefore, I viewed every slight to my honor and respect as a situation that I needed to correct.*
>
> *"I would frequently repeat to myself, 'I will only have self-respect if I teach this person a lesson on how to give me the respect that I deserve.'*
>
> *"My friends asked me, 'Why in the world do you get so angry over trivialities?'*
>
> *"'There are no trivialities,' I responded, 'Any slight to my honor is a major thing to me.' The ironic thing about the situation was that people had much less respect for me because of the way I reacted when I was angry.*
>
> *"Someone who once saw me in a verbal dispute with my relative told me strongly, 'You kept screaming that you demand to be treated with respect, but the way you said it just got this person angry at you in return. You didn't get the respect you claimed you wanted. Be smart! Have real self-respect. Get greater control over your character traits. This will give you greater self-respect and in the long run you will be more respected.'*
>
> *"I realized that this person was right. I made an intense commitment to myself to conquer my anger. I felt much better about myself. I did feel greater self-respect. And my composure in the face of challenges got me greater respect from others."*

On Being Self-Conscious Around Other People

People with a low self-image tend to be more self-conscious around other people. They keep wondering what others think about them. Because they don't think of themselves as positively as they could, they easily assume that others are judging them and thinking negatively about them.

As you build your self-image, you will be less self-conscious around other people. You will become more aware of your strengths and positive qualities. You will not get upset even if someone is judgmental.

Truthfully, most people think of themselves most of the time. They are more concerned about what you think of them than about what they think of you.

Develop a greater awareness of the Almighty's kindnesses to you throughout your life. Then your first thoughts will be of the constant flow of positive things the Almighty sends your way. A mind full of gratitude and appreciation will be free from self-conscious thoughts.

Mentally wish other people well. Since every person has needs, pray that the Almighty should send each person what he needs the most. This way when you are around other people your mind will be focused on caring for their welfare. This will free you from self-consciousness.

I have met people who are totally free from self-consciousness. They tell me that they always assume that others will like them and think positively of them. As one person told me, "I decided to be the opposite of someone who is paranoid. A person who is paranoid always thinks that others are against him. Unless I have reason to believe otherwise, I always think that others will like me. Of course, I am careful to protect myself and don't do anything stupid. But assuming that others will like me has worked wonders for me throughout my life."

> Someone who makes new friends wherever he goes told me: "I am never self-conscious around others. When you know that someone is a good friend of yours, you are happy to see him. I always assume that every person I speak to will be a friend of mine. I know that I have faults and shortcomings, and it doesn't bother me if anyone else knows about them. I never claim to be perfect. But I do want to be kind and considerate when interacting with others.
>
> "I know that if anyone knew what I thought about them, they would like me. I want them to have a good life. I want to help others in any way that I can. I look at everyone as a person I would be happy to do things for, and I assume that the vast majority of people will reciprocate. And even if someone won't be kind to me, I still want to be kind to him. So I find it easy to smile to others and be cheerful. Wherever I go, I meet others who are cheerful when interacting with me. I feel grateful to the Almighty for filling the world with so many people to enhance my life."
>
> This fellow was following King Solomon's principle for getting along with others: "As in water, face to face, so too is the heart of one person to another." When you send out positive energy to others, others will send back positive energy to you.

Forgiveness Releases Resentment

When some people remember what others have said and done to them, they feel resentful and even angry about their lowered self-image. Holding on to this resentment creates negative feelings towards those people.

When you feel angry and resentful towards someone who said and did things in the past, only you suffer. The perpetrator doesn't. He might not even recall what he said or did. Even if he does remember, very likely he doesn't realize how much you suffered. He probably doesn't realize that his words and actions caused you to have a lowered self-image.

It can be very challenging to forgive. Even very great people might find it difficult to forgive someone who wronged them in a serous way. But there are many psychosomatic physical ailments that are caused by resentment and anger: Failing to forgive causes stress and tension. A person who has enlightened self-interest will forgive to protect his own health.

Forgiving someone who has wronged you is spiritually elevating. The Almighty deals with us measure for measure. When we forgive others, we, too, are forgiven.

When we forgive, we do not justify or condone the wrong that was done to us. It does not mean we now must respect the person who intentionally set out to harm us. On the contrary, when we forgive we are acknowledging that the person did something wrong — but we say that we are above allowing that to pull us down.

Forgiving does not mean that we cannot, or should not, pursue halachically justified remedies to redress what was done. On the contrary, apologies or restitution may very well be in order. Forgiving means only that I will not allow what happened to torment me.

Having the compassion and spiritual strength to forgive others can build one's self-image. We know that it's difficult to forgive someone who has lowered our self-image. Therefore the act of forgiving is a great spiritual accomplishment. This itself can greatly raise one's self-image.

Forgiving others is an act of kindness. And it can be a kindness that is very difficult to do. The more difficult something is, the greater the reward for doing it. So the more difficult it is for you to forgive a specific person, the greater you become by forgiving.

After you forgive someone for saying or doing something that lowered your self-image, whenever you remember what that person said or did, also remember that you forgave him. Whenever you remember the incident, or in some instances many incidents, you will be able to include the memory of forgiving that person. Each time you recall those memories from now on, they will continue building your self-image.

> Someone told me that he resented a teacher he once had. That teacher had repeatedly made fun of him in class. Whenever he hadn't known an answer, that teacher had been sarcastic and biting. That teacher had enjoyed his ability to make the rest of the class laugh at this boy. The victim of this teacher's put-downs felt that he had suffered greatly from what this teacher did to him.
>
> "I can't get what he did to me out of my mind," the young man said. "It happened a number of years ago, but the memories are fresh in my mind. He made me feel stupid and hopeless. I suffered from what he did for a very long time. I'm still not over it. My self-image would have been much better if I had never met that teacher."
>
> I spoke to that fellow about forgiving the teacher, who was no longer teaching.
>
> "But I can't forgive that teacher! He totally ruined my self-image!" he protested.
>
> "If you refuse to forgive that teacher for ruining your self-image, you are making a very powerful, limiting statement to yourself. You are saying that your self-image is ruined and you

can't do anything about it now. By doing this you yourself are lowering your self-image.

"Now let's see what will happen if you build up the inner strength to forgive him. You will realize that you can build up your self-image from now on. You will see yourself in a much more positive light. You will be making a statement that you can choose your thoughts yourself. This will put you on the path to keep building your self-image from now on. Think it over and see if you can do it."

A week later the fellow called me and said, "I feel so much better than I've felt in a long time. Releasing the resentment has opened my mind to many new possibilities. I regret holding on to the resentment for so long. But I'm not going to let it cause me more distress. I'm resolved to let this memory serve as a constant motivator to gain greater mastery over my own thoughts."

Changing Your Memories of the Past

The memories of the past create our personalities. The past is our life history.

Since we are blessed with the gift of imagination, however, we can always recreate our mental version of the past. This doesn't change the reality of what was, but it can change how we feel about what happened. And we can create imaginary mental pictures about things we wished had happened. We know that the new mental pictures didn't "really" happen, but we can pretend to have lived through those positive experiences. Using this ability wisely can be a very helpful and useful tool. This tool can help a person enhance his self-image. It gives a greater awareness of what we can do to keep improving ourselves.

For example, let's say that someone wants to build up his level of courage. He searches his memory bank and doesn't see those specific acts of courage. Now he can create imaginary scenes of having had tremendous courage. He knows that these scenes didn't actually happen in the past, that he is creating these mental videos of courage as a tool to use in the present. Now he can watch these mental pictures of courage over and over again. When he needs to have more courage in the future, he can access some of these mental pictures of having courage, and then feel courageous. He can talk and act with the courage that he created through the power of imagination.

The same principle applies to creating joyful memories, creating calm and serene memories, creating enthusiastic memories, and creating patient memories.

Some people find this tool easy to apply, but others don't see mental pictures that easily. Keep practicing until it works for you.

Some people ask, "Why not create all of these inner resources right now and then imagine having them in the future? You can do this to create more courage, to create more joy, to create greater calm and serenity, to create more enthusiasm, and to create more patience."

The answer is that yes, you can. It's just that some people find that it works better to create these states and patterns as imaginary past memories. Storing them as memories makes it easier to access these states when they need them.

Some people are much more into their version of reality and might be critical of using the power of imagination. Since it is just a tool and a technique, if it works for you, great! Use it. If it doesn't work for you, try other approaches.

Changing the nature of distressful memories is a similar tool. It is like editing a video film. For example, someone might remember a childhood scene when other children laughed at him and made fun of him. He might be able to create a mental video of those children realizing that they were wrong and apologizing to him. He might be able to see those children compensating for the distress they caused. He might be able to see himself forgiving those children, and then seeing a great Torah scholar praising him highly for his willingness to forgive. He might be able to mentally imagine himself radiating great light as a reward for being so elevated and forgiving. When he remembers this scene again, the edited version will change his current feelings about those memories. He still realizes what actually happened, but changes the feelings towards those memories.

As part of this technique, you could review stressful scenes of the past and add Purim music to them. You can even add Purim clowns when appropriate. It is highly empowering to know that you can create the emotional state of a memory so that you can transform past distress into present humor and good feelings.

> *Someone who complained that he had many past memories of being considered "a nobody" now found it very difficult to have a positive self-image. It was suggested to him that he create imaginary scenes where he "remembers" doing many heroic things. He should see himself speaking and acting with tremendous courage and with tremendous empowerment. He should visualize himself as having been fearless in dangerous situations. He should see himself speaking up in situations where it would take tremendous courage to say what needed to be said.*
>
> *The idea was to create mental movies of being powerful and important, not a nobody. As he would see these great scenes in his mind he would feel great. Even though he was just creating these feelings in his imagination, he was really building up an image of who he could be.*
>
> *The Rambam states that the way to overcome a negative trait is to act for a while in positive ways that are just the opposite of the negative trait. This will eventually get a person more in line with a balanced way of being. By making extreme mental pictures of your being all that you would have wished to be, you are creating a vision of potential for yourself.*
>
> *A word of caution: This technique is not suggesting that one live in a fantasy world or a world of pure daydreams. Rather, it is a tool that, when used properly, builds up the mental vision of*

many more possibilities of how one can create oneself in better ways. So instead of having a true past that limits, one is creatively making it more likely that one will do more in his actual life.

"I'm Glad You Have Feelings"

When I was a young boy, my mother read a story to me that had a sad part. I began to cry, feeling sorry for the child in the story.

"I'm glad you have feelings," my mother said to me.

This memory became part of my self-image. Crying is a sign that someone has feelings.

Being compassionate is a highly valuable Torah attribute. Feeling the pain of another person is distressing. This kind of distress is spiritually elevating. This quality of compassion was a key element in why Moshe Rabbeinu was chosen to be the leader who would take the Children of Israel out of Egypt.

I have heard various people describe someone who cried over tragedies as, "He broke down and cried." Crying for others is a sign of empathy and feeling the pain of another person. This isn't a weakness but a strength. There's no "breaking down" involved.

If someone cries for the suffering of others, his self-image can be: "I am a person who cares strongly for the pain of others. I appreciate that I feel their pain to such an extent that I cry."

Some people feel embarrassed when they cry. "This might cause others to think that I am weak," they might say to themselves.

If someone feels that he is weak, it could be highly beneficial to strengthen himself to be able to stay strong in the face of challenges. People who are able to stay calm in the face of serious challenges are often said to have "nerves of steel," but nobody's nerves are really made out of steel.

The goal is to have a balance, to feel the pain and distress of others in order to help them when you can, and to empathize with them to lighten their emotional burden. At the same time, increase your level of inner strength to be able to handle challenges with a clear mind.

> *I once spoke to a kind person who was highly empathetic when other people suffer. "How did you develop this quality?" I asked him.*
>
> *"My father was outstandingly kind," he told me. "The distress of other people bothered him greatly and he used to do all he could to help alleviate their distress. When I was growing up, whenever I felt bad about anything, he would say to me, 'Remember these feelings. Whenever others suffer, they are feeling similar feelings. Let these feelings remind you to do or say something kind to help them out.'*
>
> *"Because of this repeated message, every time I experienced any distress for any reason, my mind repeated, 'These feelings will make me a kinder person.' Since feeling bad was another building block to becoming kinder, it gave a stronger meaning to my feelings of distress. I have told this to a number of people so that they, too, can view their own distress as a tool to become kinder.*
>
> *"I have been asked, 'But won't feeling the pain of others take away your own joy of living?' When you realize the value of being a compassionate person, you feel good because you feel for others. People who run marathon races suffer a lot of pain. Each step can become painful. But the people who run these long races feel good about the pain. They have a goal and they are reaching their goal. The pain they feel gives them a sense of becoming a stronger person. To them, their physical distress means that they are becoming tougher, and pain won't stop them. I have found that willingly choosing to feel the pain of others gives my life more meaning and depth."*

How African Violets Transformed Someone's Self-Image

In my book *Marriage* I cite one of my favorite case histories: A deeply depressed elderly woman. She lived by herself and didn't have any special talents, skills, or intellectual pursuits. She was socially isolated and wasn't involved in any activities.

Her psychiatrist, Dr. Milton Erickson, was famous for his brilliant solutions. He found that this woman did have one special interest: She loved African violet plants. He suggested that she buy 200 flowerpots of African violets and cultivate them. Making certain that they had sufficient water and sunlight would take a lot of work. After each plant matured, she was to give it as a gift to anyone who was celebrating a special occasion. She followed this suggestion.

She became known as "The African Violet Queen" of her city. She was frequently invited to special events where she was always greeted warmly. She was constantly busy with an activity she found enjoyable, and she regularly met people who were happy to see her. Her depression disappeared after following the recommended homework assignment of her sole therapy session.

There are, of course, people who might need medication. Others might need many more sessions. Many people don't like to cultivate plants, so this would not be an appropriate solution for them. But at times, even a problem that is chronic can have a creative solution that might be resolved in a fairly short amount of time.

Before this woman was involved with the African violets, her self-image was that she was an elderly woman who wasn't doing anything with her life. After cultivating the African violet plants and giving them to many people as gifts, her self-image reflected that she was an African Violet Queen, that she was busy with activities she enjoyed, and that many people were happy to see her.

Please note what Dr. Erickson did not do. He didn't give a negative diagnosis. He could have said: "This woman is severely depressed. She is not doing anything constructive with her life, and has a very low self-image." Viewing this woman in that problematic way would have made it much more difficult to help her.

Dr. Erickson knew what he was looking for: An ongoing activity that would engage this woman. She needed an activity that would enable her to become involved with other people in a positive way, one that others would recognize and appreciate. Somehow I doubt if even Erickson knew that she would be called the African Violet Queen by others. Maybe I am wrong. Perhaps he did realize it; maybe he made certain that others would call her by this title.

What is the principle we see here? If a person who is currently not functioning on a high level can find an area of strong interest to excel in, the person will have the skill and enthusiasm necessary to excel.

Once individuals excel in an area of high interest, they will be able to accomplish in ways that build their self-image.

Even if that area of interest is not recognizable right now, a person might find it on his own, or someone else might creatively think of what that person could do.

Even before people know what they can do to excel, they can have a self-image of: "I am just one step away from finding what I can excel in that will make a major difference in my life."

Respect the Elderly — Even When It's You

It's common to have issues with our self-image while growing up, but our self-image isn't set in stone when we become adults. In fact, new issues may develop as we become elderly.

Elderly people frequently aren't able to accomplish and achieve the way they did when they were younger. It's common for the elderly to have various health challenges. There is a tendency to slow down mentally and physically. Sight and hearing are not as strong as they once were. A number of elderly people begin to lose their ability to remember facts and data, and even basic information becomes forgotten. Some elderly people lose their ability to walk and need wheelchairs.

For many elderly people, self-image can become an issue.

They might say to themselves, "I'm not what I used to be." "Who am I now that I can't be as productive as I used to be?" "I hate being a burden to my children and others."

Some elderly people might have had many plans, goals, and dreams that never turned out the way they were hoping. They can feel disappointed with how they ended up.

Every single human being has a unique mission. Our life mission continues for as long as we are alive. Every elderly person has tremendous value. Regardless of what one can and cannot do as one becomes elderly, one's infinite value and worth always remain. Life is a gift. Life is precious. Someone who is totally handicapped and just barely stays alive has immense value.

Someone who needs constant help from others is bringing more compassion and kindness into the world. The self-image of someone who needs this help can be, "My very being is making the world a kinder place. Everyone who is kind to me is emulating the Almighty because of me."

Awareness of the Almighty and His kindness is an elevating consciousness. As long as one is breathing one has the ability to be grateful for each and every breath. The Almighty supplies each of us with the oxygen that is right in front of our mouth and nose. Therefore as long as we are breathing we are recipients of the Almighty's kindness. Hence our self-image can always be: "I am a recipient of the Almighty's kindness. And I am forever grateful."

Appreciating life and breathing when we are young will make it easier for us to appreciate the Almighty's kindness for as long as we live.

You deserve self-respect from the moment you were born. This stays with you for your entire life.

> *I remember a discussion I once had with an elderly man. He told me that he recently had his seventieth birthday. Family members congratulated him and seemed happy, but he was full of anxiety.*
>
> *"I have become more aware of the difficulties that elderly people suffer from. I dread being old. It's not the fear of dying that weighs on my mind," he said. "Rather, it's the fear of being helpless. After all I've done and accomplished in my life, I can't believe that I will one day be as unable to do things for myself as a young child."*
>
> *"It looks like you are taking the worst-case scenario and worrying about that," I said to him. "There are many older people who maintain good health even in their old age. Some people do have a much easier time towards the end of their life than others."*
>
> *"But the picture of myself being weak and unable to do things for myself shakes me to the very core. I know I can't predict how the later years of my life will be. But just the thought of the possibility of my being a nothing and a nobody scares me."*
>
> *"I can see from what you are saying that the core issue for you isn't just lacking the strength that you used to have," I said to him. "From what you are saying it appears that your main concern is your self-image. You are a dignified person with a high level of balanced self-respect. It seems that you view being older and unable to function like before as a heavy blow to your self-image."*

"That's definitely correct. I feel that it's almost as if I've wasted my entire life if I end up living without dignity."

"The Torah concept of "kavod haadam" — respect for humans — is valid our entire lives. Even after death, there is a high obligation to treat the departed person with the greatest respect and dignity. All the good that you have done your entire life is a reality that stays with you for all eternity. Even someone who has totally lost his ability to function in any capacity still maintains his infinite value and worth.

"I suggest that you mentally increase your respect for any elderly person you encounter. The essence of a person is his soul, not his body. Even if someone can't function at all, the soul is still there. Just as it is forbidden to shorten the life of an infant or a young child, so too it is equally forbidden to shorten the life of an elderly person whose body is not functioning well. When you internalize the Torah concept of life, you will be able to maintain a positive self-image as long as your mind is working on even the most basic level."

I could see from this person's reaction that he welcomed this entire concept.

Limited Education

Did you ever benefit from a light bulb or a fluorescent light? Of course, we all did. The person who perfected the light bulb had a total of three months of formal education in an elementary school.

As a young child, Thomas Edison didn't get along with the schoolmaster of the small school he attended. So after three months of schooling, he dropped out for good. When I first time heard this from Napoleon Hill, I found it hard to believe. But Hill, a famous motivational author, had met Edison and used him as one of his role models for accomplishing. The next time I was in a public library, I found a biography of Edison. There it was: Edison had only three months of formal schooling. He spent the rest of his life studying and researching on his own.

Some people with a limited formal education might have a self-image of: "I'm not that educated."

But Edison never let his short "proper" education get in the way. He kept reading. He kept speaking to people who had the knowledge that he wanted to gain. You can do the same.

Every time you see a light bulb, let it remind you to gain more knowledge, on your own or from speaking to knowledgeable people. Let it motivate you to keep learning more, even if you do not yet have your ideal education.

As long as you continue reading books and listening to others share their knowledge, you are a person who is continuing a lifelong quest for more knowledge.

You can have a self-image of: "I am a person who continues to gain more knowledge my entire life."

Once we've mentioned Edison, it's worthwhile mentioning one of the classic reframes of history. When Edison was working on inventing the light bulb, he tried one filament after another to find one that would work. He tried thousands of experiments. When asked about his feelings towards his failures, he commented, "I didn't fail. Each experiment that didn't work successfully taught me another way not to make a light bulb."

Every person who tries to do positive and constructive things will find that many things won't work out as planned. You build your self-image by viewing this as part of the process of gaining more knowledge and wisdom. As quoted in *Chochmah Umussar*, "There is no one wiser than someone with experience." As you accumulate more experience, you become wiser. So you can frequently say, "This, too, is making me wiser."

A fellow in his twenties spoke to a major scholar and complained, "I wish I had more education."

"I, too, wish I had more education," the scholar said, to the fellow's surprise.

"But you have been studying for many years," the fellow replied.

"Yes, I have," said the scholar. "But no amount of education is sufficient. We need to constantly review what we have already learned. When you study at the age of twenty, you see the information in a totally different light than when you studied it at age ten. And when you are thirty, you see it totally differently than when you were twenty. And when you are fifty, everything you study is much deeper and more profound than when you were only thirty. The more I learn, the more I know that I need to improve the understanding that I already have.

"Don't just wish you had more education," the scholar concluded. "That might imply that you have given up on gaining more knowledge. It's much wiser to spend your time studying more."

The Dave Farrow Story and Your Memory

How well someone remembers is often an important part of his self-image. The better his ability to remember, the better he does on tests that require memory. Many people talk about "having" a memory. They will say, "I have a good memory," or "I have a bad memory."

Compare these two self-image statements:

"I have a great memory. I easily remember what I study. I get great marks on my tests. I consider myself to be bright, and so does everyone else. People are very impressed when I show them my test scores. I see myself having a bright future because I am a person with a great memory."

"I have a very poor memory. It is difficult for me to remember what I study. I get poor marks on my tests. I don't consider myself very bright, and neither does anyone else. I am embarrassed to show my test scores to others. I see myself having a bleak future because I am a person with a poor memory."

Don't think of "memory" as a noun. It's not something that you "have" or "don't have." Rather, it is a function of the brain and mind. "You remember now" or "You don't remember now."

You, like everyone with a normally functioning brain, have the ability to improve your ability to remember. Many tools have been developed to help people remember better. When you study some of those tools and apply them, you will find yourself remembering better. You will do better on tests that depend on memory. And you will be building your self-image.

Once when I was in New York, I saw a notice that Dave Farrow, an expert on memory and mental focus, was in New York for a few days and was giving a lecture. He was going to speak about building up one's visualization ability and on improving one's ability to remember.

Dave's life history is what motivated me to attend the lecture. When he was a student in school, his teachers told him that he was mentally deficient and he should never think of going for higher education. Because he felt the pain of embarrassment, he was strongly motivated to study memory techniques and even developed some himself. Not only did he become an outstanding student who did go for higher education, he became an expert on the ability to remember.

When he was in New York that time, he was in the *Guinness Book of World Records* for remembering the order of 2,704 playing cards. That's 52 decks shuffled together!

I wasn't at all interested in remembering orders of cards. That skill wasn't the focus of the class that I attended. But I did want to speak to someone who had developed his ability to remember so much more than when he started. He proved that the experts with a limited view of his ability to study and remember were wrong.

It would be wonderful for teachers to develop their own abilities to remember better and then teach their students how to do this.

In general, all experts on the process of memory agree that when you are enthusiastic and excited about what you are studying, you will remember it better. I remember that I once met a fourteen-year-old boy who had trouble remembering what was taught in class, but had no trouble remembering the batting averages of American professional baseball players. Every day the three digits of those batting averages changed, and each day he would update his memory with the new numbers. He got a lot of admiration from other students for his amazing ability. This made him excited about the boring numbers. If he had found a way to get equally excited about what was studied in school, he would have remembered his schoolwork much better.

To improve your ability to remember, try these techniques:

• Practice seeing mental pictures of what you hear and what you see. Make the mental pictures colorful, interesting, outlandish, ridiculous, and amusing.

• Practice looking at words, sentences, and pages of a book, and then look away from the page. Then test, little by little, what you can remember seeing on the page.

• Some suggest that when people look up and to the left, they have an easier time visualizing what they say. For some people, it's up and to the right. And for others, eyes are unfocused and straight ahead. Try it out and see what works for you.

• Being able to mentally picture words will help improve your spelling ability, since the ability to spell well depends on having a visual memory of what you've seen. Spelling well can help a person raise his self-image. This is especially helpful for students who are graded on their ability to spell. They're not yet the highly successful business executives who can pay for secretaries who spell well, or who are able to look up words and use spell-checkers.

• When you meet people who remember well, interview them. Ask them about any tools and techniques that they have found beneficial. Some people find it very natural and easy to visualize what they see and hear. They have an easier time remembering. But this is a skill that everyone can improve. I have a friend, Rabbi Avraham Goldhar, who has an amazing ability to make mental pictures of what he studies. A number of years ago, he helped me improve my ability to do this, and today he teaches this skill to many others.

• Memory works by association. Therefore, when you want to remember something, find ways to associate it with others things that you remember. Going down the alphabet from A to Z can help you recall better.

• Reviewing ideas and pages builds up your brain's pathways. So when you want to remember something, review what you heard or read.

• Take notes, and review your notes.

• When you need to remember something to do, write it down. This approach isn't very impressive, but it works. So instead of having a self-image, "I always forget things," one will have a self-image of: "I have found ways to help me remember better."

Brains automatically store information that they see and hear. There have been studies of electrodes placed on brain neurons to stimulate them. The individuals who experienced this were able to see and hear with total clarity everything they ever saw and heard. I have always found this experiment highly motivating to help believe in one's mental potential.

Keep in mind that even if someone does not build up an ability to remember better, the basic value of every human being is immense. Each human being has infinite worth, regardless of the state of his ability to remember.

Keep a Victory and Success Journal

Keeping a "victory and success journal" is a great tool for building your self-image. All you need to do is write down your victories and successes! Then you can see your successes and reread them as often as you wish.

Victory and success journals give you inspiration for the future. By writing down what you've accomplished, you have a much clearer message that you have already done many positive things. This helps you realize that you can do many more throughout your life.

Write down past victories and successes. Everyone who reads this will certainly have had many hundreds of victories and successes, including you. Your goal is to include at least two hundred items on your list. Be patient. Depending on what you have already done and accomplished in your life, it might take some time to have two hundred items to write down. To start your list, go out of your way each day to say and do things that would be examples of victories and successes.

Every time you say or do something positive that was difficult for you to do, you have another victory and success to add to your list.

Don't take any of your past victories and successes for granted. You learned how to read, didn't you? Add it to your list. You learned how to write, so that's another success to include.

Make a commitment to build your self-image. That itself is a victory. Go out of your way to say and do things that will help others build their self-image. That is a victory.

Some People Enjoy Finding Weaknesses in Others

Some people enjoy finding weaknesses in others. They try to build up their own egos by pushing others down. It gives them a sense of power to observe faults, mistakes, errors, weaknesses, deficiencies, and the negative patterns of others. Then it gives them an even greater sense of power to tell their prey that they have noticed many things wrong with them.

People who do this have a mean streak. They lack kindness, compassion, and a sense of goodwill. It gives them a sense of power to see other people feeling uncomfortable, even embarrassed, because of their comments.

Some people who have this pattern don't view themselves as mean or cruel. Rather, they might claim that they are just telling the truth. "It's important to tell the truth, isn't it?" But it's even more important to be kind and compassionate. It's even more important to learn to bring out the best in people.

There are people who put others down and point out their faults and deficiencies with what seem to be good intentions. But good intentions don't allow someone to go against the Torah prohibition of causing pain with words. Good intentions don't give someone permission to ruin someone else's self-image instead of helping him build himself and his self-image.

If someone really means well, he will recognize the need to sincerely apologize when you point out the distress he is causing you. He won't make fun of you for feeling distress. He won't respond with sarcasm. He won't continue to say even more insults and putdowns. He won't repeat what he said before to prove that he was right. He will be authentically motivated to refrain from any further distress and damage.

If you have to interact with someone who seems to get pleasure out of making you feel bad and trying to lower your self-image, don't allow this person to have power over you. Only you can control the thoughts that go through your mind. He can't lower your self-image unless you let him. You still have your basic value as a person because you are created in the image of the Almighty and are a child of the Creator.

See mean and cruel people for what they are. Realize that this person is being mean and cruel, regardless of how he sees himself. It might make it easier for you to think of him as a baby. He is acting immature now, so seeing him as he was in diapers isn't so far from the reality. People with this verbally abusive pattern often view themselves as intelligent, as insightful, as sophisticated, as above-average mortals. But what they are doing is definitely wrong. At times this could be considered a crime. Stealing money from others is a crime in any court of law. Robbing someone of a positive self-image is a worse crime (*Baba Metzia* 58b).

If the person is not potentially dangerous and you are physically safe, you might be able to point out, "It's not right to speak that way."

If someone sincerely doesn't want to do something wrong, he is likely to ask you to clarify what you would want him to refrain from.

If, however, someone derives pleasure from making people experience distress, he will view this as a wonderful opportunity to say another thing with the intention of causing you more distress.

Sometimes it's wiser to just ignore what some people say. If you keep ignoring their negative statements, they won't get any fun or illusions of power, and eventually they will stop because of the lack of emotional payoff.

If you feel safe enough, however, you might say, "It seems to me that you get pleasure from saying hurtful things." A person who likes to say spiteful, hurtful things will try to say another hurtful thing. If you still feel safe enough, you might say, "Your game is quite clear. I hope that you can build your own self-image so you will get more pleasure out of being kind and compassionate. Then you won't feel a need to do this."

Realize, however, that this person probably feels a need to get in the last word. Let him. But the very fact that you explicitly called him on what he was doing will make it more likely that he won't repeat this pattern with you.

If he does repeat it anyway and you are not in physical danger, you might say with a cheerful tone of voice, "There you go again."

We hope that one day this person will gain the spiritual awareness and emotional maturity to refrain from speaking in ways that cause distress to others.

If you, the reader, enjoy finding weaknesses in others, the end of this section is for you.

Throughout life you make many choices. Some choices elevate you and some choices lower you. Finding the weaknesses in others and using your observations to lower others really lowers you. This would be manifesting a lowly character trait even if you get temporary emotional gratification.

Make the wise and compassionate decision to begin a career of building other people up. Apply your insights to use your power of words as a means of making people feel good about themselves. Use your power of words as a tool to enhance the lives of others. Find ways of speaking that inspire and motivate others to improve and grow. You have the free will to choose to be a source of good in this world. The good feelings that you may attain by being a source of kindness, compassion, wisdom, and goodness will ensure that you are living your life in a more elevated way, which will benefit many people.

> *Someone told me, "There were a few people who enjoyed saying things to me to make me feel bad. I developed the habit of saying to them, 'Thank you. You just gave me another illustration of what the Sages say, that people who find faults in others do so with their own faults.' Knowing that I will say this to them takes away some of their fun. For some people this is a strong enough motive to avoid hurting me again. And even if they don't totally stop, it minimizes the number of times that they do it."*

People Who Are Angry and Blaming

The Talmud states: "When a person becomes angry, he forgets what he has learned and he increases foolishness" (*Nedarim* 22b). And: "Even if a person is extremely wise, he loses his wisdom when he gets angry" (*Pesachim* 66b).

This universal principle can help us transcend the potential effect of statements shouted against us in anger. The angry person lost his temper when he screamed at you and said the negative things that he said. This makes it easier to disregard the way he said what he said, and not let it negatively affect your self-image.

He might have had a valid reason for being angry. You might have made a mistake that you shouldn't have made. But he should have spoken to you more respectfully. You always deserve to be spoken to with respect. Don't allow this person's anger to lower your self-image.

Someone who has the tendency to blame others is likely to blame you and other people for his faults. If he gets angry, it's always someone else's fault, not his own. All of his mistakes and errors are because of others. They distracted him. They upset him. They didn't let him think as brilliantly as he would have if they hadn't gotten in the way. Whenever something goes wrong when you are in the presence of a person with a tendency to blame, he'll always consider it your fault.

"Successful" blamers tend not to correct their faults and limitations. Since they think it's always someone else's fault, they never think that they have to do anything to improve themselves. Therefore, they tend not to improve.

Being around a person with a tendency to blame has the potential to lower your self-image. Knowing that the blamer is wrong to have this totally one-sided, biased view of reality can help you overcome the verbal knocks to your self-image. "I'm not totally to blame," is the freeing attitude.

Repeat to yourself, "This person is blaming me now. If I contributed to what I am being blamed for, I am resolved to improve. The fact that I want to improve myself will raise my self-image. Even if I did do something wrong, I still should be spoken to with respect. If this person were calmer and thinking clearly right now, he would be speaking to me in a way that is mutually respectful." This is one way to grow if you are frequently blamed by a habitual blamer.

If you are interacting with a non-dangerous habitual blamer, you might want to ask him, "If you were at least partly to blame, would you want to correct yourself?"

If he says, "Yes, of course, I know I make mistakes, and when I do I am always ready to improve," that's great.

If he says something like, "It's never my fault. It's always your fault. You have problems, go get them fixed," let that diminish the negative implications of his blaming. He is being defensive. This pattern is not the sign of a person with a truly high but modest self-image. Either he is being insecure, or arrogant, or both. Arrogance itself is an error. So, too, is his pattern of speaking. He is not an objective judge of who you are.

When you interact with a person in an angry, blaming state, try to access a calm, centered state for yourself. Try to view him from a place of understanding and compassion. People who are frequently angry and blaming are in an unresourceful, distressed state. They are suffering. Ideally, they would want to discuss the issues involved in a calm and mutually respectful manner. But if you stay calm and don't escalate the situation even when they are in a highly agitated state, you might be able to say something that will help the other person access a calmer state.

Even if someone is now angry and blaming, there is always hope that he will change. Maybe he'll wake up one day and realize that he needs greater mastery over his emotional states and over what he says and how he says it.

See the spiritual essence of this person. View him as someone who deep down would like to interact harmoniously with others.

"I grew up in an angry home. I was blamed for all kinds of things. This had a very negative effect on my self-image," a successful businessman told me. "From what I had heard about the negative impact of being angrily blamed throughout one's childhood, I wasn't certain that I would be able to develop a truly positive self-image. I was told by a number of people that such a childhood would leave scars for the rest of my life.

"A major turning point in my life came when I met another businessman at a convention and we traded life stories. His childhood had been much rougher than mine. He grew up in a dangerous neighborhood, and putting other people down was the norm.

"I asked him, 'But don't you have scars?'

"He answered, 'I have plenty of scars. Knives were the weapon of choice where I grew up. Fistfights were common, and needing stitches wasn't considered a big thing. But those cuts healed. I have a bunch of scars to prove that I've healed.

"'But how I view myself depends totally on my own thoughts. I had a great teacher in high school. My teacher said to me, "Other people might say anything they want about who you are. But it's your own choice of words and actions that creates who you really are. Your character is up to you. The only thing that counts is what you say to yourself about who you are. What others say to you is just their opinion. Their opinion is their thoughts. It's your own thoughts that lead to your words and actions that count."'

"He concluded, 'I know deep inside that I have the potential for greatness. Every human being does. My teacher was much wiser than all of those who put me down. I accepted that wise teacher's attitude as the basis for my own thinking. You should also adopt my teacher's attitude. Through me, my teacher is now your teacher also.'"

Note to People Who Are Frequently Angry and Insulting

If you are frequently angry and insulting to others, this section was written especially for you. Actually, even if you are angry only once in a while but your words tend to cause others distress, this note could be beneficial.

Parents and teachers who are frequently angry and insulting cause their children and students to suffer a lot from those angry outbursts. They suffer in the present and they might have to work very hard to build up a crushed self-image in the future. Teachers with this angry and insulting behavior pattern embarrass their students in front of their friends and classmates. This can be highly painful and damaging to a developing self-image.

Someone with a frequently angry and insulting spouse will experience much distress and suffering. The anger and insults can easily lower the self-image of the suffering spouse.

To benefit yourself and others around you:

• Develop your own happiness and joy. A happy person is usually calmer to be around and is more respectful to others.

• Gain greater mastery over the ability to stay calm and centered, even if you have valid reasons for being irritated, frustrated, and angry.

• Master the ability to consistently speak with self-respect and respect for others. If you need to correct someone, do it in a way that they feel respected. Have the self-mastery to refrain from speaking in ways that cause distress to others. Words that cause others pain are considered *onaas devarim*. The Talmud states that causing someone pain with words is worse than cheating them financially. Make a strong commitment to be careful with what you say and the way you say it.

- Gain such a positive sense of self that you accept feedback. Then people could tell you that your anger and insults cause them high levels of distress. Instead of arguing, seriously listen to what they say. Respond to such feedback, "Thank you for pointing this out. I am resolved to conquer my anger and speak to you more pleasantly."

As you improve your self-image, you will start to realize on your own if you need to make conquering your anger a high priority. Even when you are angry, make it a high priority to watch what you say. Every single human being deserves to be spoken to respectfully. I'm almost certain that there are many people to whom you do speak pleasantly and respectfully.

Some people who tend to get angry easily and insult others also tend to blame the victims of their anger and insults for being too sensitive. "If you wouldn't be so sensitive, you wouldn't feel hurt just because I raise my voice and criticize you."

If someone is more sensitive, we have a greater obligation to be more careful when we speak to him.

It is very important that you realize that your words can be very powerful. It is often easier to lower the self-image of others rather than to build it. Those who suffer from your anger and insults might be afraid to tell you how much suffering you have caused them.

It is very important to apologize and ask forgiveness from those who suffered from your anger and insults. This takes inner strength and courage. By apologizing, you raise your own spiritual and emotional level.

Some people deny being frequently angry and insulting. Denying an angry or insulting pattern doesn't make it go away. How can you know if you have this pattern? Ask those on the receiving end. They will know. Create a safe environment for them to be honest with you. They might be afraid that you will just get angry at them and then cause them more distress. Give them the reassurance that you are truly interested in improving yourself.

Developing your character is one of the most important things you can do. Develop a greater amount of inner calm and serenity. Develop a greater degree of respect for others. Develop a greater amount of self-respect and dignity, to hold yourself to a higher standard of interacting with others. Develop more kindness, compassion, understanding, and sensitivity. You and everyone you interact with will gain together.

As you develop your character and become a happier, calmer, and kinder person, you will find yourself living a much better life, and you will enhance the lives of others around you. Your self-image will be much higher than ever before.

> Someone who used to angrily put down and insult his family members eventually saw how much pain and damage he was causing them. We spoke after he realized how wrong he had been to speak the way he did.
>
> He said, "I had a very sharp way of speaking. Even when I wasn't especially angry, I would speak in a condescending manner. I had a low level of tolerance for frustration and I was frequently in a bad mood. I didn't mean to hurt anyone, but what could I do? This was the way I was spoken to when I was growing up, and this was the pattern that I was familiar with.
>
> "One day my wife told me that she was no longer able to tolerate the way I spoke to her. Her self-image was crushed. She had tried not to show how much emotional pain she was in, but now she couldn't cope with the stress any more. She had many aches and pains, very high blood pressure, and was beginning to have problems with her heart. Her doctor told her that the stress she was under was dangerous to her health.
>
> "She gave me an ultimatum. I would either learn to conquer my anger and speak to her with respect, or else she didn't feel she would be able to continue the marriage. It wasn't just that she was a little unhappy. Rather, her high level of stress was killing her. She had a choice: To save her life and leave the marriage, or become chronically ill.
>
> "She didn't want either of these two options. She wanted me to change my entire pattern of speaking to her and the children. She wanted me to learn how to be calm and speak respectfully.
>
> "The truth is, I wanted the same thing that she wanted. I knew that my anger and verbal abuse were wrong. But I didn't fully realize the extent of the pain and suffering I was causing.

"I was totally resolved to make greater mastery of my emotions a high priority. This was going to be more important to me than having things 'my way.' I was also determined to speak pleasantly to my wife and children.

"I had heard from some people that people with my pattern aren't able to change. This is the way there are used to being, and this is the way that they will stay. But I was fully resolved to develop my character. I was fully resolved to learn to be calm in the face of potentially frustrating situations. I came to realize that my thoughts about what was going on were what caused my anger. It wasn't the situation itself. This greater awareness, that my thoughts caused my reaction, gave me the belief that I would be able to improve greatly.

"I went out of my way to be especially kind and sensitive, understanding and compassionate. Fortunately I was able to make positive changes. It was very difficult for me and I had ups and downs. But my total commitment to improve my emotional states and my way of talking bore fruit. I feel so much better about myself for becoming the kind of person that all along I wished I was."

Just Plain Stubborn

Some people are just plain stubborn when it comes to changing their self-image. They don't have logical arguments to explain why they can't view themselves in a more positive way. They don't have an especially abusive or traumatic background. They aren't really deficient in any obvious or major ways. They don't have any special health or physical challenges. They just make a statement: "I don't have a positive self-image and that's just the way I am."

They refuse to speak to someone who might help them build their self-image. "Nothing anyone says will change the way I view myself. This is the way I am and that's it."

They refuse to read anything that might help them see themselves in a more positive way. "Nothing that anyone has ever written will change the way I view myself, so I don't want to waste my time."

They refuse to try any tools or techniques that might help them. "These tools and techniques are superficial. No mental tricks will make a difference."

They will make statements such as, "You're just saying that if someone has a negative self-image all he has to do is have a positive self-image. That's ridiculous." He's right. The way this sentence is worded, it certainly won't work for most people.

He is wrong, however, when it comes to people who are very flexible and open to new ideas. Even though the previous statement does not present a valid argument, it can help very flexible people. They will be able to say, "Yes, I have had a negative self-image. Now I will choose to have a positive self-image. Why not?"

This doesn't seem possible to a person who is stubborn. Even the average flexible person doesn't think it's likely to happen. I just wrote this here because, in my experience, people are different from one another. And something that won't work for many people will still work for some people.

Now back to our stubborn person. Perhaps he is a person with a polarity response. What is a polarity response? Responding with the opposite of what people say. You can test it out by challenging him, "So you think that nothing anyone says to you could possibly change your self-image? And you are also saying that you couldn't change your own self-image, even if you were totally motivated to do so?"

If the person you are speaking to tends to react with a polarity response, he is likely to respond, "No, I'm not claiming that nothing could work. And I'm also not claiming that I will never change my self-image."

Great. This is progress. It could still take a very long time to get this person to develop a more positive self-image, but at least he is saying that he is open to the possibility.

But some people might respond, "Yes, I am saying that nobody can change my self-image and even I won't change my self-image."

What can you do then?

Imagine asking one of the best dentists in the world, "How do you fix the teeth of someone who stubbornly refuses to come to your office? Nothing anyone says motivates him to come. How do you help him?" The dentist will answer that he can't help unless the man shows up.

The same with trying to help someone build his self-image: A person has to want to improve. If he refuses, you will have to wait until something happens to help him change his mind and agree to try.

Some people have a self-image that enables them to stubbornly refuse to make positive change. "I am a person who thinks of myself in a negative way. If I change my self-image, then I will no longer be me. I will have to be someone else, and I don't want to be someone else."

I once had a discussion with someone who used this argument. I finally was able to show him that his core essence wouldn't be changed if he thought about himself in more positive ways. I reminded him that at one time he was five years old. Five years later he was ten years old. Five years later he was fifteen years old. His self-image changed about how old he was, but he was essentially the same person at each age, just five years older. The fellow agreed, and then he agreed to make some positive changes.

A person who seems "stubborn" might view himself as being "consistent." He might have a greater need to be consistent than to have a positive self-image. If that is the case, maybe he is truly better off being consistent rather than flexible, because just as a person is rewarded for doing something positive, a person is also rewarded for refraining from doing something negative.

When we realize that our thoughts change the way we experience life, we can be more aware that seeing someone as "stubborn" is just our subjective way of looking at him. He has his reasons for not being more flexible. He might even wish he were more flexible in his thinking, but he just isn't able to change.

We might be able to influence "stubborn" people when we realize how much of our own thinking is arbitrary, and that as we change our thinking about something, we change our feelings. Even if we can't get such a person to see himself in a positive light, we can challenge his negative view of himself. "The negative way you are looking at yourself isn't based on the total reality of who you are. It's just based on the arbitrary thoughts that you are thinking about yourself. Even though I can't prove that you should see yourself positively, you can't prove that it's currently impossible to see yourself in a better light. Maybe you can think of reasons to view yourself in a more positive way. Think it over. Let's see what happens."

For some people, presenting a positive perspective as a possibility and not the absolute reality might be more effective.

> *One of the most negative thinkers I have ever met used to argue that he wasn't a negative thinker. "I am just a realist," he claimed. "I see others negatively because that is their reality. And I see myself negatively because that is my reality."*
>
> *I tried different approaches with him and didn't get anywhere. Finally I said to him, "Your negative thoughts about everyone are just your thoughts. You don't have any valid proof that what you say is true. You are just making statements, but not proving anything. Challenge your negative thinking about yourself with, 'Perhaps my negative thinking about myself is just a bad habit I picked up years ago. Whether or not what I thought then was valid, right now I can choose to look at myself positively or negatively. Even if I'm not ready to see myself in a positive way, I have no valid argument to prove that my negative view of myself is really true.'"*
>
> *The fellow smiled when he heard this. "I have to admit that you have a good point. I have to think about it more; maybe my negative attitude is just a problem with the way I think , not a reflection of the reality."*

Boosting Yourself by Lying and Exaggerating

Some people who crave the admiration, respect, and esteem of others might greatly exaggerate or even lie about their achievements and accomplishments. They love to boast, but they don't feel that they have enough to boast about. So they make up stories about themselves in order to appear better to others.

Besides the problems caused by not telling the truth, this pattern also has a very basic problem: it is tremendously destructive to the speaker's own self-image. The very fact that a person has to make up stories to appear better than he is sends a message to himself, "Your true self isn't good enough."

A person who exaggerates or makes up positive stories about himself for some practical gain, like getting hired for a job, is doing the wrong thing, but he is not trying to fool himself. He is trying to deceive someone else for his own personal benefit. But when a person fabricates positive things about himself in order to make a better impression, he is really adding a negative impression of himself to his self-image.

The antidote to this pattern is to be resolved to be absolutely honest when talking about yourself. If you want others to admire you, respect you, and hold you in positive esteem, actually *do* things that others will admire and respect. Even more important: Do things to gain your own respect. When you have a high level of self-respect, you won't have such a strong need to gain the admiration, respect, and esteem of others. You certainly wouldn't want to attain them with lies and falsehoods.

Lying about oneself to gain more self-esteem can't possibly work. You would know the truth. This would be similar to a person printing up forged money, but not to deceive someone else financially. The person is too honest to do that. And the person doesn't want to go around with the fake money just to show off to others that he has a lot of money. Rather, the person wants to feel wealthy. So he prints fake money to convince himself that he is wealthy. Who is he trying to fool when he tries to do this? Himself? But, ultimately, that's really impossible to do. Even when we feign positive self-image, it is primarily for the purpose of shaking our false negative self-image.

The need to appear in a positive light can be used to motivate a person to do positive things. These are things that one should do anyway, for the right reasons. But if a person isn't doing them for the best reasons, doing them to gain the respect of others is a step in the right direction. Eventually a person could do the positive things for more elevated motivations.

> *Someone once told a rabbi that he frequently made up stories about himself. He would tell people about his heroic actions, his many acts of kindness, and his intellectual achievements. The common factor in all of his stories: They weren't true. He felt that he was almost a pathological liar. Even though he had no practical benefit from making up these stories, he felt a strong urge to make himself sound so much better than he actually was.*
>
> *Now he was feeling totally awful about himself because he was such a liar. His self-image was zilch, absolutely zero.*
>
> *"It's just the opposite," the rabbi told him. "Before, when you tried to make yourself sound better by telling lies about yourself, you felt good but really you had reason to feel bad about yourself. You were making up a fantasy and trying to pass it off as the truth. Now that you are facing yourself as you really are, and you feel bad that you lied, you are really being truthful about yourself. This is a courageous step. You now do have a reason to see yourself in a more positive light. You are a person whose self-image is on the way to being healed. You are acknowledging the real you. And as you keep speaking and acting with this honesty, you will have many valid reasons for feeling better about yourself."*

"Albert Einstein Never Won Any Football Games"

A sports writer once wrote: "Albert Einstein never won any football games."

This is a true statement. It's a statement that might seem absurd at first. That statement is being taken out of its context here because of its value in the context of self-image.

Before explaining how that statement can be helpful for self-image, it's worth mentioning another fact about Albert Einstein. When Einstein was in high school, he didn't do very well in his Greek grammar class. His teacher was frustrated with him and told him that he would be a failure in life because of his lack of intellect.

That teacher is now infamous because of his pessimistic prognosis for his now world-famous student.

Einstein's sister later commented, "That teacher was partially right. My brother never did become knowledgeable in Greek grammar."

Einstein was brilliant in physics. He creatively came up with theories and the formula $E=MC^2$. The name and image of Einstein are synonymous with genius.

What is the lesson here? That people can do poorly in some areas yet excel in other areas. People can be highly knowledgeable and skilled in some areas and not in others.

Don't allow lack of talents, skills, and abilities in certain areas define who you are as a total person. Find your own strengths. Look for ways to have a positive sense of self.

As a child, someone might not know what other children know. He might not have developed skills and talents that his classmates, friends, and relatives have developed. But over time he will be able to gain the knowledge that he is motivated to master and develop the skills and talents that are important to him.

Even people who don't have a natural ability can learn to excel if they put in the effort. Every time we use our minds to learn something, we build up our brains. Repetition is the key.

Keep your major focus on what you already know and can do. Let this be a key element in your self-image.

> *Someone once told me that he wasn't very smart. He actually considered himself stupid. The way this person was talking, I thought he was going to tell me that he dropped out of high school, so I asked him, "What is your level of education?"*
>
> *He surprised me when he said, "I graduated college."*
>
> *"In what area was your degree?" I asked.*
>
> *Again, he surprised me when he said, "In Math and Science."*
>
> *"How well did you do?" I asked.*
>
> *"I got a perfect 4.0 average, and I graduated number one in a graduating class of over 800 students," he replied.*
>
> *"I don't understand," I said, puzzled. "How can you consider yourself stupid when you did so well in difficult subjects?"*
>
> *"You see," he replied, "I have a brother who is a few years older than I am. He is a creative genius. I'm not. I've always considered myself to be stupid, and I still do."*
>
> *This conversation happened many years ago. It sticks out in my mind as a situation when someone who is objectively very bright and has a great memory consistently put himself down because he compared himself to a brilliant brother.*
>
> *Everyone else considered this person bright. He could do things that his brother wasn't able to do. But because he had thought of himself as stupid when he was young, he kept repeating this thought even after he grew up and excelled.*
>
> *Always keep in mind that you are unique. You can do things that others can't. Even if you've put yourself down for what you couldn't do and didn't know, this very moment you can begin to see yourself in a more positive light.*

If a Jewish Doctor From Vienna Would Have Spent a Month in a Yeshiva

In the early 1900's, a Jewish doctor living in Vienna wanted to understand the human mind. He knew nothing about the science of the brain's biochemistry. He also had no idea that the brain contained over 100 billion neurons (according to the current scientific estimate, but the number could be much greater). He didn't know anything about the ability to scan brainwaves and how, based on what you were thinking at a given moment, your brainwaves would change.

He also didn't know that if someone went to a professional who analyzes dreams, that person would eventually dream dreams consistent with his theories. Analyzing dreams doesn't prove anything about anyone's inner mind, since it's relatively easy for authorities to program one's dreams. On the other hand, thinking and talking more about gratitude, happiness, and joy will make you a happier person and will eventually improve the quality of your dreams.

Without the benefits of later technology, this Jewish doctor asked why some people are depressed and suffer from anxiety, and similar questions. He had good intentions but, compared to what is known today, he knew very little. Although he was Jewish, this doctor hadn't studied in a yeshiva. Therefore he wasn't familiar with much universal wisdom that can be found in Torah writings.

If someone wanted to become a great chef, what kind of person should he study? A great chef, of course. And if someone wanted to become a great musician, what kind of person should he study? A great musician, of course. And if someone wanted to become a great salesperson, who should he study? A great salesperson, of course. And if someone wanted to become a great quarterback, what kind of person should he study? A great quarterback, or at least a coach who knows what a great quarterback needs to know and do.

Now let me ask you another question. If someone wanted to become a joyful person, someone who radiates joy, someone whose mind is full of appreciation and gratitude and happiness, what kind of person should he study? (This is not a trick question.) If you answered: "A joyful person," you are correct.

Unfortunately for many people, this doctor made an important mistake. He was the first of many psychoanalysts who didn't study the most joyful people in Vienna. Nor did he travel far and wide to find people who knew how to be joyful from morning to night despite many life challenges.

If he had studied joyful people, he could have asked how they were able to master joy. He could have asked them about the thoughts, words, and actions that led to joy. He could have found out about the positive approaches their parents used to teach them how to live a joyful life. Then he could have taught his patients and those who would read his books.

His patients already knew how to be depressed, how to be anxious, how to have fears, how to be miserable. They didn't need to learn how to focus on all that was wrong with their thoughts and actions. They did need to learn the skills required to create a mind full of thoughts of happiness, of inner calm and serenity, of confidence and courage.

Now let's imagine what this doctor would have learned had he studied in a special yeshiva for beginners.

He would have learned about making 100 blessings a day. Each blessing is a reminder that the King of the universe gives us something to be grateful for. There are blessings before and after eating. There are blessings for being able to see and for being able to walk. Throughout each day, we add thoughts and words of gratitude, which leads to happiness.

In the morning, the first thing we say when we wake up is that we are grateful for being alive. This is the *Modeh Ani* prayer. It starts the day with an amazingly positive thought.

The Midrash to the last verse in Psalms teaches us that we should praise our Creator for each and every breath. That increases our level of gratitude throughout the day.

In Proverbs 15:15, King Solomon teaches us that when we are grateful for all the good in our lives, we live a life of constant parties.

One day a week we celebrate the creation of the universe. This is what Shabbos is all about. Everything we do for Shabbos is part of this weekly celebration. Everything studied about Shabbos is part of the process of gaining a greater appreciation for the Almighty's creation of the world.

There is potential for much joy in Torah study and in the fulfillment of the mitzvos. If the Austrian doctor had studied in a yeshiva for much longer than a month, he would have been able to develop his Torah knowledge. He would understand why a great Rosh Hayeshiva, the late Rabbi Mordechai Gifter, once said, "The *mashgiach* (rabbinical supervisor) in a yeshiva should have one purpose: to tell the students who are so enthusiastic about learning new ideas and thinking of creative ideas themselves that they are celebrating too loudly, and they should lower their voices so as not to disturb the other students."

He would have learned about the importance of developing a love for doing kindness. Every act of kindness we do helps others feel better, and gives us positive feelings. This has been proven with brain scans of people doing and receiving kindness. This technological proof didn't exist yet in the early 1900's, but people throughout the ages have experienced the benefits of creating happiness for themselves and others through their kindness.

But what if he didn't feel joyful and enthusiastic when he applied what he was studying?

Then he could have studied the wisdom of Rabbi Moshe Chaim Luzzatto in his classic text, *Mesilas Yeshorim* (*Path of the Just*), published in 1740. In Chapter Seven he would have learned, "External movements arouse inner feelings." That is, act as if you had strong levels of joy and enthusiasm, and then your inner feelings of joy and enthusiasm will increase.

If the doctor would have argued that these weren't his real feelings right then, he probably would have been correct. But in the 1980's it was scientifically proven that when someone acts joyful and is able to emotionally get into this role-playing, his inner biochemistry will actually produce authentic positive feelings. The doctor would not have known of that research, but if he would have benefited greatly by trying out Rabbi Luzzatto's advice. He would have started to see how much more joyful he could be by continuously speaking and acting with greater and greater levels of joy.

The doctor from Vienna would have learned more about the great Talmudic scholar Rabbi Akiva, and how he taught us to realize that even problematic and difficult situations are eventually for our benefit.

He would have learned that one of the highest priorities of life is to continuously develop our character. Every difficult life situation is meant to challenge us, to help us develop ourselves, which changes our emotional experience of the situation.

He would have learned more about the power of prayer. He would have learned that every time we pray, we connect with the Creator. This expands our self-image and elevates each day.

He would have learned more about the meaning of life. He would have understood that this sense of meaning enhances every moment of life.

When the doctor from Vienna would think about his self-image, he would have learned in yeshiva that he, like every other human being, was created in the image of the Creator. He would have realized that every patient he had ever spoken to had immense worth. He would see the great potential of each person, just as Rabbi Yochonon saw the great potential of Reish Lakish.

And if he had studied Torah in a yeshiva, he would have had all the Torah that he studied in his own subconscious mind. Every holy book that he read would have been stored in his inner mind. Every Torah lecture he listened to would have been stored in his inner mind. His entire view of what is in our subconscious minds would have been more elevated.

Even though this doctor didn't merit studying in a yeshiva, you, the reader, can study what he would have studied. And then your self-image could be, "The Torah knowledge I have about gratitude and joy, about viewing life with wisdom, and about my self-image, will give me more joy and a higher self-image than I would have gained from studying the Viennese doctor's books. All the Torah knowledge that I have read and heard is in my brain, and my brain is always with me."

A Formula for Self-Development: G.T.S.S.=B.R.A.I.N.

The field of self-development is so vast and deep that it can seem overwhelming. I have summarized key elements of this book in the following mnemonic device: G.T.S.S.= B.R.A.I.N.

The first part of the formula stands for: **G**oals, **T**raits, **S**tates, **S**elf-image.

The second part of the formula stands for: **B**eliefs, **R**ight way, **A**ction, **I**magination, **N**ow.

Now let's look at the four factors that are in the first part of the formula.

Goals: Your goals are all that you want to accomplish and achieve. Your goals include your mission statement about your life. Your goals include your dreams for yourself.

Traits: Your character traits are the essence of who you are. Your traits are the patterns of your thoughts, feelings, words, and actions. Identify with your positive traits, and overcome your negative traits.

States: You are always in a mind/body state of being. This is more than the words and concepts of feelings, moods, or emotions.

The states of your emotions and thoughts at any given time decide how you experience any given moment.

Your positive states give you a higher quality of life. Greater mastery of your states, which is a long-term, lifetime goal, means that you will be able to experience more happiness and joy, more confidence and courage, more inner calm and serenity, greater concentration and focus, and more elevated and spiritual feelings. It is one of the most important skills that you can master.

Self-Image: The way you view yourself decides what you can do and accomplish in life. Building your self-image enables you to make and reach greater goals. Building your self-image gives you a greater ability to develop and refine your character traits. Building your self-image will enable you to gain greater mastery over your mind/body states.

Now let's look at the five factors in the second part of the mnemonic formula.

Beliefs: Your beliefs are your thoughts, your attitudes, your mindsets, your concepts, your cognitions, and your perspectives.

Your self-image consists of beliefs about yourself. Your beliefs about setting and reaching goals can either help bring out more of your potential, or needlessly limit you. Your beliefs about your character traits will help you continue to develop them — when you believe in your ability to choose the thoughts, feelings, words, and actions that comprise the ideal traits and attributes. Your beliefs about your ability to master your emotional states can either help you gain greater mastery or can limit you.

Right way: The words "right way" refer to two points.

• Go in the right direction to bring out more of your potential.

Go in the direction of building yourself, go in the direction of health, go in the direction of developing positive character traits, go in the direction of greater mastery of positive emotional states, and go in the direction of building your self-image.

• Know the right way to do things to reach the positive outcomes and results that you seek.

When it comes to self-image, it is very important to know specifically how to build a positive self-image and how to keep traveling in the right direction.

Action: Taking action is the only way to make and reach positive goals, to achieve and accomplish, to do acts of kindness, or to make positive things happen in the world.

A person may have great ideas, great aspirations, great wishes, and great hopes; only by taking action will they become reality. You need the energy to take action to actualize ambitious plans.

Imagination: Visualize yourself having the character traits that you want. Visualize yourself reaching your goals and dreams.

Visualize yourself experiencing the positive emotional states that you want. Visualize yourself being kind and compassionate, or having confidence and courage. Visualize yourself reaching your goal as you continue to build your self-image.

When you think about the past, you use your imagination. Use it wisely and beneficially. When you think about the future, you use your imagination. Use it wisely and beneficially.

Now: You are always in the present. In the present, you make all your choices and decisions. Choose wise thoughts, feelings, words, and actions now. This builds your life and builds your self-image.

The final part of this self-development formula is: Continuously improve your Beliefs, Right way of doing things, Actions, Imagination, and focus in the here and Now, and then you will continue to reach your Goals, and you'll continue to improve your positive Traits, emotional States, and Self-image.

I wish you tremendous success in applying this formula for your own personal development and in being able to help many people throughout your life.

I strongly recommend that you read this book a number of times. Each time you read it, you will understand the ideas and concepts in a new, more advanced light.

Positive Play-by-Play Self-Commentary

Our minds often keep running a self-commentary. That is, we keep talking to ourselves about what we are saying and doing, what others are saying and doing, and what we are experiencing.

Some people aren't aware that they often run negative self-comments. This self-commentary is automatic. When things don't go the way they would wish, when they make mistakes, or when they see other people saying and doing things, they make negative comments to themselves.

They even make negative comments about something positive they just did. They might say, "I was just lucky." "This good thing won't last." "Others do much better than I do." "I should have done a better job on this." "I hardly do anything right."

Make a strong decision to consistently run a positive play-by-play self-commentary. By keeping this up, you will be conditioning your mind in positive ways. This is a fantastic way to build a positive self-image.

If you do this many times throughout the day, you will find that your entire life will improve. You will be improving your entire self-image: "I am a person who consistently makes positive comments on what I do and what is happening to me."

Consistent positive self-commentary will enable you to build up your level of gratitude and joy, your level of confidence and courage, your level of enthusiasm and passion, your level of calm and inner peace, your level of kindness and spirituality, your level of resilience and persistence, and your level of growing from challenges and adversity.

1. "I am grateful that I have food to eat. And I am grateful that I am grateful. This builds my gratitude."

2. "Right now I am going to make a blessing before I eat this food. This builds my connection with the Creator."

3. "As I eat, I will be happy that I have this food to eat. Being happy for the food I eat gives me many opportunities to increase the amount of happiness stored in my brain."

4. "I just finished eating, so I will joyfully make a blessing after the food. Saying the blessing before and after eating the food, and appreciating the food, make me a more spiritual person."

5. "I hear the telephone ringing. I am joyfully grateful that I can hear and that I am alive. I will repeat this pattern a number of times, and then I will automatically be happier and grateful whenever I hear a telephone ring."

6. "The caller asked me to do him a favor. I appreciate the opportunity to do an act of kindness for someone. This increases my level of love for kindness."

7. "The kindness was more difficult than I had thought it would be. But, the more difficult the kindness, the greater the act. Doing it makes me a kinder person."

8. "Right now I have to do something that I don't feel like doing. In the beginning I wanted to push it off, but I decided that since I have to do it, I will do it with joy. Deciding to do something even when I don't feel like doing it builds up my self-mastery muscles."

9. "I have to buy something now. I am grateful that I have the money to pay for it."

10. "I just began to worry about having more money in the future. I will go from a place of worry to a place of trust in the Almighty. And I will think in terms of abundance. I see that when I start worrying, I have the ability to move my thoughts to a place of trust. This is a great pattern that I am building up right now."

11. "Whenever I have the money that I need, I will increase my sense of abundance. Right now, I am able to manage. I feel great about that. This reminds me to be grateful."

12. "When I worry about how I will manage in the future, I will focus on potential solutions."

13. "I have a good friend who will help me think of solutions. I am grateful for my friend. My friend has done many things for me over a long period of time. I appreciate him and I am grateful that my mind is focusing on thoughts of appreciation."

14. "My friend helped me. I would love to do something positive for my friend. I am grateful that I can reciprocate."

15. "I have to take care of some trivial matter, and it's taking longer than I thought it would. This is another opportunity to build up my patience."

16. "While I wait in line, I will use my mind in ways that will build up my sense of happiness and gratitude, self-confidence and courage, and empowerment and inner strength. I will visualize myself building up my skills and talents."

17. "I see an elderly person over there. I will cheerfully ask if I can do anything to help."

18. "I just thought of my grandparents. I will call them up and ask them if I can do anything for them. One good deeds leads to another. My thinking of being kind in one way reminds me to be kinder in other ways also."

19. "I just remembered a mistake I made yesterday. I will think about ways I can correct that mistake. I learn from mistakes to keep on developing myself. Mistakes are learning experiences."

20. "Right now I have a few extra minutes; what is the wisest use of my time? Every time I ask how I can use my time wisely, I improve the use of my time."

21. "I am going to read more of the inspiring book that I received as a gift. Every time I read good ideas, I have more knowledge and wisdom stored in my brain, and my brain is always with me. I am grateful to the relative who gave me that book."

22. "I just heard an important concept. Let me think of ways I can apply it. Every time I apply what I read and hear, I build my self-image."

23. "I hear that person over there talking enthusiastically about a hobby. I will increase my own enthusiasm about doing good in the world."

24. "I just heard about a potential problem that might arise in our city. I will increase my feelings of courage to be able to handle it. Every difficulty I face is an opportunity to keep developing myself. I appreciate it when things are going smoothly, but it's not realistic to expect everything to go the way I want. Each and every day, I grow from the challenges that I face. I will enjoy the process of growing from each challenge."

25. "Things didn't work out the way I was hoping they would. I am grateful that they did work out better than they might have. I see that I am finding a positive way of looking at the situation. Every time I see a situation in a positive way, I develop my ability to see things with a positive perspective."

26. "That setback was rough. I am now going to bounce back. I see that I am increasing my level of resilience."

27. "For the last ten minutes I was daydreaming about worst-case scenarios. I feel awful now. I will come back to the present and be grateful that what I imagined is not true. I am feeling relieved. I am

building up my realization that my thoughts create my feelings. I will focus my mind on thoughts that enhance my life."

28. "Right now, I will ask myself, 'What is the wisest thing for me to think, say, and do right now?' This is one of the best questions I can ask myself throughout the day. Every time I ask it, I am making this question a greater part of who I am. I am building my self-image as a person who frequently asks, 'What is the wisest thing for me to think, say, and do right now?'"

110
Positively Alphabetical

Your patterns of thinking create the way you think about yourself. Although we have repeated this idea many, many times throughout this book, we need to repeat it yet again.

The more times you repeat a pattern, the easier that pattern is to access from your memory bank. The more you associate words with positive thoughts, the more automatically those positive thoughts come to the forefront of your mind.

For example, let's say you would like to associate the word "positive" with the sentence, "I consistently become more positive in my thinking, speaking, and acting." Now, let's say that this is important to you because you strongly, very strongly, want to behave in positive ways. Therefore, you will frequently say, "Every time I read, hear, or think about the word 'positive' I will immediately think of the sentence, 'I consistently become more positive in my thinking, speaking, and acting.'" How many times will you have to repeat the sentence?

I don't know how long it will take for this pattern to become automatic for you. But since this is a very valuable "positive" association, it's worth repeating a number of times a day over a long period of time. Allow yourself to celebrate and feel joy each time you repeat this sentence, since you are building yourself as you do.

The easiest way to remember positive patterns of thinking is by using the order of the alphabet to list important positive words. Then associate those words with sentences that build your self-image.

Here is a list of positive words in alphabetical order. Sentences that build our sense of self follow each word. The words and sentences are just a beginning. Keep adding more and more words and positive sentences to your own list. Read this list many times, and these image-building sentences will eventually become your automatic way of thinking.

These patterns are a bit repetitive, and that is why they will eventually become automatic after you read this list many times.

One last comment before you read this list of words and related sentences: Read this list as if you were totally joyful and enthusiastic. Even if you don't start out being enthusiastic, as you regularly read this with joy and enthusiasm, you will find yourself becoming a much happier person.

A

ABLE: "There are a lot of positive things that I am *able* to do. I am deeply grateful."

ABUNDANCE: "I have the self-image of a person who knows that the Almighty is constantly bestowing *abundance* upon me, and I am grateful for all aspects of this *abundance*."

ACCEPT: "I *accept* the Almighty's Will for me in all ways, and this gives me inner peace and a life of appreciation and gratitude."

ACCESS: "Every positive emotional state I have ever experienced is stored in my brain. I will continue building up my expertise in *accessing* these states."

ACCOMPLISHMENTS: "Every *accomplishment* builds my self-image and enables me to *accomplish* more and more."

ACTIONS: "The more positive *actions* I do, the more I build myself."

ADD: "Every positive thought I think, word I say, and action I do *adds* up. All the knowledge and skills that I gain *add* up, too. Therefore I am always in the process of building my self-image."

ADVERSITY: "*Adversity* will make me wiser and better and will keep developing my character."

ALERT: "I allow myself to access a state of having an *alert* mind and relaxed body. This enables me to use my mind in the most optimal way."

ALIVE: "As long as I am *alive*, I will keep developing my character and continue to build my self-image."

ALL: "*All* strengths in *all* contexts. Every time I experience any inner strength, that pattern is stored in my brain. My inner mind will become more aware of when I haven't applied my strengths, and then automatically apply *all* strengths in *all* contexts."

AM: "I *am* developing my entire self more and more all the time. I *am* more today than I ever was before, and I will keep on growing and developing who I *am*."

AS: "*As* I choose wiser thoughts, words, and actions, I keep building my self-image."

APPRECIATION: "I *appreciate* all that I can *appreciate*. Every thought of *appreciation* makes me a more grateful person."

ATTITUDE: "Every positive thought that I think strengthens and builds my positive *attitude*."

AUTOBIOGRAPHY: "Every positive thing I say and do is added to my virtual *autobiography*. I keep adding positive words and actions each and every day."

AWARENESS: "I will keep gaining more and more *awareness* of my inner strengths and talents."

B

BE: "I am resolved to *be* and *become* more and more of what I can *be*."

BEST MOMENTS: "As I recall my *best moments*, I will be able to access them by remembering what I thought, said, and did during those *best moments*. My *best moments* build my self-image every time I recall them."

BETTER: "I am becoming *better* and *better* each and every day in every way."

BLESSING: "Every *blessing* that I say connects me to the Creator. I keep looking for opportunities to *bless* other people. I have experienced many *blessings* in my life and I am grateful for each and every one."

BOOK: "All the positive ideas that I've ever read in any *book* are stored in my brain, and my brain is always with me. I remember many of the positive ideas that I've read."

BRAIN: "I am grateful for my magnificent *brain*. Every positive thought, word, and action is stored in my *brain*, and my *brain* is always with me."

BREATH: "I am grateful to my Creator for each and every *breath*. Since I appreciate each *breath*, I always have something to be grateful for."

BUILD: "Every positive thought, word, and action *builds* me, and I keep *building* myself throughout my life."

C

CALM: "Every moment that I am *calm* gives me more *calm* moments to store in my brain. I will become *calmer* in more and more situations. Whenever I need to become *calmer*, I will *calmly* breathe slowly and deeply and repeat the word *'calm'* over and over again."

CAN: "I will keep focusing on what I *can* do; not on what I can't do."

CARING: "Every *caring* word that I say to others makes me a more *caring* person."

CELEBRATE: "I *celebrate* every personal victory of developing my character."

CHALLENGES: "Every *challenge* I face helps me grow and develop myself. I see myself handling each and every *challenge* in ways that build my self-image."

CHARACTER TRAITS: "My positive choices of thoughts, words, and actions keep developing my *character traits*."

CHESED: "Every act of *chesed* (kindness) that I do for others makes me a kinder person and gives me more joy."

CLOSE: *"Close* your eyes and visualize yourself being the way you wish to be. See yourself speaking and acting in ways that build your self-image."

COMPOSURE: "I am building up my ability to keep my *composure* even when things are not going the way I wish."

COMPUTER: "My brain is an amazing *computer*. Every positive thing I've ever done is stored in my brain. Every positive inner strength and all the positive things I've ever heard or read are stored in my brain. My brain is always with me, and I can access my best ways of being whenever I choose."

CONFIDENT: "Each and every day I am more and more *confident*. Every moment of *confidence* is stored in my brain, and my brain is always with me. I learn from other people who are *confident*. I am much more *confident* now than I was when I first started out in life."

COURAGE: "I have already spoken and acted with *courage* many times throughout my life. Every time I speak and act with *courage*, I become a more *courageous* person. I will frequently visualize myself speaking and acting with *courage* in more and more situations. The more times I practice speaking and acting *courageously*, the more *courageous* I become. I will imagine what it will be like to be a tremendously *courageous* person with a wise balance. Just thinking about this stores the pattern in my brain. My *courage* is becoming stronger and stronger all the time."

CREATE: "I *create* myself with every positive word that I say and action that I do."

CREATOR: "The *Creator* loves me, and I love the *Creator*. I have inherent worth because I am created in the *Creator's* image."

D

DAY: *"Day* by *day* I am growing and developing myself in important ways."

DETERMINATION: "I keep increasing my *determination* to do much good in my life."

DIFFICULT: "The more *difficult* something is, the greater I become if I do it anyway."

DIFFICULT PEOPLE: *"Difficult people* are my partners in helping me develop my total self."

DIGNITY: "I will maintain my *dignity* whether or not things go my way."

DISAPPOINTMENTS: "I will grow from *disappointments* and keep developing my character, which is what life is all about."

DO: "Every positive action I *do* builds me. I will keep *doing* many positive things each and every day."

DON'T YET KNOW: "Whatever I *don't yet know*, I can learn."

DREAMS: "In my *dreams* I will see myself becoming more and more like the person I wish to be."

E

EACH: *"Each* and every day I keep developing myself more and more."

ENERGY: "My positive *energy* will keep increasing and this will enable me to do many positive things."

EMPOWERED: "Each time I speak and act in an *empowered* way I become a more *empowered* person. I will think of *empowered* role models from whom to learn. I visualize myself thinking, speaking, and acting in more *empowered* ways."

ENCOURAGEMENT: "I appreciate everyone who ever *encouraged* me. Those words of *encouragement* keep *encouraging* me throughout my life. I will *encourage* others to keep developing themselves."

ENJOY: "I will *enjoy* the entire process of developing my thoughts, words, and actions. If I have to do something anyway, I will find ways to *enjoy* doing it."

EXCELLENCE: "I strive for *excellence* in my own unique way."

F

FASCINATED: "I am becoming more and more *fascinated* with how I keep gaining more knowledge and how I keep developing my character."

FEAR: "I will go from thoughts of *fear* to thoughts of courage, empowerment, joy, and serenity."

FEEDBACK: "All *feedback*, positive and negative, helps me develop myself."

FIND: "I will *find* what I'm looking for, and I will consistently look for ways to upgrade my thoughts, words, and actions."

FOCUS: "Whatever I *focus* on gets stronger. I will *focus* on happiness and gratitude, and I will become a happier and more joyful person. I will *focus* on improving my thoughts, words, and actions, and this enables me to improve what I do and who I am."

FRIENDS: "I will view each person I encounter as a *friend* who will enhance my life. I will think, speak, and act in a *friendly* manner to everyone. This will upgrade my self-image as a person who finds it easy to make friends."

FUN: "I will have *fun* being all that I can be."

FUTURE: "I will frequently see myself speaking and acting in the *future* the way I wish to speak and act. Each time I do this, I build myself and my self-image."

G

GIFTS: "The Almighty has given me many *gifts*. I will appreciate them greatly."

GIVING: "Every act of kindness makes me a more *giving* person."

GO: "The word 'go' will remind me to think about the positive goals that I would like to be motivated to GO FOR!"

GOALS: "I have already reached many *goals* in my life. Each *goal* I reach makes it easier for me to reach more *goals*. I visualize myself reaching more and more positive *goals*. I keep building the inner resources that will help me make and reach many more *goals*."

GOOD: "I keep asking myself, 'What is a *good* thing to do now?'"

GRATEFUL: "I become more and more *grateful* each and every day. I have much to be *grateful* for. I am *grateful* to the Creator. I am *grateful* to all the people who have helped me throughout my life."

GREAT: 1. "Each *great* moment is added to who I am. Each *great* moment makes it easier for me to speak and act in *greater* ways."

2. "I will learn from every *great* person I meet and read about."

3. "I will think about some *great* things that I can say and do."

H

HABITS: 1. "As I think about the positive *habits* that will enhance my life, I visualize myself speaking and acting in ways that are consistent with those positive *habits*."

2. "As I think about the negative *habits* that I would like to stop, I increase my motivation to stop doing what is best for me to stop."

HAPPINESS: "Every *happy* moment I've ever experienced is stored in my brain. And each *happy* moment makes me a *happier* person. Every time I choose to be *happier* it makes it easier for me to choose to be *happy* again."

HARD: "If a positive action is *hard* for me to do, I develop my character and build my self-image as I do it."

I

I: "*I* am created in the image of the Creator. *I* am a child of the Creator. *I* am valuable. *I* will think, speak, and act in ways that build me. *I* will treat others with respect. *I* keep developing myself more and more all the time."

IF: "*If* I can do something once, I can do it again. *If* anyone else can do something, I too can learn to do it. *If* I can imagine doing something positive, I can eventually do it."

IMAGINATION: "In my *imagination* I see myself speaking and acting at my best, and this builds my self-image."

IMPROVE: 1. "I will frequently ask myself, 'What can I do to *improve* today?'"

2. "I will keep *improving* my self-image by *improving* my thoughts, words, and actions."

INNER STRENGTH: "My *inner strength* gets stronger and stronger all the time. This will enable me to speak and act with more *inner strength*."

INSPIRATION: "I keep being *inspired* by the words and actions that have already *inspired* me. Each moment of *inspiration* is stored in my brain and my brain is always with me. I talk to myself in ways that *inspire* me."

INTENSIFY: "I will *intensify* my will to have great self-mastery and this will build my self-image."

J

JOY: "Every *joyful* moment makes me a more *joyful* person. I create more and more *joy* in my life with the positive thoughts that I think, the positive words that I say, and the positive actions that I do."

JOY OF LEARNING: "My *joy of learning* enables me to experience tremendous joy throughout my life."

JUST ONCE: "Whenever I need to gain greater self-mastery, I will make it easier by telling myself, "I only need to do it *just once*."

K

KIND: "Every one of my *kind* acts or thoughts makes me a *kinder* person. Every *kind* word that I say makes me a *kinder* person."

KNOWLEDGE: "I gain more and more *knowledge* each and every day."

L

LET GO: "I *let go* of all negative thoughts and move my thoughts to positive, life-enhancing thoughts."

LITTLE: "*Little* by *little* I will upgrade my thoughts, words, and actions. As I do this I build my self-image."

M

MEMORY: "My ability to access what is stored in my *memory* is getting stronger and stronger. The more I use my *memory*, the easier it becomes for me to access more of what I have stored in my magnificent brain."

MIDDOS (character traits): "Each and every life event and situation is an opportunity for me to continue developing my *middos*."

MIND: "My *mind* is precious. With the thoughts that I think in my *mind*, I create my life. I will fill my *mind* with positive and elevated thoughts."

MIRROR: 1. "I smile and wave at every *mirror* to increase my level of happiness and joy."

2. "I will *mirror* excellence to excel."

MINDSET: "I will continuously develop the *mindsets* that I wish to develop. This will enable me to think, speak, and act the way that I wish."

MISTAKES: "I will learn from each and every *mistake* to continue improving."

MORE: "I will do *more* and *more* good all the time."

MY: "*My* thoughts, words, and actions are becoming more and more the way I wish to be. Knowing this keeps building *my* self-image."

N

NEVER: "I will *never* allow the negativity of others to become my reality. The negativity of others will serve as a reminder for me to be more positive."

NEXT: "Whenever I needlessly think negative thoughts, I will say the word, *NEXT*! and choose more positive thoughts."

NO: "I will say 'NO' to negativity."

NOTHING: "*Nothing* anyone says or does will lessen my awareness of my tremendous intrinsic value."

NOW: "I am always in the *now*, and *now* I choose positive thoughts, words, and actions."

O

ONCE: "As soon as I do anything positive just *once*, it is stored in my brain and my brain is always with me."

ONE: "The Holy *One* is my Father, my King, Creator and Sustainer of the universe. He wants me to recognize that He loves me and that I am created in His image."

OPPORTUNITIES: "I will seek and find *opportunities* to keep developing myself."

OPTIONS: "I keep asking myself, 'What are my positive *options* for now?' As I choose positive *options*, I build my self-image."

OTHERS: "I will think of more and more positive things that I can do for *others*. Every time I do something for *others*, I build my self-image."

OUTCOME: "I will think and speak about the *outcomes* that I want, and this will enable me to accomplish more."

OUTSTANDING: "Every time I say or do something *outstanding*, it builds my self-image."

P

PAST: "When I think of the *past*, I will recall the positive events of my life and the strengths and inner resources that I have gained. I will keep building on what I did properly in the *past*. The good and positive I do in the present upgrades who I am from now on."

PATIENCE: "Every time I am *patient*, I have more *patience* stored in my brain. I am becoming a more *patient* person each and every day. Thinking about being *patient* builds my *patience*."

PERSISTENCE: "I think about how much I will gain by being more *persistent*. Every time I *persist*, I see myself as being a more *persistent* person."

POSITIVE: "Every *positive* thing I say and do builds me. I say and do more *positive* things each and every day."

POWER: "I will keep using the *power* of my amazing brain to become the way I wish to be."

PRESENT: "I am always in the *present*. In the *present* I choose my thoughts, words, and actions wisely. This keeps building my self-image."

PRESSURE: "When I am under *pressure*, it brings out the best in me. I access a state of being centered, focused, and flowing, and handle it all with an inner self-confidence. I will read this over and over and visualize this pattern until it becomes my automatic reaction."

PRETEND: "Whenever I need to do something that I find difficult to do, I will *pretend* that I can do it. Whenever I am able to do something by *pretending* that I can do it, I will actually be able to do it."

PRIORITIES: "I am aware of my *priorities* and think, speak, and act in ways that are consistent with my priorities."

Q

QUESTIONS: "I frequently ask myself questions that bring out my best. A question I often ask myself is, 'What would be a wise question to ask now?'"

QUOTATIONS: "What are my favorite wise *quotations*? I will ask others: 'What are your favorite wise *quotations*?' Every wise *quotation* I have stored in my brain adds to my self-image."

R

REACH: "*Reach* for the stars. I might not catch any, but at least I won't get my hands in the mud. I'll enjoy the process of *reaching* high."

RECORDINGS: "All the positive ideas that I've ever heard in *recordings* are stored in my brain, and my brain is always with me. I remember those ideas better all the time."

RESPECT: "I will think about other people with *respect*. I will talk *respectfully* to and about everyone. The more I *respect* others, the more *respectful* of a person I become."

ROLE MODELS: "Every time I see or read about a *role model* who acts the way I wish to be, I will integrate that person's pattern into my mind and brain. The more I do this, the easier it will be for me to speak and act with those patterns."

S

SEE: "I will keep *seeing* myself being the way I wish to be. This raises my sense of self. I know that I am conditioning my mind in great ways."

SELF-IMAGE: "Each and every day I will say and do things that build my *self-image*. My *self-image* is great because I am created in the Almighty's image and I am the Almighty's child. I have tremendous worth and inherent value."

SELF-MASTERY: "Every time I experience *self-mastery* by refraining from saying or doing anything, or experience *self-mastery* by saying or doing something that is difficult for me, I am building my *self-mastery*. I have already had a multitude of *self-mastery* experiences, and I will continue to have more and more each and every day."

SELF-RESPECT: "I will consistently talk in ways that are *self-respecting* and respectful of others."

SELF-TALK: "My *self-talk* encourages and inspires me to be and do my best. My *self-talk* is going to make me a more joyful person with a positive self-image."

SERENE: "Each and every moment that I am *serene* makes me a more *serene* person. I frequently recall other moments that I have been *serene*. As I become more and more *serene*, my mind works better and better and it becomes easier for me to develop my entire self."

SHABBOS: "Every time I say or hear the word *Shabbos*, I gain a deeper appreciation for the Creator and His Creation. The world was created for me and I am grateful for all that I benefit from the world."

SLEEP: "Before I go to *sleep* I will think of positive ideas and statements."

SLOW: "*Slow* and steady leads to great things."

START: "Whenever I hear and read about positive patterns, I will *start* thinking, speaking, and acting that way. What are some of the positive patterns that I would like to *start*?"

STOP: "I will *stop* the thoughts, words, and actions that prevent me from being all that I can be. What are some of the negative patterns that I would like to *stop*?"

STORIES: "The *stories* I hear about the positive words and actions of others builds my self-image as a person who wants to emulate positive patterns."

STRONGER: "My inner strength is getting *stronger* and *stronger* each and every day."

SUCCESS: "Each *success* I have teaches me more about my inner strengths and capabilities. Each small *success* helps build my self-image."

T

TALK: 1. "I will *talk* in ways that bring out the best in myself and others."

2. "All the positive *talks* that I have heard are stored in my brain. My brain is always with me. I remember the essence of those positive *talks* and they have a positive influence on my thoughts, words, and actions."

THIS: *"This*, too, will upgrade my self-image."

THOUGHTS: "My *thoughts* create the entire quality of my life. I will keep *thinking* with the patterns of *thoughts* that enhance my entire life. I will *think thoughts* that increase my inner joy and build my self-image."

TIME: "I keep asking myself, 'What is the wisest use of my *time* right now?'"

TODAY: *"Today* I will make wiser choices of thoughts, words, and actions."

TOMORROW: *"Tomorrow* I will continue to improve myself. I will visualize myself being all that I wish to be *tomorrow*. As I live today in the best possible way, I will be preparing for *tomorrow*."

TORAH: "My goal is to make the *Torah* concept of the inherent value of each person my self-concept, and view everyone as children of the Almighty."

TRUST: "I will keep increasing my level of *trust* in the Almighty. This will enable me to experience more inner peace and greater happiness."

U

UNDERSTANDING: "I gain greater *understanding* of what I need to think, say, and do to bring out the best in myself and others."

UNIQUE: "I am *unique*. I am one of a kind. Therefore I don't need to compare myself to anyone else."

V

VALUABLE: "I am a *valuable* human being. My *value* as a person is a gift from the Creator and no one can take it away."

VALUES: "I am aware of my top *values* and consistently act according to those *values*. My self-image is that I have important *values* and this is who I want to be."

VICTORIES: "I will celebrate each personal *victory* of character development. Each spiritual *victory* raises me spiritually."

VISUALIZATION: "I keep *visualizing* myself speaking and acting the way that I wish to be. I use my power of *visualization* to make and reach great goals."

W

WHAT: "*What* can I say and do now to develop my self-image?"

WHATEVER: "*Whatever* I can do once, I can do again, because all that I can do is stored in my brain."

WHEN: "*When* I apply more and more of what I know, I will be a happier and more joyful person with refined character traits, and will achieve and accomplish much in my life."

WISDOM: "I gain more and more *wisdom* with all that I study and learn. I become wiser with each life experience."

WISEST: "I keep asking myself, "What is the *wisest* thing to say and do now?"

WORRY: "I will go from thoughts of *worry* to thoughts of joy and courage."

Y

YES: "Every time I say the word *yes*, it reminds me to say 'yes' to becoming better and better.

YET: Whenever I think about any knowledge, skill, or talent that I don't have, I will realize I just don't have it *yet*.

YOU: "*You*, too, are created in the Almighty's image and I will have self-respect and respect for *you* whenever I interact with *you*."

Z

ZEST: "I will live my life with *zest*. This will enhance the entire quality of my life."

ZRIZUS (alacrity; being proactive): "My quality of *zrizus* will give me the energy to use more and more of my potential all the time."

Daily Affirmations to Build Your Self-Image

Affirmations are powerful. As you frequently repeat image-building affirmations, you build your self-image.

Twice a day, once in the morning and once at night, repeat the affirmations listed below. Observe the beneficial ways that you develop your mind and your entire way of being as you say them for thirty days.

People without a positive self-image think limiting thoughts about who they are and what they can do. Nobody purposely repeats image-defeating thoughts in order to condition their own mind negatively. Rather, those limiting and insecure thoughts came about without a conscious decision or effort. But anyone can consciously decide to repeat the following image-building thoughts!

As you repeat these image-building statements frequently, these thoughts become integrated and internalized. After just one reading, they will be stored in your brain, and your brain is always with you for easy access. As you repeat them many times, the neural pathways of your brain that lead to these thoughts will become stronger and stronger. The more often you repeat the affirmations, the easier it will be for you to think of them automatically.

Repeat these messages gently in the beginning, to condition your mind. Then repeat them with extreme enthusiasm and enjoy the entire process. Have fun.

Be patient with this process. Be persistent. Anyone who repeats these messages frequently will eventually find that they have a positive effect.

Some people repeat affirmations just a few times and then wonder why they haven't worked. "I guess I'm not the kind of person that self-statements work for," they state to themselves. They don't realize that saying that conditions their minds to keep the positive messages from working for them! Everybody's self-statements conditions his mind; it's just a question of the content of those statements. It makes sense to repeat self-statements that build your self-image.

The benefit of having these statements in your inner mind is so great that it is worth the time and effort to repeat them many times a day in the beginning. After you integrate these patterns of thought, one or two daily repetitions will keep them fresh in your mind.

Repeating these messages before going to sleep will allow your mind to repeat them without external interruptions.

Some people find it beneficial to record these messages and then listen to them over and over again while they are involved in various activities throughout the day. Some people have their favorite music play in the background as they record these messages.

I wish you tremendous success in conditioning your mind in ways that enable you to live a better life and to have a positive impact on the lives of others.

Repeat these daily affirmations:

- "I keep building and developing my character and my self-image each and every day."
- "Every positive thought I think, positive word I say, and positive action I do is stored in my brain, and my brain is always with me."
- "Every positive action I've done even once, I can repeat again and again."
- "I am gaining greater mastery over my thoughts. I think more thoughts of appreciation and gratitude."
- "I become happier each day as I spread happiness to others."
- "Every positive inner resource I have experienced in any context is always with me and I can access it at any given moment."
- "My choices create me. I will choose my thoughts, words, and actions wisely."
- "My thoughts enable me to become happier and more joyful, calmer and more serene, more confident and more courageous."
- "I have immense value."
- "My immense value is a Divine gift. I have had immense value from my first moment of life and it stays with me my entire life."

- "Nothing anyone says to me can take away my immense value."
- "I am created in the image of the Creator."
- "I am a child of the Creator and Sustainer of the universe."
- "The world was created for me. Therefore I can appreciate the entire universe and I will think, speak, and act in ways that will make the world a better place."
- "Every time I treat another human being with respect and honor, I become a more honorable person myself."
- "Just thinking about how I will speak and act with respect and honor to other people makes me a more honorable person."
- "I will maintain my self-respect in all situations."
- "I will always speak to other people in ways that are self-respecting and respectful."
- "I choose to view myself as a person who is a 10 out of 10. This automatically gives me more confidence and courage."
- "I will speak and act in ways that are an expression of my awareness that I am a 10 out of 10."
- "I will speak and act in the positive ways I wish to be. Every single time I do this I am building myself."
- "All needless limitations and blocks melt away."
- "Since all needless limitations are just from my imagination, in my imagination I will imagine going way beyond those imaginary limitations."
- "My self-talk will consistently build my self-image."
- "My self-talk will consistently build up my level of gratitude and happiness."
- "My self-talk will consistently build up my ability to be calm and serene more and more frequently."
- "When I see my reflection in a mirror, I will point to myself and say, 'You are tremendously valuable.'"
- "When I see my reflection in a mirror, I will say to myself, 'Each and every day you will choose great thoughts, great words, and great actions.'"
- "My thoughts are the key to my self-image and my emotions. I will focus on joyful and empowering thoughts."
- "I will gently move my thoughts to thoughts that enable me to grow and develop myself joyfully."

- "I am a person who is always in the present moment. I presently choose positive thoughts, words, and actions."
- "I am a person who grows from each and every challenge."
- "Every challenge I experience builds my character."
- "If I like the skillful way I handled a challenge, the skill becomes stored in my brain to access whenever I need it."
- "If I'm not satisfied with the way I handled a challenge, I will visualize myself handling challenges better in the future, and this improved way will become my reality."
- "I am a person who bounces back. I bounce back easily and quickly."
- "Everything I do well shows me that there are many more things I can learn to do well."
- "I will automatically learn from someone who has a positive quality and pattern."
- "Every person I ever saw, met, and read about can serve as a positive role model in some way. I can speak in the positive ways that anyone else has ever spoken. I can do the positive things that anyone else has ever done."
- "I will see the positive in other people, and will say and do what I can to build their self-image."
- "I will catch people doing things right and I will enjoy giving positive feedback."
- "My memory is getting better and better all the time."
- "Every positive thing I have seen, read, and heard is stored in my brain and my brain is always with me."
- "When I see something that I want to remember, my inner mind will mentally take a picture and that will be stored in my brain. It becomes easier and easier for me to recall whatever I want to remember."
- "Whenever challenges arise, my mind focuses on solutions and outcomes."
- "My creative mind comes up with wonderful solutions."
- "Every act of courage is stored in my brain. I gain more and more courage each and every day."
- "Whenever I need courage to speak or act, my inner mind easily accesses the courage I need."

- "I mentally see myself being tremendously courageous."
- "I have a core of well-being. My thoughts create my present moment-to-moment experiences. I release thoughts that cause distress and free my mind for calmer and happier thoughts."
- "I am kind. Every kind word and action makes me a kinder person."
- "I am becoming more and more patient."
- "Every time that I am patient makes it easier for me to be even more patient. I think joyful thoughts when I am patient."
- "I am becoming more and more self-confident all the time."
- "I think more and more self-confident thoughts."
- "I speak with self-confidence and I act with self-confidence."
- "Every self-confident person I meet shows me how to be more and more self-confident."
- "I have tremendous joy every time I am self-confident."
- "I am becoming more and more empowered all the time. I think, speak, and act the way an empowered person thinks, speaks, and acts."
- "I am resolved to be joyful."
- "Every joyful moment makes me a more joyful person."
- "I think, speak, and act the way a joyful person thinks, speaks, and acts."
- "I apply the wisdom I have stored in my mind more and more each and every day."
- "I make and reach great goals."
- "I enjoy the entire process of making and reaching goals."
- "Every success and personal victory expands my self-image."
- "It becomes easier and easier for me to create positive habits of thoughts, words, and actions."
- "It becomes easier and easier for me to overcome negative habits."
- "My self-mastery is becoming stronger and stronger."
- "Each experience of self-mastery strengthens my ability to have self-mastery."
- "I will choose to speak and act in positive ways. I will repeat these patterns over and over again and they will become part of me."
- "Every situation and occurrence will help me develop my character."

- "Each day of my life will be a meaningful day for me."
- "I continuously strive to keep improving and developing myself."
- "I am always in the present. That means that as I read this I am in the present. I presently resolve to keep increasing my level of happiness and joy; my level of being calm, relaxed, and serene; my level of being self-confident and having courage; and my level of being kind and compassionate."
- "I feel wonderful and terrific; good and great! I feel wonderful and terrific; good and great!"
- "Each and every day I will fill my mind with thoughts of gratitude and happiness."
- "Each and every day I will choose to speak and act in ways that keep developing my self-image."

Index

A.D.D., positive aspects 253
Able to persevere 91-93
Abraham, guest of 68
Absent minded remember brain 76
Accents 103
Accepted me the way I was 159
Access inner strengths 78
Access positive states 269
Accomplishment oriented 111-112
Accomplishments 30
Accurate self-knowledge 136-141
Achieve all that you would wish 39
Achievement of conquering anger 281
Achievements for happiness 267
Acknowledging the truth 134
Act as if you had a positive self-image 53-58
Act joyfully 268-269
Act like a confident person 224-228
Act the way you wish to be 53-58
Acting in Purim play 110
Acting joyful to experience joy 322
Action to accomplish 325
Actions influence us 53-58
Actions, choosing 84-85
Add the word "yet" 107-108
Add to meaning of what you do 81
Adding wisdom to mental library 83
Adversity, greater than Superbowl victory 268
Affirmations to build self-image 345-50
Afraid to refuse requests 155
African Violets built self-image 292-3
Aharon, happy for Moshe 177
Aharon of Karlin, Rav 30
Aharon treated people with respect 123
Airplanes were a goal 73

Akiva, Rabbi, all for the good 217
Akiva, Rabbi, and the rock 92
Akiva, Rabbi, meeting 67
Aleph bais 82-83
Alert mind, relaxed body 213-214
Algebra as anchor 275
All aspects of life 19
All I need to do 183
All inner strengths in all contexts 76-79
All or nothing attitude 99
All start as newborns 184-185
All you need 76-77
Almighty loves you 19, 32-34
Almighty's perspective 17-18
Alphabet 82-83
Alphabet, positive conditioning 330-344
Already doing many positive things 88
Already thought positive thoughts 117-119
Alzheimer's disease of a president 135
Ambition and energy 73
Anchors, negative to positive 274-278
Anger anchors 274-278
Anger and arrogance 134
Anger and positive self-image 280-282
Anger, memories of 234
Anger: the Inner Teacher 281
Angry and blaming 306-308
Another way to view 143
Any time in your life 78
Applause 125-127
Apply your knowledge and wisdom 42-43
Appreciation, gifts and strengths 133
Appreciation leads to happiness 263-270
Appreciation of our planet 68-69
Approval of others 125-127
Arousing envy 135

Arrogance and humility 132-136
Arrogance leads to anger 134
Article to help you improve 42
As a newborn baby 121-122
As long as it takes 94
Ask questions 73
Ask respectfully 191
Asking for a favor 191
Asking for what you want 190-192
Aspirations and dreams 39
Aspirations, highest as prayer 70
Assertive once 98
Assertive respectfully 190-192
Assertive when wants to be 190-192
Association for memory 301
Associations, creating positive 330-344
Assume others will like them 283
At any given moment 41
At least I made them feel bad 199-200
Athletes breaking records 64
Attaining goals 73
Attitude, all or nothing 99
Attitude, if anyone can do it, so can I 101-105
Authentic change of mind 120-122
Authentic modesty 135
Authentic self-image 125-126
Authentic wish to be kind 155
Authority figure 246
Autobiography, writing all the time 41
Automatic value 19
Automatically putting self down 86
Aware of self-worth 29-32
Awful, not as much as you fear 251
Bad feelings about self 244-246
Baharan, Rabbi Avraham 214-215
Balanced attitude towards expectations 235-236
Balanced in all ways 135
Balanced self-knowledge 136-141
Baltimore 268
Bank account and personal value 193-194
Bank robbery witnesses 143-144
Banks, robbing 78
Bannister, four minute mile 77
Basic building blocks 83
Be realistic 99
Become part of worthwhile organizations 218-219
Beeps of car as anchors 277-278
Beginning of the day 163

Believe in ability to attain goals 72-75
Believe you can do things 59-63
Believing in other people 160-162
Believing in your product 186-189
Beneficial impact on son 158
Beneficial thoughts, words, actions 84-85
Benefits of low self-image 145-147
Benefits of self-mastery 128-129
Best in class 195-196
Best in other people 73
Best interests 247
Best moments are best teachers 64-66
Best, the need to be 176
Better than you realize 55
Better to focus on gratitude 114
Beyond initial dreams 103
Beyond wildest imagination 248
Biggest deficiency 252-254
Biochemistry, happiness 265
Biofeedback machine, EMG 115
Biofeedback machine, mirror as 271-273
Biographies, read 66
Bite, one at a time 93
Blaming and angry 306-308
Blaming the student 170
Blaming the victims of anger and insults 306-312
Bless people 177
Blocks, imaginary 59-63
Blood pressure, happiness 264
Boasting 27
Boasting versus sharing success 133-134
Bob Burg 191
Body image 35-36
Body, Soul with a 35-36
Book, didn't get published 215
Book to help you improve 42
Boosting self by lying 316-317
Bored, don't focus well 253
Born with confidence, no one 224-228
Bouncing back 208-209
BRAIN, mnemonics 324-326
Brain stores every positive pattern 98
Brain waves, happiness 264
Breakthroughs 65
Breathing, happiness 264
Brilliant brother 319
Bring out the best 40, 164
Brother is creative genius 319
Build from inside out 245
Build on what you did right 37-40

Build self-image 86-87
Build up strengths 159
Building self-image, high priority 116
Building self-image with stories 172-173
Building your confidence 224-228
Business consultants 59-60
Calm role models 102
Calm, thoughts, words, actions 90
Calm under pressure 232-234
Calming imaginary drink 233
Calming student 169-170
Can do it sometimes 99
Can learn and do more 108
Caring for others' welfare 283
Celebrate small successes 72
Celebration, ultimate 68-69
Centered, focused, flowing 259
CEO of ICFSW 179-181
Certainly be successful 73
Challenge of money 193-194
Challenge of rejection 247-249
Challenge to help us grow, everything 263
Challenges of life 20
Challenges strengthen 142-145
Challenging life 72
Champion 23
Change entire lifestyle 163
Change of schools 124
Change self-concept 30
Change versus Choosing wisely 84-85
Change what can be changed 265
Charitable organizations, feeling better 146
Chazon Ish and alphabet 82-83
Chazon Ish, harm of excessive modesty 31
Chazon Ish, noticing faults in others 201
Cheerful, thoughts, words, actions 90-91
Child of the Almighty 17
Child with a lot of energy 158
Children listening to you 281
Children, wake up 28-29
Chofetz Chaim, Almighty's love 32-34
Chofetz Chaim and my father 67-68
Chofetz Chaim, aware of own greatness 32
Choices every moment 41
Choose life 84-85
Choose to do more good 41
Choose to make world a better place 79-81
Choosing thoughts, words, actions 84-85
Choosing wisely versus Change 84-85
Chutzpah, positive aspects 253
Clarify your goals 74

Climbing Mount Everest 64
Climbing mountain 40
Clown on screen 233
Club, low self-image 145-147
Coach, believed in people's abilities 106-107
Coach for confidence 224-228
Coach for self-knowledge 141
Coach to reach goals 74
Coach, tough 258-259
Collecting positive states 51
Committee not source of your worth 181
Compared to brother 319
Competitive game, life isn't 174-178
Completing the task 82-83
Complexity of self-knowledge 136-141
Compliment lasting two weeks 27
Computer erased 217
Computer with all inner resources 223
Conceit and humility 132-136
Concentrate once 98
Concentrating in some contexts 76
Concentrating when distracted 170
Concentration camp survivor 203
Concerned about other people 130-132
Concise list of happiness formula 270
Condescending, never 133
Conditioned 263
Confidence, act as if 79
Confidence building 224-228
Confidence, excessive 230-231
Confident in some contexts 76
Confident role models 102
Consider yourself 10 out of 10 186-189
Considering self stupid 319
Considering self valuable 196
Considering yourself important 29-32
Consistently bring out best 40
Consistently feeling bad about self 244-246
Consistently negative thinking 47
Constantly strive to be better 251
Consult someone who will encourage you 216
Context, each idea has 241-242
Contexts, all inner strengths in all 76-79
Continue practicing 57
Continue to do great things 80
Control what you say 201
Convinced yourself you can't 57
Core issue: feeling bad about self 244-246
Correct your faults 41

Courage, act as if 79
Courage, improving your 221-223
Courage in some contexts 76
Courage to acknowledge mistakes 250-252
Courage to ask for what you want 190-192
Courageous role models 102
Courageous thoughts, words, actions 90
Creating happiness 263-270
Creative, being told, "You are," 158
Creator's image 17-18, 23
Credible people who believe in you 62
Crime to lower self-image 157
Critical parents 60
Critical person, being around 113-116
Crying shows feelings 290-291
Current self-image 41
Daily affirmations to build self-image,
Daily do the difficult 204-205
Daily question, improvement 70
Dealing with disappointment 217
Declare you have high self-image 195-196
Dedicated to have high self-image 195-196
Deep down wanted to be good 169
Deep resolve 125
Defective, believed self to be 159
Deficiency's positive aspects 252-254
Deming, Edward 71
Dentist, patient doesn't show up 314
Determination motivates 207
Detrimental thoughts 42
Develop a life mission 72
Develop character when facing challenges
  268
Develop greater confidence and courage
  108
Developing yourself by doing the difficult
  204-5
Diamond's value 17-18
Did you change already 85
Difference in someone's life 237-239
Different choices 84-85
Different versions of what happened 143
Difficult things 204-205
Dilemmas 35
Diploma of self-worth 181
Direction, right 325
Direction you are headed 41
Directions, not asking 230
Dirt in mouth 163
Disappointments 215
Disappointments, keep going 91-93

Discounting positive statements 61
Discouragement 260-261
Discouragement, keep going 91-93
Discuss disagreements 245
Distress, needless 266
Distress of rejection 247-249
Distressful memories 288
Divide tasks into small segments 253
Divrei Hayomim, first verse 65
Do things that are difficult 204-205
Do you know the alphabet? 82
Doctor from Vienna 320-323
Doctor with excessive confidence 230
Does what's difficult 231
Doesn't yet believe in own potential 161
Dog as anchor 274-275
Doing a lot for lazy person 109-110
Doing even more kindness 154
Doing what you love to do 75
Doll contest, winning 147
Don't know that yet 107-108
Don't need external factors 195
Don't needlessly limit yourself 20
Don't persevere, won't reach goals 91-93
Don't put yourself down 95
Done right already 157
Donkey sees a great person 202-203
Dreams and aspirations 39
Drink imaginary, for more courage 222
Dripping water 266
Drop in the bucket 83
Drops of water 92
Each drop does something 92
Each human unique 174-178
Each person own version 143
Easier than imagined 192
Easier to look at 85
Easily come to mind 86-87
Easily thrown off balance 232-234
Easy, not 115-116
Eating elephant 93
Eating healthy 210
Edison and light bulb 93
Edison, Thomas 296-297
Edit mental pictures 288
Education, limited 296-298
Education not the key in selling 186-189
Ego driven makes mistakes 134
Einstein, Albert 318-319
Elderly person, sad 239-240
Elderly, respect 294-296

Elephant, eating 93
Elevate the story of your life 41
Elevated and forgiving 289
Elevated for not speaking against others 201
Elevated moments 64
Elevated, thoughts, words, actions 90
Embarrassing others 27
EMG machine 115
Emotional pickup 81
Emotional state, mastered 108
Emotional state to understand 170
Emotional states go up and down 49-52
Emotionally stuck 81
Emperor's son 96
Empowered, thoughts, words, actions 90
Encyclopedia, reading 93
End of the day 163
Energy, doing what you love to do 75
Energy level, Happiness 264
Energy, send positive 284
Energy to study Torah 162-164
English, various accents 103
Enjoy the entire process 235-236
Enjoy the process 191
Enjoy today 270
Enjoying finding weakness 303-305
Enthusiasm, keeping up for four hours 65
Enthusiastic, truly 75
Entire journey 255
Entire picture of your life 41
Entirely new level 152
Entrepreneurs and rejection 249
Erickson, Dr. Milton, Flowers 292-293
Erickson, Dr. Milton, Teaching reading 165-166
Essay on Repentance 121-122
Eternal love of Almighty 32-34
Evaluate situations positively 266
Evaluation of what happened, personal 266
Evening mental exercise 89-91
Evening on a higher path 163
Eventually 256
Everest, climbing 64
Every bit of improvement 145
Every moment make great choices 41
Every positive thought, word, action, builds you 86-87
Every single time 98-99
Every situation is a challenge 142-145
Every small strength 86-87

Everyone has all inner resources 73
Everyone has something you can learn from 133
Everyone has ups and downs 125
Everything external is on the screen of my mind 233
Everything wrong with me 87
Exaggerating about self 316-317
Excessive confidence 230-231
Excessively dependent on reactions of others 125-127
Exercise 210
Exercise to build self 89-91
Existence, therefore you have value 17-20
Expand beliefs what is possible for you 105-107
Expectations 235-6
Experience makes one wise 297
Expert at putting self down 18
Expert at seeing benefit 266
Experts at bringing out best in people 73
Experts at handling disappointment 217
Experts at not reaching goals 74
Express your true belief in people 160-162
External movements, internal feelings 322
Extreme joy, waking up 268
Extremes harmful 139
Fail, if you knew you couldn't 73
Fake money 316-317
Falling, and getting up 208-209
Farrow, Dave and your memory 298-301
Father, and Chofetz Chaim 67-68
Favorite memories 124
Fear anchors 274-278
Fear of disapproval, kindness 155
Fear of making mistakes 250-252
Fear of success 152
Fearful wimp 108
Feel good because of how you want to be 39
Feeling bad about self 244-246
Feeling good a number of times a day 88
Feeling good about kindness 155
Feeling good about ourselves 25-28
Feeling good about self 123-124
Feeling good 246
Feeling worth 26
Feelings and thoughts 51-2
Feelings fluctuate 49-52
Feelings from external movements 322
Feinstein, Rabbi Moshe 32

Felt totally different 152
Fiction, truth stranger than 149
Fifty on a test 37-38
Financial mindset of wealth 63
Find people who do what you want to do 75
Finding solutions 144
Finding weakness in others 303-305
Fines for self-mastery 128-129
Finger snapping to become calm 233
Fingers pressed the wrong computer button 217
First murder 174-175
First step of happiness 265
Five things each day 239-240
Fixing wrong way 25
Flexible people change easily 313
Flowerpots 292
Fluctuation of feelings 49-52
Focus exercise 89-91
Focus on accomplishing 111-112
Focus on improvement 42
Focus on improvements 70
Focus on positive aspects 265-266
Focus on reaching goals 41
Focus on soul 35
Focus on the good 169
Focusing for short amounts of time 253
Focusing in some contexts 76
Focusing on mistakes and errors 250-252
Focusing on shortcomings 157
Food for thought 22
Fooling myself 19
Football games and Einstein 318-319
For a lazy person, you do a lot 109-110
Forgiveness releases resentment 285-287
Formula for creating happiness 265-270
Formula for self-development 324-326
Foundation on which to build 126
Four choices 89-91
Four hundred repetitions 169-170
Four minute mile 77
Fragile self-image 134
Frame of reference 246
Free from arrogance 133
Free from self-consciousness 283
Free will 56
Frequently angry and insulting 306-312
Friendly attitude 191
Friends to reach goals 74
Friends 195-196
Friends, making easily 284
From here not to future 255
Frustrated when trying to help others 71
Function best when happy 264
Fundraiser, isn't 167
G.T.S.S. 50-51
G.T.S.S.=B.R.A.I.N. 324-326
Gain and benefit 266
Gaining more knowledge 82
Game, life isn't competitive 174-178
Game of staying calm 233
General sense of identity, upgrading 59-63
Get together with friends 74
Getting rid of negative thoughts 113-116
Giant, imagine being a 233
Gift, all is a 31
Gift, value as 19
Gifter, Rabbi Mordechai 322
Ginsburg, Rabbi Gavriel 235
Give positive feedback 157
Give the matter thought 110
Giver, not taker 154
Glad you have feelings 290-291
Global positive effect 59-63
Go beyond what we can usually do 64
Goal to gain greater mastery 108
Goals and self-image 50-51
Goals for happiness 267
Goals, making and reaching 72-75
Good about this 266
Good at 124
Good news 248
Good, this is for 266
Grateful that unharmed 143
Grateful thoughts, words, actions 90
Gratitude leads to happiness 263-270
Great four 89-91
Great motivator 83
Great thing about journey 255
Great things in my life 238
Great thoughts, words, actions 89-91
Greatest pleasure in life 71
Greatness of your thoughts 80
Greatness stored in you 20
Greet people joyfully 157
Grew up with low self-image 110
Guest of Abraham and Sarah 68
Guinness Book of World Records 65-66, 299
Handicaps not stopping 103-105
Hands in the mud 235

Happiness, developing 263-270
Happy moments 64
Harm of excessive modesty 31
Harmony with others 264
Harsh pattern of speaking 198
Having a low self-image 43-47
Having versus thinking pattern 43-44
He might have been correct 161
Healing way of talking 198-199
Health, a challenge 142
Health oriented choices 210-211
Healthy self-image with modesty 135-136
Healthy sense of self 28
Heartbeat, happiness 264
Help out positive cause 167
Help people believe in themselves 160-162
Help people raise self-image 156-160
Helping humanity 80
High expectations 235-236
High level of courage 221-223
High priority to build self-image 116
Highest dreams and aspirations 39
Hill, Napoleon 297
Hillel, bathhouse 210
Hillel, meeting 67
History of your life 65
Hobbies 74
Honest when talking about self 316-317
Honking of car as anchors 277-278
Honor and glory 195-196
Honor from others 125-127
Honor others 22-25
Honorable person 22-25
Hormones, happiness 264
How long does it take 94-98
How we see ourselves now 163
How would you be? 39
Human beings have intrinsic value 196
Humanity, helping 80
Humans infinitely changeable 62
Humble 248
Humility, all is a gift 31
Humility and arrogance 132-136
Humility, conceited for studying 141
I am building my self-image 86-88
I am grateful to Rabbi Pinkus 158
I am my choices 182-183
I am no longer this person 121
I am servant of Almighty 121
I can's 64-65
I can'ts 64-65

I don't know that much 82-83
I don't like myself 182
I understand if it's too difficult 191
I will live my life with a high self-image 195-197
I.Q. not the key in selling 186-189
I'm never wrong 134
I'm not all I want to be 182
I'm nothing 18
ICFSW 179-181
Ideal way of being 125-127
Ideals to live up to 126
Identify with positive qualities 41
Identify with positive 59
Identify with soul 35
Identity 51
Identity, best moments 65
Identity change 121
Identity upgrading 59-63
If don't try to accomplish 111-112
If I can do it once 98-101
If only 256-258
If someone else can do it 101-105
If you knew that… 255-256
If you knew you couldn't fail 73
Ignored suggestions 71
Illness, a challenge 142
Image defeating statements 115
Image-building notes 168-169
Imaginary blocks and limitations 59-63
Imaginary courage drink 222
Imaginary mental picture 287
Imaginary video screen 233
Imagination, beyond wildest 248
Imagine being calm 233
Imagine being the way you wish 42
Imagine great coach 58
Imagine you are assertive 190-191
Immature ways of thinking 113-116
Immune system, happiness 265
Impact your life 41
Imperfections, identifying with 157
Importance of considering yourself important 29-32
Important person 30
Important, you are 29-32
Impossible expectations 235-236
Impossible to forget brain 76
Improve level of choosing 89-91
Improve mindset who you are 59-63
Improved mind and outlook 121

Improvement, focus on 42
Improvements, small and tiny 70-72
Improving general sense of identity 59-63
Improving my entire life 251
Improving self-image, how long? 94-98
Improving your courage 221-223
Incapable 30
Increase sense of value and worth 44
Inferior attitude 60-61
Inferior 30
Inferiority complex 58
Infinite love of Almighty 32-34
Infinite value 18
Influence of positive stories 172-173
Influence on you 89-91
Morning mental exercise 89-91
Influence others 20
Influenced by our actions 53-58
Influencing others with intensity of will 206-207
Information that you need 73
Inner attitude of confidence 224-228
Inner good feelings 57
Inner mind, speak to 78
Inner resources 73-74
Inner security 135
Inner value 191
Insecurity 245
Inside out 245
Inspiration, some benefits stay 164
Inspiring approach 38
Inspiring life mission 72
Inspiring music 269
Inspiring suggestions 122
Inspiring thoughts 118
Insufficient to say, "Feel good about self" 24424-6
Insulting and angry 306-312
Insulting people 26
Integral part of greatness 256
Intelligent for avoiding mistakes 231
Intensity of will 206-207
Interact best when happy 264
Interests and hobbies 74
International Committee for Self-Worth 179-181
Interrupt negative thoughts 117-119
Interrupting pattern of thinking 249
Interview for job 249
Interview people to find out how they did it 102

Intimidated around people 190-192
Iron man 135
It hasn't worked 116
It's not over 237-238
It's not who I am 109-10
Jewish doctor from Vienna 320-323
Job, didn't get or lost 215
Job interview 249
Journal 302
Journal for self-mastery 128-129
Joy builds self-image 263-270
Joy coach 270
Joyful life focused on progress 40
Joyful moments 64
Joyful person, no competitors 178-129
Joyful person, study, to learn joy 321
Joyful pessimist 278-280
Joyful role models 102
Judging oneself favorably 139
Judgment Day 148-153
Just acting as if you can't 57
Just plain stubborn 312-315
Just saying 241-242
Kamenetzky, Rabbi Yaakov 32
Keep developing good points 157-160
Keep going 91-93
Keep up positive 55
Kind in some contexts 76
Kind role models 102
Kind thoughts, words, actions 90
Kindness, a life of 153-155
Kindness consciousness 130-132
Kindness each day 267
Kindness, many acts 80
Kindness when assertive 191
Knowing dreams 72
Kohain 17-18
Kvetching 24
Lashon hara 200-201
Laughed at as child 287-288
Laughing in class 215
Laughing to feel better 248
Lazy person doing a lot 109-110
Leader of gang of robbers 163
Learn from everyone 101, 178
Learn from goal-setters 73
Learn something valuable 42
Learning to walk 209
Lesson, repeating 400 times 169-170
Letters of Talmud 82-83
Library, reading entire 93

Life, a process of making and reaching goals 72-75
Life enhancing thoughts 113-116
Life experiences get in way 97
Life giving choices 84-85
Life has disappointments 215
Life histories, unique 263
Life history, I can's 65
Life isn't competitive game 174-178
Life mission 17, 72
Life of constant parties 263, 322
Lifelong positive influence on me 158
Lifesaver advice 122
Lifestyle change 163
Lifetime project 41
Lifetime quest for self-knowledge 136-141
Liked and respected, modesty 136
Limitations, imaginary 59-63
Limited education 296-298
Limited self-image and discouragement 261
Limiting beliefs limit 105-107
Limiting role 57
Limiting thoughts, stop thinking 113-116
Lion, upgrade to 152
List of inner strengths 74
List of problematic patterns 87
List of things to be grateful for 265
Logic, changeable 62
Long as it takes 94
Long time ago 74
Long time for words to enter heart 159
Long time to improve 96
Long way to go 71
Longer than you thought 91-93
Looking back 256
Loss of lack of self-mastery 128-129
Love being kind 156
Love for kindness 155, 322
Love to do 75
Love your neighbor as yourself 31
Loves you, Almighty 32-34
Low expectations of self 235-236
Low self-image, benefits 145-147
Low self-image club 145-147
Low self-image created by thoughts 113-116
Low self-image, having 43-44
Low self-image, reasons for 45-47
Luzzatto, challenges 142
Lying about self 316-7

Maintaining old perceptions 109-110
Major difference in someone's life 237-239
Major service to person receiving kindness 80
Make me a Kohain 17-18
Make people feel valued 157
Make the world a better place 79-81
Make the world a kinder place 80
Making and reaching goals 72-75
Making choices 84-85
Making up stories about oneself 316-317
Manhattan, selling of 21
Many forms of accomplishing 111-112
Many opportunities each day 86-87
Many years later 123
Master at focusing on the wrong 263
Mastered emotional states, yet 107-108
Mastermind groups 74
Math as anchor 275
Mature, real you 156
Mean streak 303-305
Meaning of life 28
Meaning of what you do 81
Meaning to life 72-75
Meaningfulness of kindness 130-132
Meditative exercise 89-91
Meet the challenges of life 20
Meeting Hillel and Rabbi Akiva 67
Memories, favorite 124
Memories of the past 287-289
Memory and self-image 298-301
Memory of becoming angry 234
Mental library, adding wisdom to 83
Mental note, alert mind, relaxed body 214
Mental photo album 269
Mentor to reach goals 74
Metamorphosis of turtle 152
Mezuzah 33
Middle of life story 41
Might have been 256-258
Mind's self-commentary 326-330
Mindset who you are, improve 59-63
Mindset, if anyone can to it, so can I 101-105
Mirror confident person 227
Mirror, practice assertiveness 191
Mirrors, smile at 271-273
Mistaken about self 131
Mistakes and errors because of others 306-312
Mistakes because of excessive confidence 230

Modeh ani 265
Model everyone who can do things 102
Moment, each, choosing 84
Moment, new 117
Momentum to continue 73
Money and self-image 193-194
Money and worth 177
Money as a tool 193-194
Money from what you love to do 75
Morning mental exercise 89-91
Moshe's humility 133
Most battered doll 147
Mothers lifting cars 64
Motivate to grow 247
Motivated, being, changes us 163
Motivated, determination 207
Motivated to build self-image 113-116
Motivating approach 38
Motivators as role models 102
Mountain climbing 40
Multitude of things can learn from others 101-105
Murder, first 174-5
Muscle tension, happiness 265
Music, inspiring 269
My true value 18
Natural abilities, lacking 318-319
Need to be the best 176
Need to feel good about self 28
Needless expenses 75
Needless fear 190-192
Needless putdown statements 86
Needlessly low self-image 60
Negative anchors to positive 274-278
Negative feelings towards self 33
Negative message about self 201
Negative self-commentary 327
Negative thoughts, getting rid of 114-115
Negative thoughts prevent happiness 256
Negotiating under pressure 232-234
Nervousness when taking test 214-215
Neural pathways to positive thoughts 114
Never assertive 191
Never feel good about myself 87
Never would have believed 111-112
New choice each moment 84
New, every moment is 117
New inner strengths 78
New mental picture 287-288
New patterns of thoughts, words, actions 163

New York Times photograph 177
Newborns, all are 184-185
Next time 119-120
Next, to thoughts that build self-image 117-20
Nine happiness-creating formulas 265-270
NLP anchors 274-278
No, and self-image 247-249
No guarantee that will accomplish 111-112
No idea what was possible 152
No is just a delay 248
No longer be me 314
No, saying respectfully 155
Nobel Prize 23
Nobody, I'm a 18
Nope 241
Not a matter of time 94
Not certain it will work for me 97
Not claiming it's easy 115-116
Not easy 115-116
Not having thought and acted the way you wished 86
Not intelligent enough 101
Not over until it's over 237-238
Not required to complete 82-83
Not thinking about self-image 47-48
Notes from you 168
Notes, self-image building 168-169
Nothing will change my self-image 313
Notice what you do well 39
Nourish body 35
Now in present 326
Now, what can you do 256-258
Now, what is wisest to do 215-217
Number one 195-196
Observe assertive person 192
Obsessing about what you can't change 261
Occurrences, focus on positive aspects 266
Off balance 232-234
Official looking certification 181
On being kind person 153-155
Once, if I can do it 98-101
Once in a while 77
One act of confidence, courage 55
One bite at a time 93
One hour at a time 93
One of the greatest skills 118
Optimist, joyful 278-280
Organizations, become part of worthwhile 218-219

Others cause of mistakes 306-312
Others try to discourage you 91-93
Out of context 241-242
Outlook 121
Outstanding feat 64
Over 261
Over only when it's over 237-238
Overall progress 71
Overcoming arrogance 140-1
Overcoming discouragement 260-261
Overeating 128-129
Overwhelming 71
Paintings 78
Parable, Purim 148-153
Paranoid, opposite of 283-284
Parents, angry 306-312
Parents believed in me 160-162
Parents, build on what's right 37-40
Parents changing approach 169
Parents' view of their child 168
Parents with low self-image 281
Parties, life of constant 263, 322
Patience and persistence 19
Pattern of thinking 43-44
Patterns of thinking, alphabetical 330-344
Patterns of thinking, happiness 263-270
Patterns of worry 144-145
Patterns, positive, stored in brain 76-77
Peace and prosperity 81
Peak performances 105-107
Pen, unable to hold 135
People aren't born with self-image 184-185
People love stories 172
People pleasers 155
People who make you feel good about self 123-124
Perfect environment 264
Perfect self-knowledge 136-141
Perfect, this is 217
Perfectionism 250-252
Performers 125
Perseverance 91-93
Persistence 91-93
Personal coach 105-107
Personal joy coach 270
Perspective of Almighty 17-18
Pessimist, joyful 278-280
Photo album 269
Picking up litter 80
Picture benefits of goals 73
Picture reaching goals 74

Pillar of the world, kindness 153-155
Pinkus, Rabbi Avraham 158
Pinkus, Rabbi Shimshon 202-203
Pioneer for others 209
Pitfall of excessive confidence 231
Planet, maybe on different 169
Play by play self-commentary 326-330
Play the role 57
Played powerful role 110
Pleasure making people feel bad 303-305
Point right direction 73
Polarity response 313
Polio, Roosevelt didn't let it stop 104
Popular 195-196
Positive anchors 274-278
Positive approach 169
Positive aspects of a deficiency 252-254
Positive associations, create 330-344
Positive influence on you 89-91
Positive patterns in brain 76-77
Positive self-commentary 326-330
Positive statements, discounting 61
Positive stories stored in brain 172-173
Positive things people said about you 124
Positive things you do now 41
Posture, happiness 265
Potential of each person 24
Potential to be a scholar 162-164
Poverty, a challenge 142
Power of Teshuvah 120-122
Powerful attitude and mindset 101-105
Powerful statement to Almighty 121
Pray for Almighty's help 39
Pray for needs of others 283
Prayer, highest aspirations 70
Precious 18
Preida, Rabbi, repeating 400 times 65
Preida's, Rabbi, student 169-170
Prerequisite 196
Presence of people who make you feel good about self 123-124
Present, all choices in 326
Present vantage point 256
President, arrogance 135
President Roosevelt, didn't let polio stop 104
Pressure caused by your thoughts 232-234
Pressure, calm under 232-234
Prestigious job 195-196
Pretend 55, 78
Pretend memories 287-288

INDEX / 361

Priority to build self-image 116
Priority to feel good about self 245
Problems, go to solution thinking 267
Procrastination, focus on improving 43
Profound decision 20
Programmed 263
Progress, focus on 40
Progress from day one 184-185
Progress, teachers focusing on 83
Projecting an image 125-126
Psalms stored in your brain 220
Public speaking as anchors 274-278
Public speaking, confidence 227
Publisher didn't accept book 215
Purim music 289
Purim parable 148-153
Purim play, acting in 110
Purposefulness of kindness 130-132
Putting oneself down many times 86
Putting others down 201
Putting yourself down 145-147
Putting yourself down, don't 95
Quality and quantity of kindness 155
Quarterback won Superbowl 268
Quest to build self-image 91-93
Rabainu Yonah, start new 121-122
Raising self-image with one sentence 237-238
Rambam, act the way you wish to be 53
Rambam, becoming kind 154
Rambam on anger 281
Reaching for the stars 235
Reaching goals 72-75
Reaction to disappointment 217
Reactions of others 125-127
Read this book a number of times 326
Reading Talmud without understanding 171
Reading, teaching 165-166
Real estate trends 230
Real me 156
Realistic 99
Realistic and possible 71
Reality from now on 121
Really change 85
Really doing 80
Really kind 154
Reasonable goals 115
Reasons to justify a low self-image 45-47
Reasons why feel bad 245
Record breaking 64

Refrain from negative speech 201
Refraining because of pain 128-129
Reframing rejection 247-249
Refresh my brain 78
Refusal, fear of 192
Refusing to speak to someone 313
Regal lion 152
Reish Lakish 162-164
Rejection and self-image 247-249
Rejoice with all the good 265
Rejoice with final results 248
Relaxed body 213-214
Remember encouraging words 161
Remember goals you reached 74
Repeat self-image building sentences 345-350
Repeat to yourself 89-91
Repeating lesson 400 times 169-170
Repeating negativity 57
Repeating old perceptions 109-110
Repentance 120-122
Resentment and forgiveness 285-287
Resilience, bouncing back 208-209
Resistance, transcending 165-167
Resolve to correct your faults 41
Resolve to do good 26
Resources, you have all inner 73-74
Respect elderly 294-296
Respect others 22-25
Respected and liked, modesty 136
Respectful chutzpah 253
Respectfully assertive 190-192
Respectfully say, "No" 155
Rested mind 211-212
Revise the picture of your life 41
Rewards for self-mastery 128-129
Rewriting 217
Right, build on what you did 37-40
Right now 261
Right to be assertive 190-192
Right to have a high self-image 195-197
Right way 325
Robbery witnesses 143-144
Robbing bank once 78
Rock and Rabbi Akiva 92
Role, limiting 57
Role models of confidence 224-228
Role models, everyone who can do 102
Roosevelt had polio, was president 104
Root cause of anger 281
Rough life 87

Rudeness, imitation of strength 135
Rule in school 215
Running four minute mile 77
Sad elderly person 239-240
Sad reality 164
Salanter, Rabbi Yisroel 92
Salanter, Rabbi Yisroel, self-knowledge 137
Sandler, sales trainer 186-189
Sarah, guest of 68
Saving self-image building notes 168-169
Saving someone from rejection 248
School, not accepted in 215
School with great atmosphere 124
Schools as goals 73
Schwardron, Rabbi Shalom 171
Search for and find self-image building 86-87
Secret of speaking and acting 57
Secret of wealthy entrepreneur 249
Security, inner 135
Security, marriage problems 245
See people as they will be 164
See yourself in greater light 81
See yourself in positive light, 37
Seeing self in negative light 139
Seeking honor 28
Self-centeredness 130-131
Self-commentary 326-330
Self-concept determines ability 30
Self-confidence 224-228
Self-confident moments 64
Self-confident thoughts, words, actions 91
Self-conscious around people 283-284
Self-defeating thoughts 113-116
Self-development formula 324-326
Self-discipline for self-knowledge 136-141
Self-discipline not to speak against others 201
Self-fulfilling prophecy 30
Self-hate 33
Self-image building with choices 86-87
Self-image is an issue of thought 43-44
Self-image lowering thoughts 113-116
Self-image, not thinking about 47-48
Self-improvement, lifetime 41
Selfish 130-131
Selfish, told as child 155
Self-knowledge, accurate 136-141
Self-mastery builds self-image 128-129
Self-mastery, greater 39
Self-respect and respect for others 191

Self-respect at all times 20
Self-talk, joyful 268
Self-worth, ICFSW 179-181
Selling 186-189
Send out positive energy 284
Sense of perspective 251
Sense of relief, great 88
Sense of self, healthy 28
Servant of Almighty 121
Serving Almighty with joy 264
Shabbos can build your self-image 68-69
Shabbos guest believed in host 162
Sharing success with others 133-134
Shortcomings, focusing on 157
Show people they have strengths 157-158
Shy person, not really 109-110
Shyness to confidence 227
Sign, treat with respect 24
Sincere change of mind 120-122
Sincere effort to improve 39
Sincerely want to know yourself 136-141
Singing, learning 95
Situations, focus on positive aspects 265-266
Skills, keep building 267
Skills, one of greatest 118
Slights, calm about 134
Small improvements 70-72
Smile at mirrors 271-273
Snapping fingers makes you calm 233
Solomon, King, patterns 198
Solutions, focus on 267
Solve what can be solved 265
Someone else can do it 101-105
Something is wrong with me 182-183
Sometimes can do it 99
Song that raises consciousness 118
Soul wants me to choose 36
Soul with a body 35-36
Source of light 26
Speak and act pleasantly 135
Speak as if you had a positive self-image 53-58
Speak joyfully 268-269
Speak like a confident person 224-228
Speakers as role models 102
Speaking against others doesn't build you 200-201
Speaking and acting with courage 222-223
Speaking in public as anchor 274-278
Special moments in our lives 64-66

Special Purim law of turtles 152
Special reason 196
Specific skills 74
Spiritual moments 64
Standing up after falling 208-209
Start anew 121-122
Starting as newborns 184-185
State collecting 51
State of alert mind, relaxed body 213-214
States, access positive at will 269
Steipler's humility 132-133
Step at a time 70-72
Steps of repentance 120-122
Stock market trends 230
Stop calling self a worrier 145
Stop limiting thoughts 113-116
Stop playing limiting role 57
Store Psalms in your brain 220
Stored in brain 76
Stories of people who grew from challenges 144
Stories raising self-image 172-73
Story of your life 41
Strategy failing 24
Strengths in all contexts 76-79
Stress, needless 266
Strive for greater accomplishments 30
Stroke 135
Strong negative feelings 245
Stronger from challenges 144
Stubborn 312-315
Stuck in a rut 81
Students of Vilna Gaon 65
Study for short segments 253
Studying in yeshiva 320-323
Stupid and hopeless 286
Stupid, considering self 319
Subconscious, Torah knowledge 323
Subjective view of yourself 186-189
Success and rejection 249
Success journal 302
Success stories 161
Successes 124
Successes, self-mastery 128-129
Successful 60
Successful beyond initial dreams 103
Successful blamers 306-312
Successful persuading 186-189
Successful teacher's approach 39
Suggest a bit of improvement 71
Superbowl quarterback 268

Super-confident 57, 227
Surprising yourself about what you can do 105-107
Survived one hour at a time 93
Sword way of talking 198-199
Systematic belittling 203
Taking things personally 280-282
Talents, keep building 267
Talking about great things isn't doing 237-238
Talking to yourself 326-330
Talmud test 37-38
Tape recorder to sound confident 226
Teacher calming student 170
Teacher focusing on progress 83
Teacher for self-knowledge 141
Teacher, insightful and clever 37-38
Teacher, resenting 286
Teacher, tough 258-259
Teacher, you will be a great 162
Teachers give positive identity 124
Teachers notes' to parents 168-169
Teachers, angry 306-312
Teachers, best are best moments 64-66
Teaching reading 165-166
Telephone ringing 278
Telephone was a goal 73
Ten out of ten 186-189
Ten years from now 255
Tense situations 232-234
Tension when taking test 214-215
Teshuvah, power of 120-122
Tests in school 171
The way you think about yourself creates you 20
Think your way to better self-image 44
Thinking about yourself 130-132
Thinking, not, about self-image 47-48
Thinking pattern versus having 43-44
This time 119-120
This, too, is for the good 266
This, too, will build my self-image 86
This won't work 19
Thought creates self-image 43-44
Thoughts about rejection 247-249
Thoughts are just thoughts 118-119
Thoughts, choosing 84-85
Thoughts that lower self-image 113-116
Thousands of thoughts every day 265
Thrown off balance 232-234
Time and effort 241-242

Time, how long to improve self-image 94
Timid, not really 109-110
Tiny step at a time 70-72
Tone deaf 95
Tone of voice, happiness 265
Tongue of wise heals 198
Too bad you don't have father's intelligence 228
Too much confidence 230
Tool, money as 193-194
Torah knowledge in subconscious 323
Torah perspective 17-18
Total process of self-knowledge 136-141
Totally committed 116
Tough coach 258-259
Train ride analogy 132-133
Training to learn things 101-105
Transcending resistance 165-167
Transforming an "I can't" to an "I can" 64-65
Travel in right direction 325
Treat every person with respect 192
Treat with respect 23
Treated with more respect 152
Tremendous inner value 191
Tremendous value 17-18
Trick of your mind 191
Trivial victory 147
True humility 132-136
Truly in best interest 247
Truly the ideal 125-127
Truth stranger than fiction 149
Tshuvah, feeling better about self 26
Turning yourself to be a kind person 154
Turtle story 148-153
Ultimate celebration 68-69
Ultimate perspective 17-18
Unable to hold a pen 135
Unasserted 192
Unbelievable ways 64
Unconditional kindness 153-155
Unconditional worth 181
Understand in new light 326
Unimportant 30
Unique, each human 174-178
Unique life histories 263
Unique way each day 86-87
Uniqueness of every person 137
Universe created for you 68-69
Unlimited value 19
Untalented 30

Until now 108
Up and down of emotions 49-52
Upbeat self-talk 268
Upgrade to be a lion 152
Upgrading your identity 59-63
Ups and downs, life 263
Upset over what was 261
Using your full potential 105-107
Valuable 32
Valuable ideas 242
Valuable suggestions 122
Value and worth always high 51
Value because you exist 17-20
Value, tremendous inner 191
Verse, repeating 400 times 65
Version of reality 288
Versions of what happened 143
Victories, self-mastery 128-129
Victory journal 302
Vienna, Jewish doctor 320-303
Viewing self as unassertive 190-192
Vilna Gaon, two patterns 198
Vilna Gaon's students 65
Visualize doing the difficult 204-205
Visualize goals 74
Visualize self calm under pressure 232-234
Visualize yourself 42
Waiting, the great four 89-91
Wake up in the morning 265, 268
Walking, the great four 89-91
Wanted to be a teacher 162
Wasserman, Rav Elchonon 32
Water dripping on rock 92
Water dripping 266
Water, face to face 284
Way you treat others 23
Weakness in others 303-305
Wealth, a challenge 142
Wealthy businessman 177
Wealthy mindset 63
Well meaning mother 228
Well nourished mind 211-212
Well rested mind 211-212
What can I do to help you? 219
What can I do to improve today 41
What do others like about you? 39
What inner strength do I need now? 78
What is good about this? 266
What is important for you? 41
What is possible for you 105-107
What is turtle thinking? 150

What is your vision 72
What might have been 256-258
What really happened? 143-144
What would motivate me? 128-129
What would you need to feel good about self 157-160
What you can't do 113-116
What you did right 37-40
What you don't ask for 190-192
What's the matter with you? 38
Whining 24
Whispering of your inner mind 58
Who am I? 51
Who am I to argue with Almighty? 33
Who are you? 17-19
Who can catch on faster 171
Why me? 151
Why people have a low self-image 45-47
Why we need to feel good about ourselves 25-28
Will grow up to be someone special 158
Will, intensity of 206-207
Will to do Almighty's will 121
Willpower, increasing 128-129
Winning doll contest 147
Wisdom lost when angry 306-308
Wise choices 84-85
Wise pattern of talking 198-199
Wise person learns from everyone 101, 178
Wise suggestions 122
Wisest thing I can do now 215-217
Wisest use of time 261
Wish other people well 283
Wish people well 177
Wish the world well 81
Wished to have thought and acted 86
Wishy-washy 116

Witnessing a bank robbery 143-144
Wolbe, Rabbi Shlomo, self-knowledge 138-139
Wonderful, thoughts, words, actions 91
Won't be me 314
Won't reach goals without persevering 91-93
Words, choosing 84-85
Working out differences 280-282
World a better place 79-81
World created for me 17, 30
Worrying is a pattern of thinking 144-145
Worth less because of ways other view 125-127
Worthless 20
Worthwhile organizations 218-219
Worthy cause 167
Write new sentences 41
Write self-image building notes 168-169
Wrong with me, everything 87
Years later after positive encounter 123
Yeshiva, studying in 320-323
Yet 107-108
Yetzer hara, don't think about virtues 114
Yochonon, Rabbi, and Reish Lakish 162-164
You are creative 158
You become the way you act 58
You can do a lot more 105-107
You can learn to do anything 73
You never get what you don't ask for 190-192
You will be a great teacher 162
You're right 56
Your own beliefs about yourself make the difference 160-162
Zaitchyk, Rabbi Chaim 173

This volume is part of
THE ARTSCROLL SERIES®
an ongoing project of
translations, commentaries and expositions
on Scripture, Mishnah, Talmud, Halachah,
liturgy, history, the classic Rabbinic writings,
biographies and thought.

For a brochure of current publications
visit your local Hebrew bookseller
or contact the publisher:

Mesorah Publications, ltd
4401 Second Avenue
Brooklyn, New York 11232
(718) 921-9000
www.artscroll.com